The Byronic Byron

LONGMAN ENGLISH SERIES

This series includes both period anthologies and selections from the work of individual authors. The introductions and notes have been based upon the most up-to-date criticism and scholarship and the editors have been chosen for their special knowledge of the material.

General Editor Maurice Hussey

*Available in paperback

The Byronic Byron

a selection from the poems of Lord Byron

edited by

Gilbert Phelps

Longman

LONGMAN GROUP LIMITED
London

*Associated companies, branches and
representatives throughout the world*

First published 1971

ISBN 0582 34169 8

NOTE ON THE EDITOR

Gilbert Phelps, writer and lecturer, has published a number of critical
studies and made many contributions to BBC educational and other pro-
grammes, having been for some years a Talks Producer. His most recent
series of talks has been in 'Reading to Learn'. He has written seven novels,
of which the most recent are *The Winter People* (Bodley Head, 1963;
Penguin) and *Tenants of the House* (Barrie & Jenkins, 1971), as well as
The Last Horizon, a book about his travels in Brazil (Bodley Head, 1964;
Charles Knight, 1971) and poems in various magazines and collections.
Having taught English in Portugal, at Blundell's School and in the
universities of Cambridge and Oxford, near which he is now living, he
has also published *Question and Response* (Cambridge University Press,
1969), a critical anthology of English and American poetry.

Contents

To 'Meem'
(Mabel Batchelor)

Preface and Acknowledgements

The term 'Byronic Byron' is meant to indicate that part of Byron's poetic output upon which his reputation among his contemporaries largely rested and which was most characteristic of him – but which recent literary fashion has tended to devalue in favour of his more satirical work. This selection seeks to redress the balance by switching the emphasis in the other direction – though without neglecting the other aspects, and comes out of my work for the BBC/National Extension College, Cambridge course 'Reading to Learn', broadcast in 1970–71.

I am, of course, indebted to a number of biographers and students of Byron, and I have included the books I have found most useful in the section 'Further Reading'.

I am also greatly indebted to the General Editor, Maurice Hussey, who has guided the book from its inception, prodded me at exactly those moments when it was most necessary, been at all times most generous with his time, encouragement and advice.

My thanks are also due to Mrs. Jessica Scholes, for her hard work in typing much of the manuscript.

G.P.

Biographical Outline

22 January 1788	George Gordon, born in London, son of Captain John Byron and Catherine Gordon of Gight.
2 August 1791	Death of Captain John Byron.
1794–8	Byron a pupil at Aberdeen Grammar School.
19 May 1798	Death of the fifth Baron Byron. George Gordon, his great nephew, succeeded to the title and to Newstead Abbey, the ancestral home of the Byrons, in Nottinghamshire.
August 1799	Byron sent to a preparatory school at Dulwich.
April 1801	Byron sent to Harrow.
October 1805	Byron entered Trinity College, Cambridge.
1806–7	Wrote most of his juvenile poems (privately printed).
June 1807	Publication of *Hours of Idleness*, Byron's first published collection of poems.
March 1808	Publication of *Poems, Original and Translated*, a revised edition of his juvenile poems.
April 1808	Byron entered upon his inheritance.
September 1808	Byron established himself at Newstead Abbey.
1 March 1809	Publication of *English Bards and Scotch Reviewers* (as a riposte to an attack on *Hours of Idleness* in the *Edinburgh Review*).
13 March 1809	Byron took his seat in the House of Lords.
2 July 1809	Byron left Falmouth on a tour of a number of European countries, including Portugal, Spain, Malta, Albania, Turkey and Greece.
3 May 1810	Byron swam across the Hellespont (an exploit of which he was very proud).
July 1811	Byron returned to England.
7 August 1811	Death of Byron's mother at Newstead Abbey.
27 February 1812	Byron delivered his maiden speech in the House of Lords.

10 March 1812	Publication of first two cantos of *Childe Harold's Pilgrimage*.
5 June 1813	Publication of *The Giaour*.
26 June 1813	Byron and his half-sister Augusta Leigh (daughter of Captain John Byron by his first marriage) in London together.
29 November 1813	Publication of *The Bride of Abydos*.
1 February 1814	Publication of *The Corsair* (10,000 copies sold on the day of publication)
15 April 1814	Birth of a daughter, Elizabeth Medora, to Augusta Leigh. Rumours that Byron was the father.
6 August 1814	Publication of *Lara*
2 January 1815	Byron married Anne Isabella ('Annabella') Milbanke.
April 1815	Publication of *Hebrew Melodies*.
10 December 1815	Birth of Byron's daughter, Augusta Ada.
15 January 1816	Lady Byron left her husband.
7 February 1816	Publication of *The Siege of Corinth*, and *Parisina*.
18 April 1816	Lord and Lady Byron legally separated.
25 April 1816	Byron left England.
25 May 1816	Byron in Switzerland with Shelley, the poet, Shelley's wife Mary and Shelley's sister-in-law Jane, 'Claire' Clairmont, who had become one of Byron's mistresses.
November 1816	Byron took up residence in Venice.
18 November 1816	Publication of the third canto of *Childe Harold's Pilgrimage*.
5 December 1816	Publication of *The Prisoner of Chillon*.
13 January 1817	Birth of Allegra, Byron's illegitimate daughter by Claire Clairmont.
16 June 1817	Publication of *Manfred*.
28 February 1818	Publication of *Beppo, a Venetian Story*.
28 April 1818	Publication of the fourth canto of *Childe Harold's Pilgrimage*.
September 1818	Byron started writing *Don Juan*.
April 1819	Byron met Teresa, Countess Guiccioli (née Gamba), who became his mistress.

28 June 1819	Publication of *Mazeppa*, and the *Ode on Venice*.
15 July 1819	Publication of first two cantos of *Don Juan*.
December 1819	Byron settled in Ravenna, to be with his latest (and most permanent) mistress, Teresa Guiccioli. Through her family, the Gambas, he became involved in an abortive conspiracy against the Austrian rulers of Italy.
21 April 1821	Publication of the *Prophecy of Dante*. Publication of *Marino Faliero, Doge of Venice*, a five act tragedy.
July 1821	Teresa Guiccioli and her family expelled from Ravenna.
8 August 1821	Publication of Cantos III, IV and V of *Don Juan*.
October 1821	Byron rejoined Teresa at Pisa (where he also met Shelley again).
19 December 1821	*Cain* published (together with two of Byron's other dramas).
16 August 1821	Byron attended the burning of Shelley's body (after his death from drowning) on the seashore near Via Reggio.
1822	Byron, Teresa and the Gambas (Teresa's family) moved to Montenero (near Leghorn), then to Genoa.
15 October 1822	Publication of the *Vision of Judgment* (in the first number of Byron's shortlived radical paper, *The Liberal*)
March 1823	Byron elected to the Greek Committee (a small body of influential Liberals in London devoted to the cause of Greek liberation from Turkish rule)
1 April 1823	Publication of a satire entitled *The Age of Bronze*.
15 July 1823 to 26 March 1824	Cantos VI–XVI of *Don Juan* published at intervals (Canto XVII was left unfinished at his death).

xiii

23 July 1823	Byron set sail from Leghorn for Greece.
3 August 1823	Byron arrived at Cephalonia.
5 January 1824	Byron landed at Missolonghi (at the invitation of Prince Alexander Mavrocordato and the rebel Greek legislative body.)
20 February 1824	Publication of *The Deformed Transformed*.
19 April 1824	Death of Byron at Missolonghi.
16 July 1824	Byron's remains buried in the chancel of the village church of Hucknall Torkard, in Nottinghamshire.

(The above brief outline does not list all Byron's publications).

Introduction

The Byronic Byron

In a wider sense, of course, all Byron's poetry is Byronic. One of the aims of this selection, indeed, is to show the continuity of his creative development. To suggest, therefore, that there is a 'Byronic Byron' as distinct from a whole one may seem something of a paradox.

It is a paradox, however, that is forced on us, for the majority of Byron's modern English critics have tended to split him into two very unequal parts. On the one side they place *Don Juan* and to lesser extent, as a kind of run-up to it, *Beppo*, together with satirical pieces like *The Vision of Judgment*. The rest of Byron's poetry, apart from a few of the songs and lyrics, a few passages from the later Cantos of *Childe Harold's Pilgrimage* and perhaps a few perfunctory tributes to Byron's narrative verve, is usually dismissed as pretentious and second-rate.

Yet it is exactly this part of his output that seemed most characteristic to his contemporaries and which made him the most popular and influential poet of his time. This was the case, moreover, not only at home but also on the Continent, where Byron was ranked second only to Shakespeare, and where it would have been difficult to find a single European critic who would not have wholeheartedly endorsed the verdict of the great German writer and sage, Goethe: 'The English may think of Byron as they please, but this is certain, that they show no poet who is to be compared with him.' Such a judgment, unless we are to assume that Goethe and his fellows were fools, justifies one perhaps in suggesting that here too is a paradox that needs explaining.

This is not to deny that Byron is a great satirist, or that *Don Juan* marks the crown of his achievement, though it is very much more than a satirical poem. But it *is* to argue that in throwing the emphasis so heavily in this direction a serious distortion and lack of balance have resulted. It is to argue, too, that the poetry that belongs most naturally to the 'Byronic Byron' is more important, both in its own right and in relation to his work as a whole, than is generally allowed.

It is for these reasons that this selection shifts the focus away from the more satirical side of Byron's genius, even in the passages from *Don Juan* itself, and why, indeed, that great poem does not figure as prominently as usual. If length were no object, then obviously the whole of Byron ought to be represented in equal proportions: in a limited space there is ample justification for the limitation proposed – it really is time the 'Byronic Byron' had his day.

Gothic Beginnings

The story of Byron's early life often reads like a Gothic novel – the term we apply to a type of fiction, first popularised by Horace Walpole's *The Castle of Otranto*, which was published in 1764 and embodied the growing romantic fondness for sinister melodrama in a mysterious medieval setting.

The Byron family in itself possessed the ancient Norman blood and dark secrets which were practically obligatory to the *genre*. Most of Byron's paternal ancestors had been as violent, bloody and dissolute as the most avid Romantic could wish. Among his immediate forebears, the great-uncle from whom he inherited the title had been known alternately as 'the mad Lord Byron' and 'the wicked Lord Byron': he had killed a kinsman in a duel, and was rumoured to have tried to murder his own wife. Byron's father was known as 'Mad Jack'; he was a profligate spendthrift who was reputed to have driven his first wife to her grave, and who probably died by his own hand (in 1791, three years after Byron's birth).

The family of Byron's mother, the Gordons of Gight, had just as romantic a heredity, claiming descent from the kings of Scotland – including, appropriately enough, Macbeth – and they had just as stormy a history. Byron's maternal grandfather was a melancholic who also probably died by suicide. His mother

('Mad Jack's' second wife) was herself unbalanced, with an ungovernable temper – and her death in 1811 was probably the result of a fit of rage over the arrival of an upholsterer's bill.

It was, in fact, as luridly 'Gothic' a heredity as could be imagined – and inevitably it raises the question as to how far Byron was its victim. He himself always believed that he belonged to 'a doomed race' and that he was subject to a mysterious ancestral curse. This, of course, was very much in the Romantic fashion, and Byron, who had a strong histrionic streak, was not averse to exploiting the fact. All the same, there is a sense in which it could be said that the legend of the Byronic Byron had begun even before Byron was born.

A Gothic Childhood

Byron's early years certainly played into the romantic pattern. His father had left England, after squandering the bulk of his wife's fortune. Byron and his mother lived in straitened circumstances in a series of shabby lodgings in Aberdeen. In addition, Byron had been born lame, and had to endure agonies at the hands of incompetent and unsuccessful doctors. Although in later life he delighted to excel at boxing, swimming, fencing and other sports, he was always deeply sensitive about his deformity. To make matters worse, in her outbursts of rage his mother used to taunt him about it. In all this there is a kind of grimly grotesque element one does not as a rule encounter outside Romantic fiction.

A similar lurid quality attends Byron's early erotic experiences. In later life he was always hinting at a 'dark secret' in his childhood—as in this passage from one of his letters: 'If I could explain at length the *real* causes which have contributed to increase this perhaps *natural* temperament of mine, this melancholy which hath made me a bye-word, nobody would wonder.'

Now a guilty secret, issuing in a romantic melancholy, was also one of the typical ingredients of the Gothic novel – and here again Byron tended to make the most of the situation. But there is no doubt that the guilty secret did exist, and we probably know from John Cam Hobhouse, one of Byron's closest friends, what it consisted of: 'When Byron was nine years old, at his mother's house, a free Scotch girl used to come to him and play tricks with his person.'

This experience (which seemed far more terrible then than it would in our more tolerant times) had a number of lasting effects on the lonely and highly-strung child. For one thing, 'the free Scotch girl' Hobhouse referred to was Byron's 'nanny', and as she was an ardent Calvinist, who preached hell-fire and damnation at him, he grew up to have a particularly bitter hatred and contempt for religious hypocrisy, together with a cynical attitude towards religion itself. At the same time he was never able to escape from a profound sense of guilt, while the histrionic streak in his temperament led him to exaggerate the importance of his 'crime'.

Byron also had a number of precocious attachments to various girl relatives of about the same age as, or a little older than, himself. These, by contrast, were of a highly idealistic nature, and throughout his life he was subject to wild alternations between cynicism and idealism in his love relationships.

It will be seen, too, that another important part of the Byronic legend, that of the great romantic lover, was also in the making from a very early age. But what was perhaps most important of all, this premature emotional and physical arousal caused him, to quote Peter Quennell, one of his biographers, 'to feel that he had anticipated life, and that he had begun to squander his capital before he had reached an age when he could gather in the interest'.

Again it has to be pointed out that a brooding sense of guilt accompanied by a conviction that life had been laid waste before it had properly begun, was an outstanding symptom of the Romantic syndrome. So, too, was a defiant attitude towards religion and morality, and (to look ahead into Byron's future) a determination to shock society by even more spectacular proofs of 'wickedness'.

4

But was it romanticism, and all the complex pressures lying behind it, that forced Byron into his particular life pattern, or was it Byron who gave romanticism its special direction? This is a question which is constantly arising.

And finally, there was a romantic, 'little Lord Fauntleroy' element about the way in which the shabby-genteel lame boy was suddenly transformed into a peer of the realm. When he was born the prospect was remote, for his great-uncle, 'the wicked Lord', had a grandson who was, of course, his heir. But the grandson was killed in battle, and when four years later 'the wicked Lord' also died (1798), his great-nephew made the dramatic transition 'from a shabby Scotch flat to a palace' (to quote Byron's own words), and became, at the age of ten, the sixth Baron Byron. The 'palace', Newstead Abbey, the ancestral home of the Byrons in Nottinghamshire, was, it is true, half in ruins – but that, after all, only added to the Gothic spell. Newstead today has become, appropriately, a Byronic museum.

Premonitions of Destiny

The feeling that he was the victim of a fate that was slowly but inexorably leading him towards some dark and mysterious destiny continued through Byron's schooldays, first at a preparatory school at Dulwich and then at Harrow. So did the intense romantic attachments, to boys as well as to girls. These were accompanied, after he went to Cambridge, by spells of debauchery followed by moods of intense self-disgust, the kind of mood that found expression in several of the poems which appeared in his first collection, published in 1807 (while he was still at the university) under the title of *Hours of Idleness*—as, for example, in the opening couplet of *Damaetas*:

> In law an infant, and in years a boy,
> In mind a slave to every vicious joy . . .

There were similar references to his wickedness in *English Bards and Scotch Reviewers*, the satirical poem which he published in 1809 as a riposte to those who had derided his earlier volume, accompanied by a good deal of braggadocio.

Shortly after the publication of *English Bards and Scotch Reviewers*, Byron, who had long dreamed of foreign travel, left England for nearly two years. At that date the Grand Tour was still an accepted part of a young nobleman's education. In Byron's case, though, there was a strangely prophetic element (as in so many of his affairs) about it, both in the itinerary and in the mood in which it was undertaken.

There was nothing particularly out of the ordinary in his visiting Gibraltar, Spain and Portugal – apart from the fact that the Peninsular War was still in progress – but the visits to Albania, Turkey and Asia Minor, and above all to Greece, were more unusual for the time. It was with Greece, then under Turkish rule, that his name was to be most gloriously associated – and you will see from the extracts in this selection from the first two Cantos of *Childe Harold's Pilgrimage* (which he wrote during his travels) that Greece had already entered powerfully into his imagination.

In addition, after a farewell carousal at Newstead Abbey with his friends (which you will also find reflected in the extracts) Byron had set out in a curiously morbid, self-accusing, and foreboding frame of mind. There is, for example, a strangely final note about the stanzas which begin 'Adieu, adieu! my native shore'. It is almost as if this first departure from England was a dress rehearsal for the one that was to come later, and as if in some way Byron's imaginative antennae registered the fact. Underlying the whole of the Byron story there is this doubt as to whether he was the victim of a fate that had singled him out to be the focus of the trends and pressures of the age, a kind of Prometheus for it (a figure from classical mythology towards which, like his fellow poet and friend Shelley, he was particularly drawn), or whether he was subconsciously engineering his own destiny. It is this kind of doubt, together with all the puzzling coincidences that attended Byron's life, that led Peter Quennell to observe: 'Having admitted that he was morbidly superstitious, we must also admit that circumstances were continually conspiring to give his superstition

6

Romantic Fame

fresh colour.' 'The effect was . . . electric, his fame . . . seemed to spring, like the palace of a fairy king, in a night.' So Tom Moore, the Irish poet and Byron's friend and biographer, described the astonishing change that came over Byron's fortunes with the publication in March 1812 of the first two Cantos of *Childe Harold's Pilgrimage*, which Byron had brought back with him from his travels. When he returned to England he was depressed, lonely, more or less isolated as far as Society with a capital 'S' was concerned, and practically unknown. Within a few months London was at his feet: he was sought after by all the most famous hostesses of the day, pursued by women of all classes, and had become the object of the kind of adulation that in our own day is usually reserved for the film star or the pop idol.

What was it about *Childe Harold* that caused such a stir? In the first place, it catered in a popular and dramatic form for many of the contemporary fashions – and at this more topical level Byron can be seen as the great 'showman' of the Romantic Movement. The taste for medievalism, for example, was fully exploited (especially in the first Canto), by the use of Gothic backgrounds and all kinds of medieval terminology – including the word 'Childe' itself, which was an archaic term for an apprentice knight – and by the poem 'Adieu, adieu! my native shore' which is roughly in the form and style of the medieval ballads. At the same time the Romantic craving for picturesque scenery and exotic, far away places was also exploited to the full.

Far more important was the powerful appeal – then as now – of 'shocking disclosures'. The liberation of the emotions and the relaxing of the old restraints brought about by the Romantic Revival had stimulated interest in autobiographies, memoirs and confessions of all kinds. But there had never before been anything so thrillingly personal and so romantically wicked as *Childe Harold*. Although Byron himself always denied it (with some justification, as we shall see) everybody assumed that he and his hero were one and the same person – and it is undoubtedly true that many of the more flamboyant aspects of Byron's temperament, together with many of his attitudes and emotions, find an outlet in the poem.

The Byronic Hero

The character type embodied in *Childe Harold* (and in verse tales like *The Giaour* and *The Corsair* which followed it and which were just as popular) was one of the most potent ever created. To do it full justice would involve a history of the entire field of Romantic poetry, fiction, painting and music. In the years that followed, the 'Byronic hero' (as it came to be known) cropped up in all kinds of guises: in Rochester, the brooding, demonic hero of Charlotte Bronte's *Jane Eyre*, for example, and in a hundred lesser romantic novels, down to our own time; in the vast, restless canvases of the French painter Delacroix; in the poetry of Frenchmen like Hugo, Lamartine and Alfred de Musset; in the music – and life – of Berlioz, as well as, more specifically, in the *Mazeppa* of Liszt, the *Manfred* of Tchaikovsky, and the *Ode to Napoleon* of Schoenberg. It reached as far afield as Russia, where Pushkin, 'the Russian Shakespeare', learned English in order to read Byron in the original, and where Lermontov, another great Russian poet, was the creator of several 'Byronic heroes' and played the part himself in his own life.

The 'Byronic hero', however, was not merely a literary type. It also had a profound political and social significance. Politically, it was a dual symbol: first, of defiance against tyranny (as in the stanzas on Greece in *Childe Harold's Pilgrimage*), and secondly, in a far more pervasive sense, of hopes and aspirations that had already been thwarted.

In order to understand this we must remind ourselves that the Europe which Byron knew was very different from that of the earlier Romantics. When the young Wordsworth, for example, wrote the famous lines:

> Bliss was it in that dawn to be alive
> But to be young was very heaven

he was expressing the feelings of elation and hope which the French Revolution (which began in 1789) had inspired among most of his youthful contemporaries. Byron, on the other hand, lived in a period when the earlier promise of the French Revolution had been blighted by the Terror, the dictatorship of Napoleon Bonaparte, the long-drawn-out Napoleonic Wars, and after the final defeat of Napoleon at Waterloo in 1815, by a long period of reaction throughout Europe in which every spark of revolt was ruthlessly crushed.

Now Byron and countless ardent young spirits like him throughout Europe hated the old reactionary regimes which Napoleon had overthrown, and which were restored when he was defeated, far more than they hated Napoleon himself; this explains why so many of them, including Byron himself, retained a sneaking sympathy for him. At the same time, they often found themselves denied any outlet for their revolutionary feelings (especially in backward autocracies like Russia), and became in consequence increasingly bitter and resentful.

In other words, the sense of blighted hopes, the disillusionment, melancholy and despair which we have noted in Byron's nature, entered into, perhaps in part derived from, and certainly when transmuted into the poetic creation of the 'Byronic hero' expressed, more powerfully than any other writing of the period, the political malaise of a whole generation.

But although the forces that had been released by the French Revolution might be dammed back, diverted or distorted, they could not be conjured out of existence. They continued to seethe beneath the surface for many years to come – and they poured into the poetry of the Byronic Byron. When you read the relevant extracts in this selection you will see that neither Byron nor his heroes were melancholy and disillusioned in a passive way: on the contrary, wrapped in their dramatic cloaks and with fierce scowling brows they wandered about the earth as if driven by furies, breathing pride and defiance; even the most turgid of the Byronic verse that depicted them conveys their unappeased energies.

The French Revolution itself, however, had really only been one of the more spectacular symptoms of the vast social changes that had gradually been taking place beneath the surface of eighteenth- and early nineteenth-century Europe – changes in thought, religion, manners, fashions, communications, technology, and in the whole pattern of social and economic organization.

This was particularly so in England, where the Industrial Revolution was already getting into its stride, and Byron was very much aware of the fact. His hostility towards the ruling classes of his own country was directed both against the fact that they supported the old regimes displaced by Napoleon and then restored to power after his defeat, and against their neglect of their responsibilities towards the victims of the new industrial processes at home. One of the contributory factors in Byron's sudden rise to fame had been a brilliant maiden speech which he delivered in the House of Lords shortly before the publication of *Childe Harold*, in which he savagely denounced the government of the day for introducing a Bill seeking to impose the death penalty for frame breaking, following a number of riots in Byron's own country of Nottinghamshire when the hungry and desperate stocking-weavers had tried to smash the new machines which were robbing them of their livelihood.

Fall of a Romantic

Byron's fall was as dramatic as his rise. In 1815, after a series of amorous escapades which enhanced rather than tarnished his romantic reputation, he married an aristocratic and serious-minded young woman named Anne Isabella Milbanke. A year later, after the birth of a daughter, Ada, a separation took place which rocked London society.

In suing for this separation Lady Byron never publicly specified the exact reasons for her action. But there were all sorts of scandalous rumours – the most persistent, and deliciously shocking, of which concerned Byron's relationship with his married half-sister Augusta Leigh ('Mad Jack's' daughter by his first marriage).

Byron had been corresponding with Augusta since childhood and had come to look on her as the only relation he had – not excluding his mother – who really understood him and whom he could really trust. They had met only rarely, however, until in 1813 they began to see a great deal of each other. Whether or not the relationship between them became an incestuous one (and the indirect evidence suggests that it did), Byron's reaction to the rumours is very curious indeed. Instead of doing his best to discourage them, he appeared to go out of his way to drop all sorts of hints, not only to his friends but also – after his marriage – to his wife, about a new 'dark secret' in his life and one far more shocking than that which had haunted his childhood. He even touched on the theme of incest in one of his verse tales, *The Bride of Abydos*, which was published in the spring of 1813 and which described the mutual passion of a boy and girl who believe themselves (mistakenly as it turns out) to be brother and sister.

Like a moth attracted to a candle-flame Byron could not seem to get away from the topic, in spite of the fact that he genuinely loved Augusta and knew that his recklessness would hurt her as much as it would him. There was some destructive impulse in him which he simply could not resist. As Peter Quennell says: 'We can only explain the remarkable lack of prudence with which he acted between 1813 and 1814 by suggesting that, far from shunning disaster, his sense of guilt enjoined that he should go out in search of it.'

No wonder that Byron later wrote in one of his poems to Augusta:

> I have been cunning in mine overthrow,
> The careful pilot of my proper woe.

This overthrow was certainly complete. From being lionised and fêted wherever he went he became, almost overnight, an object of hatred and vituperation, and an outcast from society.

And yet, bearing in mind that the society that cast him out was that of Regency England, which was hardly noted for its high moral tone and had ridden worse scandals, the violence of its revulsion against Byron makes one wonder whether political motives may not have entered into it. It was the opinion of the nineteenth century critic R. C. Jeffreson, for example, that 'had Byron voted with the Tories, treated the Prince Regent respectfully, and held his pen and tongue about matters touching the Thirty-Nine Articles* England's higher society would never for a single instant have sided with Lady Byron in her domestic troubles'.

Whatever the truth of the matter, on 25 April 1816 Byron left England, never to return.

Romantic Exile

Byron's disgrace and ostracism caused him intense suffering, and there were times in Switzerland, where he stayed for several months during the first year of his exile, when he seriously contemplated suicide. At the same time somewhere inside the very genuine feelings of loneliness, rejection and injustice, there was a sense of something almost approaching relief. After the years of gnawing guilt and foreboding, the blow had at last fallen. It was, if hardly a 'consummation devoutly to be wish'd', one that had been gathering a long time, and now at least the intolerable tension had snapped. The part of his nature that subconsciously craved punishment and expiation had been satisfied. There had, too, been a kind of inexorable logic in the train of events which chimed in with his belief that he belonged to 'a doomed race', and he could not help feeling that he was somehow fulfilling a preordained destiny. So indeed he was, in so far as the Romantic *zeitgeist* or 'spirit of the times' had found in his peculiar talents and personality its most perfect instrument. The Victorian poet and critic Matthew Arnold accuses Byron of displaying in his exile 'the pageant of a bleeding heart'. This aptly expresses the

* The Thirty-Nine Articles are those to which men taking Orders in the Church of England subscribe. One of Byron's speeches in the House of Lords had been in favour of a Bill for removing some of the disabilities under which Roman Catholics still laboured.

Byronic flamboyance, the histrionic, larger-than-life posture. But really it was no wonder that Byron was given to self-dramatisation and the actor's stance. He could hardly avoid them: he *was* an actor who had, whether he liked it or not, been cast to play a particular role in the life of his times.

It was, moreover, by no means all flamboyant posturing. For one thing, by going into exile Byron had immeasurably widened the scope of his symbolic role. The 'Byronic hero' had already made its mark, but to some extent it was still a 'literary' symbol, derived in part from Gothic romance and in part from Goethe's famous novel *The Sorrows of Werther*, which had been published in 1774 and whose romantic young hero was not dissimilar to Childe Harold. But now that Byron was not merely a 'grand tourist' commenting on the political scene, through a fictional character, but was himself a wanderer and exile, his impact was inevitably greater. He was now his own 'Byronic hero' – which was one of the reasons why, in the third Canto of *Childe Harold's Pilgrimage*, written during the first year of his exile, the Childe begins to fade into the background and Byron speaks more and more in his own voice. The old 'Byronic hero' had corresponded to a geniune and widespread mood of defiance and disillusion, but one that had so far been vague and amorphous. With Byron's exile, it took on a much sharper focus, and as a symbol of revolt against social, politi-cal and economic repression it became more challenging and dangerous.

A gradual coalescing of a hitherto confused mass of ideas, attitudes and emotions began to make itself felt in Byron's poetry almost from the moment he left England. The third Canto of *Childe Harold*, for example, reveals a new firmness of control, together with a new ability to stand aside from his sufferings, and a note, if not of hope, at any rate of a revival of energies – as when in describing the Alps he writes:

> And thus I am absorb'd, and this is life:
> I look upon the peopled desert past
> As on a place of agony and strife,
> Where, for some sin, to sorrow I was cast,

> To act and suffer, but remount at last
> With a fresh pinion; which I feel to spring,
> Though young, yet waxing vigorous as the blast
> Which it would cope with, on delighted wing,
>   Spurning the clay-cold bonds which round our being cling.

In some strange way Byron seemed to be developing an ability to split himself into several distinct *personae*. Thus when in November 1816 he settled in Venice (where he lived for the next three years) he threw himself, in a mood of savage despair, into a life of debauchery – and yet in his letters (which are among the best in our language) he was describing his amours in the most racy and detached way imaginable, as if they belonged to a comic novel the writing of which he was thoroughly enjoying.

During this period, too, he wrote some of his most important poems, discovered the merits of the Italian *ottava rima*, the stanzaic form best suited to his particular kind of genius, and published the first two Cantos of his masterpiece, *Don Juan*, at which he worked intermittently for the rest of his life and left unfinished at his death.

It is a mistake, though, to assume that the more Byronic Byron had not also been changing and developing. Here there were two main lines of development. In the first place there was a deeper and more metaphysical exploration of the typical Byronic themes, which began in Switzerland with the composition of poems like *Darkness* and *Prometheus* and the first two acts of his verse tragedy *Manfred* (completed in Venice and published in 1817), and continued in a series of dramas, among them *Cain* (published in 1821). In the second place, as Byron's awareness of his symbolic role deepened, the undirected explosion of defiance and energy gradually moved towards a political focus. There had been premonitions of this movement in the first two Cantos of *Childe Harold's Pilgrimage*. It gathers force in the third Canto, and in the fourth (published in 1818) it begins to become urgent and insistent.

When he settled in Italy Byron kept in close touch with political developments at home, but his interest was increasingly concentrated on the part England was playing in backing the Great Powers in their repressive policies. In 1822 he launched a magazine called *The Liberal* to put forward his views. Scathing attacks on Castlereagh and Wellington, whom Byron saw as the arch-reactionaries in England in the years following Waterloo, appeared in the earlier Cantos of *Don Juan* and elsewhere. In 1819 he had met a young Italian woman, the Countess Teresa Guiccioli, who became his mistress and the most stable of all his attachments. Teresa's family, the Gambas, belonged to a secret group of conspirators called the Carbonari, sworn to throw off the Austrian yoke; when in 1820 Byron moved to Ravenna in order to be near his mistress he became a member of this group, and the leader of one of its branches. He showed himself, moreover, to be the reverse of the impractical romantic dreamer, revealing a marked capacity for organisation and patient leadership, financing the purchase of arms and ammunition, and running considerable personal risk.

The Carbonari conspiracy fizzled out, but Byron had made an important contribution to the cause of Italian independence. He had convincingly demonstrated that he was no Romantic *poseur*, and from now on Europe saw him not merely as symbol of revolt against tyranny, but also as a potential leader. The Byronic hero, finally absorbed into his creator, had come of age.

Two years later the Greek rebellion against Turkish rule began. Byron and a band of friends set sail for Greece. Once again he proved himself an able organiser and negotiator and an inspired leader. But his health gave way, and after a heroic struggle to keep on his feet, he died on 19 April 1824. The cenotaph which was erected at Missolonghi in his memory became a centre of veneration for the Greeks he had helped to liberate, and for lovers of freedom throughout the world. The Byronic hero had become a martyr, and the Byronic Byron had achieved its final apotheosis.

The Universal Byron

Topical and Universal
All this only tells half the story as far as Byron's poetry is concerned. In many ways the facts about Byron's life get in the way

15

of a proper assessment. They are so fascinating and dramatic that we allow ourselves to be hurtled along by them like skaters over a frozen surface, and the helter-skelter quality of the verse contributes to this effect.

In consequence we tend to judge Byron primarily at the more 'topical' level, whereas he is in fact also a universal poet, in the profoundest sense of the term – a poet who works, to quote Professor G. Wilson Knight, 'from a vast eternity consciousness to which events, as events, are the negative symbols of its expression' – and this is applicable to the 'Byronic Byron' just as much as it is to *Don Juan*.

The Byronic Vision

Looked at from this point of view Byron emerges as a poet with a coherent and developing vision of human life and destiny, whose real pilgrimage was a search for the forms and symbols that would best express that vision, and whose work must therefore be seen as a unified whole.

This vision, lying beneath (and sometimes even apart from) the personal, political and social elements, is, it is true, in many respects a singularly bleak one in spite of the energy of Byron's verse, his frequent high spirits and his gift for comedy. Its central theme has its origin in the fascination which the Old Testament story of the 'Fall' (when Eve succumbed to the serpent's temptation and ate the apple), and the consequent expulsion of Adam and Eve from the Garden of Eden, had held for him as a child, together with the doctrine derived from it (central to Calvinist teaching) of an inherited 'original sin'. This fascination tied in with the feelings of bitterness and disillusionment and of potentialities for love and happiness prematurely laid waste commented on earlier. The Bible myth seemed to Byron a particularly apt metaphor for his own early expulsion from an imaginary Eden of love, warmth and security.

The Calvinist doctrine of original sin and of predestination, whereby men are saved or damned even before they are born, is forbidding enough in all conscience, but there is at least a place in it for God, and a God who knows what he is doing and has some concern for makind. Byron, however, does not seem to allow even that much comfort. The American critic, Professor Robert F. Gleckner, in a book suggestively entitled *Byron and the Ruins of Paradise*, argues that Byron's gradually deepening conviction was that 'Man's Fall . . . and his consequent expulsion from Eden is not totally understandable in terms of a sin, the commission of some forbidden act; rather, for Byron, man's fall is the providential act of a God who punishes as evidence of his love.' What is more, for Byron the human condition consists of a whole series of expulsions from Eden as man's high aspirations and ideals continually and inevitably crumble into the welter of a chaotic and indifferent universe.

We may not entirely agree with Professor Gleckner's formulation, but it is difficult to see how any really careful penetration beneath the top layers of Byron's poetry can fail to yield a philosophical position at any rate very similar to it and one that operates with remarkable consistency and gathering force through the whole of Byron's work.

Some Examples

This applies even to the juvenile poems of *Hours of Idleness*, where the tone is nearly always elegaic and the constantly reiterated theme is of a childhood Eden that can be momentarily recaptured through memory, only to be destroyed by the reality of the present. The first two poems in this selection are good examples.

In *Hebrew Melodies* (a volume published in 1815) most of the poems are either actual laments, hymns to the loss, by one means or another, of love and beauty, or celebrations of destruction.

It is no accident that Byron should be drawn to 'Israel's scatter'd race' forced to 'wander witheringly' (as Byron says in *The Wild Gazelle*): for the homeless Jews, wandering in strange lands, whom not even death can reunite, are powerful symbols of the condition of universal Byronic man.

As soon as we are aware of this philosophical perspective, all the typically Byronic poems reveal a new depth and subtlety.

Take for example *The Prisoner of Chillon*: its brilliant narrative qualities have been generally acclaimed, but it is usually assumed that its theme is simply that of man's defiant faith in liberty; it is this, of course, but its fundamental concern is the eternal condition of man, imprisoned by his mortality, his darkness lightened only by occasional illusory gleams of light. In other words, like so much of the Byronic Byron, it is a more serious poem than is generally realised.

'Darkness' and 'Prometheus'

Naturally enough, though, it is in the more obviously metaphysical of Byron's poems that these ideas can be best explored. The most devastating expression of the sheer bleakness of Byron's vision is probably *Darkness*, one of the poems he wrote in Switzerland during his first year of exile. It gives a terrifying picture of a world dying as the result of some cosmic cataclysm, in which all human values are destroyed and man himself has reverted to savagery – the kind of world we might envisage in our century 'after the Bomb'.

Prometheus, written about the same time, is another example. The myth of the Titan chained to a rock and tortured through all eternity because he has befriended humanity was a favourite among the Romantics. Shelley, for example, published his famous *Prometheus Unbound* in 1820. But whereas for Shelley Prometheus, released from his bonds, becomes a symbol of Romantic love and hope for the future, in Byron's poem he remains for ever the victim of an

> inexorable Heaven,
> And the deaf tyranny of Fate,
> The ruling principle of Hate,
> Which for its pleasure doth create
> The things it may annihilate.

The Titan, endlessly punished for the crime of love, becomes for Byron, therefore, a symbol both for Byron's personal tragedy, and for the condition of men in general, perpetually punished by expulsion from whatever Edens of happiness and love they may briefly inhabit during the course of their lives.

He is a 'sign', Byron says,

> To Mortals of their fate and force;
> Like thee, Man is in part divine,
>   A troubled stream from a pure source;
> And Man in portions can foresee
> His own funereal destiny;
> His wretchedness, and his resistance,
> And his sad unallied existence.

At the same time, *Prometheus*, although it is a poem about man's perpetual defeat, is not one of resignation: the rather stagey defiance of the Byronic hero in its earlier manifestations has been transformed into a principle of god-like patience and courage.

'*Manfred*'

'Man's funereal destiny' is further explored in *Manfred*, the hero of which has much in common with Prometheus, except that 'the clankless chain' that binds him is the 'fleshy chain' of his own suffering mortality, doomed for ever to wish for and yet to fear death.

He too has the attributes of a god; like all men, Byron believes, he is 'half dust, half deity'. Like Prometheus, he is 'noble', and destined for great things. Like him, he possesses the capacity for knowledge and for love. But Manfred's love has wrought destruction, and the knowledge he has acquired has merely revealed that the 'star' of earth which was once

> . . . a world as fresh and fair
> As e'r revolved round sun in air

has become nothing more than

> A wandering mass of shapeless flame,
> A pathless comet, and a curse,
> The menace of the universe;
> Still rolling on with innate force,
> Without a sphere, without a course,
> A bright deformity on high,
> The monster of the upper sky!   (Act I, sc. 1)

Manfred presents the inexorable dilemma of man, as Byron sees it, in which the infinite human mind and the finite human heart are restlessly and eternally in conflict, the one destructive of the other, and each destructive of itself. The 'fatal flaw' which brings about the tragedy of Manfred is here not so much the moral guilt of a definite act of sin, as the guilt of being, as M. K. Joseph has put it, 'a member of the human race'.

As in *Prometheus*, the only really 'free' option open to the hero is that of patience and defiance, and to keep that free and untainted Manfred must, respectfully but firmly, reject the comfort and escape offered by religion in the form of the Abbot.

The vision of the human lot in *Manfred* could hardly be more pessimistic, but in the clash between the hero's awareness of the love and beauty that *might* have been – if Eden had lasted or really had existed – and the grim reality, a tension is generated that belongs to genuine tragedy. Once again, in fact, the point must be stressed that the despair is not a passive but an active one.

This is evident, above all, of course, in the verse itself. In *Manfred* Byron is no longer using a series of masks or alternative *personae*. The Byronic Byron is in full command, creating symbols and metaphors out of the heart of his experience. The greatest achievement of this stage of his development was to have produced out of the negative of despair the postive of vital poetry.

One other point needs to be made about *Manfred*. Its hero is very much the Byronic Byron *in extremis*, but there is a hint (in Act I, scene 2) of a possible alternative to despair, whereby man might come to 'breathe'

> The breath of degradation and of pride,
> Contending with low wants and lofty will,
> Till our mortality predominates,
> And men are – what they name not to themselves,
> And trust not to each other.

In other words, man may bring himself to surrender the cherished illusion of the dominion of his mind, and the divinity of his heart, accept his mortality, and attempt to live in the world on its own terms. It is an alternative that Manfred indignantly rejects. But these lines perhaps look forward to *Don Juan*, where the vision of the world of men is no less disenchanted but is accepted with less stress, more humour and infinitely more compassion.

'Cain: A Mystery'

It is in *Cain* that Byron most directly tackles the myth that meant so much to him. Contemporary opinion was divided on the value of the 'Mystery', as Byron subtitled it. Sir Walter Scott believed that Byron had 'matched Milton on his own ground'. Shelley, too, compared Byron to Milton, declaring that '*Cain* contains finer poetry than has appeared in England since the publication of *Paradise Regained*', while Goethe wrote of Byron's 'burning spiritual vision', which 'penetrates beyond all comprehension into the past and the present'.

On the other hand the more orthodox were shocked and horrified. It is easy to see why, for whereas Manfred does at least behave respectfully to the Abbot as God's representative, there is no such concession in *Cain*, which calls in question the edicts of God, and by implication the whole moral basis of the universe.

Cain's crime in killing his brother Abel is not condoned, but it is represented as an almost inevitable consequence of the lot imposed on man after his expulsion from the Garden of Eden – far more so than as a result of Satan's intervention. In a sense, too, our sympathies are engaged with Cain from the moment when, in his first soliloquy, he challenges the justice of a God who brings suffering, evil and death to mankind:

>   Because
> He is all-powerful, must all-good, too, follow?
> I judge by the fruits – and they are bitter.

The injustice, moreover, is seen by Cain – admittedly on the demonstration of Lucifer – as existing on a cosmic scale. When Lucifer takes him on a kind of conducted tour through Space and Time, he shows him not only that other beings, infinitely more beautiful and powerful than man, have lived – and died – in the past (thereby further emphasising man's own littleness and mortality), but also that a whole series of Edens have, apparently, been mockingly created only in order to be destroyed.

Lucifer, indeed, claims that he and his followers have more in common with mankind than has God himself:

> . . . at least we sympathise –
> And, suffering in concert, make our pangs
> Innumerable more endurable,
> By the unbounded sympathy of all
> With all!

The words of Lucifer, it is true, can be seen as part of Cain's 'temptation'. It is made clear, too, that the free-ranging power of the mind that he represents is ultimately worthless, because knowledge only reveals the devastating truth about the nature of things and 'mortal nature's nothingness'.

But the God who is supposed to represent love, Lucifer argues to a receptive Cain, has nothing better to offer. On the contrary, he is an 'Omnipotent tyrant', jealous, vengeful, destructive, power-hungry, and by no means the representative of pure goodness. What is more, he is just as wretched as Lucifer and mankind themselves:

> He is great –
> But in his greatness, no happier than
> We in our conflict: Goodness would not make
> Evil; and what else hath he made?

God and Lucifer alike, that is, are no more than the state of man – heart and intellect – writ large, in cosmic and eternal terms.

Cain is not a statement of atheism, as Byron's contemporary critics declared: Byron does not doubt the existence of God, but it is not a God of whom he can approve, and we are left in little doubt that the accusations of Lucifer are substantially Byron's own. It is impossible to speak of anything approaching a spark of religious or any other comfort in connection with

Cain. The most that can be said is that it contains the same two points around which defiance and vitality can perhaps coalesce that we noted in *Manfred*. The first is the principle of creativity. For God in *Cain* is equated with the poet, in that he, too, is driven to continuous creation out of destruction and chaos –

> to make eternity
> Less burthensome to his immense existence
> And unparticipated solitude.

The second is that the 'alternative' which was contemptuously touched on in *Manfred*, exists here too, in that Cain at the end of the play apparently accepts the fate which God imposes on him, even though it implies the slavery and 'degradation' which Manfred proudly rejected, and even though it means that he is driven farther than ever from the Eden which his parents Adam and Eve once inhabited, into an exile of even greater wretchedness, which he knows will be perpetuated through his offspring.

'Childe Harold's Pilgrimage'

When once we realise that Byron offers us a unified vision, no matter how pessimistic, of man's condition, we realise that his poetry exists in its own right, quite apart from the accidents of time and place which push his life, personality, and topical significance so obtrusively into the foreground.

We can see, for example, that *Childe Harold's Pilgrimage* is much more than a collection of theatrical gestures or a glorified guidebook. It, too, is an exploration of his basic and universal theme. Fundamentally Childe Harold is a symbol of modern man expelled from an Eden which was in any case (as we have seen from *Cain*) doomed from the start, to wander lost and alienated through the world. This does not mean that the political and social factors already discussed in relation to *Childe Harold* were not powerfully at work at one level of Byron's consciousness: indeed his concept of the 'lost Eden' has itself a political connotation, in the sense that the world he lived in was, like our own, becoming increasingly ugly and materialistic, inevitably producing a dream of some earlier society, before the advent of the new economic and industrial changes and the new political forces attending them, which was more stable, more civilised and gentler. It is this, perhaps, that led the French writer Lamartine to describe *Childe Harold* as 'the only epic possible in our day'.

When, however, we approach the poem from the angle of Byron's unifed vision, Byron's use of what are virtually three narrators in the earlier Cantos (Harold, the man who narrates his adventures and comments on them, and the poet himself), and their gradual merging into one single voice, can be seen as a search for a form in which to express his vision and as the gradual formulation of the vision itself.

This matter of the different 'voices' in *Childe Harold* is important because it explains some at least of the shrillness and false rhetoric in the first two Cantos: for like a ventriloquist Byron was there trying out his various 'voices', throwing them hither and thither along an experimental scale.

The movement towards his final purpose is tentative and slow in these first two Cantos, though the central theme of man's expulsion from an illusory Eden is quite clearly adumbrated on a number of occasions – as when in the first Canto we are told that Childe Harold had a 'past' which he loved, 'Or dreamed he loved, since Rapture is a dream' – and the whole panorama against which the theme is to work itself out is laid before us, including the backgrounds of nature and history (especially ancient history), sometimes as symbols of the 'lost Eden' and sometimes as possible avenues of temporary escape from too painful a consciousness of man's condition.

The third Canto deepens and enriches the central theme. It was composed, as we have seen, during the first heat of Byron's disgrace and exile, when out of the depths of his personal unhappiness he was struggling to dredge up some elements of hope and renewal – as in the passage which opens with the lines:

> I live not in myself, but I become
> Portion of that around me . . .

But we must realise that this is the reverse of a Wordsworthian tranquility and assurance: Byron knows that, for him, escape can only be achieved at the expense of hardening his heart and losing part of his humanity, a humanity which is synonymous with suffering. Whether he likes it or not he is still: 'A link reluctant in a fleshy chain'. The whole passage is scattered with question-marks, which serve to underline the doubt lying behind it. The moment of union with nature is illusory. Far from being Wordsworth's 'nurse, comforter and friend' she remains in the last resort cold and aloof, a constant reminder of man's mortality and littleness.

In this Canto, in fact, landscape is being used more and more powerfully as a source of imagery to illustrate man's dilemma. So too, it is important to realise, are places and their historical and biographical associations. Napoleon in defeat, for example, 'Conqueror *and* Captive of the Earth', is just as much a symbol for Harold or Byron the poet or universal man, as he is a historical portrait.

Nothing could be farther from the truth than the gibe which has been directed against *Childe Harold* that it is a 'verse Baedeker'. It is true that Canto the Fourth describes with great vividness and a wealth of detail some of the most famous 'sights' in Italy, together with their historical and cultural associations, and 'anidmadversions' upon them, superficially in the manner of the old writers of 'topographical poetry', such as the Elizabethan Edmund Spenser in his poem *The Ruines of Time*. M. K. Joseph is certainly right when he says that the theme of the Canto is 'the traditional one of lament for lost empire and for the decay of love, of the triumph of time over human mortality'. But what is not at all conventional, and is often overlooked, is that in depicting these famous sites Byron is really employing a new kind of imagery: the treasures of Italian art, the monuments of Italy's former greatness, and the ruins of the past (particularly those of Rome) constitute a landscape of the mind and heart as surely as the Alps had done in the Third Canto of *Childe Harold* or in *Manfred*. But the identification has become more complete – partly, perhaps, because Harold has now practically faded away. The poet Byron absorbs, and is absorbed into the scenes he describes: he is himself, he says, a 'ruin amidst the ruins'.

This does not make for any more optimistic a conclusion, and there are none of the conventional 'consolations' usual in this kind of poetry. The ruins of a vanished glory are, given Byron's overriding sense of loss and rejection, only too apt a symbol for the 'vanity of human wishes' (to borrow the title of a poem by Dr Johnson which Byron much admired) and of the endless cycle of hope and disillusion he envisaged.

At the same time the Canto does convey the message that the assertion of man's unconquerable spirit can not only enable him to endure its desolation but can, in the words of Professor Gleckner, 'create out of universal death and chaos a coherent vision of fragments sufficient to sustain man in his dying' and it is this that makes Canto the Fourth an impressive climax and summing-up to the poem as a whole.

'Don Juan'

It also brings it close to *Don Juan*. Modern critics sometimes write as if Byron wasted the whole of his creative life until suddenly he discovered the *ottava rima* and, hey presto! everything was changed. But *Don Juan* is *not* a work written in isolation: it is, on the contrary, the culmination of a process which began with the juvenile poems, and an integral part of it. It is quite true, of course, that it is frequently very funny, but in stressing the comic-satiric aspects of the poem critics have tended to overlook the fact that at its centre lies the same grim vision of man's destiny that motivates all Byron's work – 'Men', he writes in Canto Nine, 'are but maggots of some huge Earth's burial'. Much of the laughter in *Don Juan* is, in consequence, of the kind that lies close to tragedy, the kind of laughter we afford to Rosencrantz and Guildenstern in *Hamlet* or to the Fool in *King Lear*.

It is quite true, too, that in many ways *Don Juan* is a work of resolution, almost of reconciliation: it gathers up all the previous lines of development – personal, literary, social, historical, political; and it absorbs all the various Byronic *personae* – the actor and poseur, the lover, the cynic, the idealist, the satirist, the lyricist, the Romantic dreamer, the man of action – and the Byronic Byron.

It is a great mistake, in fact, to assume that the Byronic Byron has disappeared from *Don Juan*, or that he has been completely absorbed into, or been replaced by, the young hero of the poem. He is very much in evidence in his own right, and he performs a vital creative function. Sometimes, of course, he is used for purely ironical or comic effects, as when passages of rhetoric, lush description, stagey melancholy, or Romantic over-indulgence are built up merely in order to be demolished by a caustic aside, or a sudden change of step into cynicism, stark realism or bawdry – and indeed Don Juan's 'pilgrimage' can itself be seen as in part an ironic commentary on that of Childe Harold.

But at other times the whole point is that the kind of poetry we associate with the Byronic Byron – in direct contrast to the prevailing tone of *Don Juan* – simply *must* be allowed to exist in its own right. The most obvious example is the Haidée interlude, which occupies the greater part of Cantos II, III, and IV, and which is Byronic Byron at its most fluent and romantic. It is not, however, meant primarily as an ironic contrast, though it is that as well. First and foremost it is a separate entity, an organic whole within an organic whole; for it represents one of Byron's most sustained and wholehearted evocations of the ideal vision – indeed the earlier passages are full of echoes from the descriptions of Adam and Eve in the Garden of Eden in the fourth book of Milton's *Paradise Lost* – which haunted Byron all his life and which he could never entirely abandon. He *means* this interlude to be both long and in a different key from the rest of *Don Juan* in order to register its concrete reality as a myth that is imperishable in the sense that it is for ever recurring in men's imaginations, while at the same time also meaning to end it with calculated abruptness, in order to convey his bitter sense of its impermanence or unattainability in terms of actual realisation and to plunge it, and us with it, once more into the destructive welter of violent and random reality.

The 'Isles of Greece' stanzas in Canto Three are of a similar nature, in that Ancient Greece was always for Byron one of the symbols of a nobler and purer past, a myth almost of a

Golden Age, to be contrasted immediately with the sordid reality of a present in which the Greeks were frequently, he felt, opportunists, cowards and slaves.

Byron's Versification

Long-range Effects

The sharp decline in the reputation of the Byronic Byron, as opposed to the Byron of *Don Juan* and the satires, began in the latter half of the nineteenth century. To Victorian critics and writers, with their strong views about 'pure' art and poetry, the characteristic verse methods of the Byronic Byron seemed slapdash and sadly lacking in 'craftsmanship'.

That there are serious defects cannot be denied; Byron's poetry *is* frequently crude, banal, and over-rhetorical. But there is a certain type of writer to whom the close focus of verbal analysis is not entirely applicable, and who demands the approach of the long shot and the wide-angled lens. It is a rare type, but Byron belongs to it; one at least of the Victorian poets, Swinburne, understood this when he suggested that Byron 'can only be judged and appreciated in the mass; the greatness of his work was his whole work taken together'.

Imagery

As we have already seen, many of the longer passages are in effect extended metaphors (Ancient Greece, or Napoleon, or the ruins of Rome, for example). Indeed the Byronic Byron as a whole is of this order, in so far as it is a protracted, organic image – living, changing, developing – of a certain kind of hero and of a certain kind of response to experience.

Within these extended metaphors, the smaller ones, if we look at them in isolation, often seem trite and vulgar; but caught up in the greater wholes to which they belong their defects somehow do not seem so noticeable. In the stanzas describing the battlefield of Waterloo in Canto III of *Childe Harold*, for example, rhetorical expressions like 'Earthquake's spoil' for the

French dead who, like Napoleon's hopes, are 'sepulchred below'; or the 'red rain' of blood that has made 'the harvest grow', strike one as forced and stale, but within the total image of the battle (which is in its turn part of Byron's overall vision of chaos and anarchy) they play their part and even contribute by their very stridency to the general cacophony.

Their 'badness', moreover, recedes even further – something like the rather boring catalogues of weapons and strategies in Homer's *Iliad* – if we can regard *Childe Harold's Pilgrimage* as basically symphonic or epic in structure.

This does not mean that all Byron's individual images are unsuccessful. They are at their best, though, when they partake of the same nature as the long-range imagery; when, in fact, they are microcosms of it, informed with the same restlessness and spaciousness.

The most obvious imagery of this kind is that related to the sea. Byron turns to the sea to express a whole range of moods, some tranquil but most of them stormy. Above all, he uses the sea to communicate his feelings – and those of suffering humanity in general – of violent loss and rejection, as when, in the third Canto of *Childe Harold*, he says:

> for I am as a weed,
> Flung from the rock, on Ocean's foam to sail
> Where'er the surge may sweep, the tempest breath prevail.

The imagery of the sea is often combined with that of ruin and wreckage, as when in the Fourth Canto of *Childe Harold* he wonders whether 'from the floating wreck which Ruin leaves behind' he might 'from the planks far shatter'd o'er the sea' build for himself 'a little bark of hope', in which he may be able once more

> To battle with the ocean and the shocks
> Of the loud breakers, and the ceaseless roar
> Which rushes on the solitary shore
> Where all lies founder'd that was ever dear.

Byron employs mountain scenery in much the same way. Occasionally it represents the brief intervals of calm, in which he imagines he can lose himself in Nature. But for the most part mountains are either symbols of icy indifference, or they form a background to the more violent manifestations of Nature – winds, storm-tossed clouds, torrents and so on. Thus we have, in Canto Four of *Childe Harold*, the 'banner' of Freedom streaming 'like a thunder-storm *against* the wind'. In *Mazeppa* the wild horse is like the 'torrents', and phrases like 'the lightning of the mind' frequently occur in Byron's poetry. The mountain eagle, too, figures as a symbol of defiance when Byron says (in Canto Three of *Childe Harold*) that he will

> . . . remount at last
> With a fresh pinion.

Fire, in one aspect or another, usually stands for man's defiance, aspiration or daring, or for the turmoil in the poet's mind. Thus the 'annals of Italy' (in Canto Four of *Childe Harold*) are 'graved in characters of flame'; love, the Giaour declares is 'a spark' from the 'immortal fire' of Heaven, and his own love

> . . . like the lava flood
> That boils in Aetna's breast of flame.

Man's higher aspirations and his defiance of God's decrees are also expressed in more cosmic terms: there are images of chaos, comets, meteors and planets in *Manfred*, for example. These images of fire, heat, light and cosmic phenomena are often brought into contrast with those derived from cold, ice, dust, earth, and especially clay (the Spirits, for example, speak of Manfred's 'condemmed clay').

There are many juxtapositions of life and death, growth and decay. Writing of the death of Freedom, for example, Byron says:

> Thy tree hath lost its blossoms, and the rind,
> Chopp'd by the axe, looks rough and little worth,
> But the sap lasts – and still the seed we find
> Sown deep, even in the bosom of the North;
> So shall a better spring less bitter fruit bring forth.

As this quotation with its reference to the trees of Know-ledge and Eternal Life indicates, and as we might expect from what has been said about Byron's preoccupation, imagery derived from the Bible story of the Garden of Eden often appears. In the same group of stanzas, for example, Byron suggests that the tyrannical actions of Napoleon were dis-honestly exploited by the Great Powers who overthrew him – and

Are grown the pretext for the eternal thrall
Which nips life's tree, and dooms man's worst – his second fall.

A number of other images bear on this central theme of Byron's. Mirrors, for instance, often signify man's state of unsullied innocence, but as often as not they are then 'shattered' or 'distorted'. And man's wretched outcast condition is often described in terms of prisons, dungeons, or chains.

In other contexts the 'light' or 'fire' of life and hope are placed in contrast to images derived from darkness, frost, ice, deserts, decomposition, and the blight on fruit or foliage. 'Blood' can be used both in 'good' and 'bad' contexts, and sometimes it is combined with expressions of disgust: France, for example, Byron says, 'got drunk on blood to vomit crime'.

Man's baser instincts are often symbolised by animals – wolves, bears, tigers, hyenas and so on – or by insects. Grief and bitterness, for example, are frequently compared to 'the scorpion's sting'. Man's lowly status in the scheme of things is that of the 'worm' (as on several occasions in *Manfred*). The vanity or frailty of human hopes are conveyed in similar terms: thus Childe Harold before he sets sail from England (in the first Canto),

... bask'd him in the noontide sun
Disporting there like any other fly.

In *The Giaour* Byron chooses the rare and beautiful blue-winged butterfly of Kashmir ('the insect queen of eastern spring'), which leads 'the young pursuer' on a 'weary chase' from 'flower to flower' as a symbol of the futility of the pursuit of love and beauty:

A chase of idle hopes and fears,
Begun in Folly, closed in tears.

Nearly all Byron's images, it will be seen, bear in one way or another on his central theme of exile and loss. And however stale they may seem taken in isolation they are also all of them living fragments of the Byron world.

Methods of Composition

If Byron was not the kind of artist who goes in for carefully chiselled details that does not mean that he was not an artist at all. Recent research, in fact, has thoroughly discounted the old idea (encouraged by Byron himself, who liked to pretend that he was a mere aristocratic dilettante) that he did not take pains with his work.

Those who criticise him for unsatisfactory results in the details without taking account of the whole to which they belong have completely misunderstood the kind of artist he was. In this connection there are some very revealing comments in his letters. In one of them he dismissed 'descriptive poetry' as 'the lowest development of the arts'. Now at first sight this seems surprising, coming as it does from a poet who wrote so much about 'places', but not so surprising when we reflect that none of Byron's set pieces – Lake Leman, say, in Canto Three of *Childe Harold*, or Venice, Florence or Rome in Canto Four – have any resemblance to descriptive or genre painting. They are, in fact, the very opposite to still life studies for the simple reason that they are never still: they are, on the contrary, continually being thrown into violent agitation by the poet's comments, reflections, moods and personality.

Another of Byron's remarks can be seen as even more revealing: 'If I miss my first spring I go growling back to my jungle.' Byron's natural method of composition was to write straight out from the core of his imaginative experience, and if he did not succeed he had no patience with chipping away in the hope of effecting surface improvements: he preferred either to abandon the attempt or to start all over again. Most of the alterations to his manuscripts came when he was already sure of the overall theme he was aiming at, and they were made with his eye on that goal rather than on the actual detail under his hand at the moment.

In this he reminds one of D. H. Lawrence who, if he was dissatisfied with the first draft of a novel, would usually put it aside and start all over again from the beginning, instead of struggling to recast and remould. In this way Lawrence felt he would not be interfering with the spontaneous flow of his imagination and emotions, and Byron is in some ways like him in this respect. In Lawrence's case too, it is often unfair to judge by passages taken in isolation.

Energy

There is one quality which even Byron's most hostile critics allow him – that of energy. It is a quality which nowadays tends to be underestimated: nevertheless it is an essential quality of all great poetry.

Byron's friend and fellow-poet, Shelley, said that Byron's poetry was like his talk, 'a stream, sometimes smooth, sometimes, rapid and sometimes rushing down in cataracts'. It may be a helpful idea to extend this image of Shelley's and imagine the 'stream' of which he spoke carrying along in its headlong course all kinds of boulders and pebbles, as well as mud and silt. In much the same way the impetus of Byron's energy often carries along the cruder elements in his poetry, throwing them into violent motion, and quite often the *movement* is more important than the separate components, often itself constituting the real 'meaning'.

Byron's Narrative Poetry

Naturally enough, this quality of energy makes Byron a superb narrative poet. It is energy, moreover, that is always carefully controlled and modulated in the interests of the story. It is not only that Byron keeps the plot moving at an exciting pace – even when, in *The Prisoner of Chillon*, the characters are chained in a dungeon. He has also a remarkable gift of keeping his story mobile, concrete and sensuous. Thus when there is a passage of philosophical reflection, it is supported by precise, particularised images and definite references. There is, for example, the passage in *The Giaour* we have already mentioned where the hero reflects on his lost love:

> Yes, Love indeed is light from Heaven,
> A spark from that immortal fire
> With angels shared, by Allah given,
> To lift from earth our low desire.
> Devotion wafts the mind above,
> But Heaven itself descends in love;
> A feeling from the Godhead caught,
> To wean from self each sordid thought:
> A Ray of him who form'd the whole;
> A Glory circling round the soul!

And this is immediately followed by the specific, personal reference:

> I grant my love imperfect, all
> That mortals by that name miscall . . .

In the same way, the emotions of the characters are never given in isolation, but absorbed completely and vitally into the plot. The sensations and emotions of Mazeppa, for example, when he is strapped naked to the wild horse, are conveyed in such a way that we never for a moment forget the frantic galloping of the horse beneath him:

> The wood was past; 'twas more than noon,
> But chill the air, although in June;
> Or it might be my veins ran cold –
> Prolonged endurance tames the bold;
> And I was then not what I seem,
> But headlong as a wintry stream,
> And wore my feelings out before
> I well could count their causes o'er . . .

Narrative poetry is out of fashion nowadays, but surely (quite apart from the fact that they contain the characteristic Byronic theme of wasted youth) those lines are splendid writing by any standard. No wonder that Matthew Arnold said that Byron possessed 'a wonderful power of vividly conceiving a single incident, a single situation; of throwing himself upon it, of grasping it as if it were real and he saw and felt it, and of making us see and feel it too'.

Verse Forms and Experiments

In concentrating on *Beppo* and *Don Juan* critics sometimes overlook the fact that the Italian *ottava rima* which Byron adapted for their composition was only one of many verse forms which he employed. In point of fact there are very few poets, even among the Romantics, who experimented more than he did.

His types of verse include narrative, descriptive, satirical and lyrical poetry; romance, drama, monologue, epistle, ballad and song. *Childe Harold* is composed in an adaptation of the Spenserian stanza. The narrative poems use mostly the octosyllabic couplet or, more characteristically perhaps, Byron's very personal adaptation of the heroic couplet of Pope and the Augustans. *Cain* is written in blank verse. The songs and shorter pieces use a great variety of lyrical measures and metrical devices.

The Songs and Lyrics

The attitude towards Byron as a lyrical poet has been particularly contemptuous. Thus Ernest de Selincourt declared that Byron always employed a 'familiar, hackneyed tune', and Herbert Grierson wrote: 'There are no gems of flawless art and felicitous beauty in Byron's poems. His flowers, such as they are, wither when gathered.'

There is some truth in these complaints. Byron was too fond, another critic has said, of the 'dactyllic beat', a metrical foot consisting of one long followed by two short syllables or beats, which does produce a 'dum-de-de-dum-de-de' effect. All the same it is difficult to reconcile these opinions to poems like *There Be None of Beauty's Daughters*, *When We Two Parted*, and *So, We'll Go No More A Roving* – the last of which in particular has a wry sadness and realism that puts it among the best lyrics of the period.

35

The mention of these poems is a reminder that their methods are in a different tradition from that of most of the lyrics of the Romantic Revival. Byron's natural poetic predilections were for the Augustans (as the poets of the 'classical' eighteenth century were known); his lyrics have a good deal in common with those of Dryden, and through Dryden with those of seventeenth-century poets such as Ben Jonson and Marvell. In consequence their language and imagery are more rounded and classically formed, and their effects more like bell-notes – very different from the fluid, breathless music of Shelley, for example. They have what Herbert Read called 'an explicit felicity', and a way, he says, of deliberately using 'the obvious cliché' to telling effect.

There are plenty of examples of this in *There Be None of Beauty's Daughters*: obvious phrases such as 'like music on the waters', and Augustan epithets, as in 'sweet voice', 'charmed ocean', which nevertheless do not produce a banal overall effect. The overall effect, indeed, is just as important in Byron's lyrics as in his other poetry. So, too, is the energy, and quite often what binds the various elements together is a kind of impressioned rhetoric.

Rhetoric is a poetic device which is very much frowned on nowadays, though it was a compulsory study for the Elizabethan, Jacobean and Augustan poets and is still understood and practised by continental poets; this may be one of the reasons why Byron ranks higher in foreign estimation than he usually does in ours. If it comes to that, rhetoric is still understood by ordinary people in this country. The exciting drum-beat of *The Destruction of Sennacherib*, for example, has appealed to generations of schoolboys and others who have come new to poetry, though they have tried to repress their liking of it because their teachers usually tell them that it is 'crude' and 'vulgar'.

But rhetoric does not necessarily mean lack of content, and if we look more closely at this poem – as often happens with the Byronic Byron – we find that it is deeper and more subtle than the first hypnotic gallop through would suggest. For one thing, it is curiously ambivalent in its attitudes and in the

36

responses it invites. The stirring rhythms make one feel that one is caught up in the Assyrian army, charging with them to glorious victory – but this of course is dead against the moral and religious drift, for the Assyrians are the enemies of the Lord, and we should be on *his* side, not theirs. Then again, most of the beauty, colour, brightness, life – the 'purple and gold' the 'sheen of the spears', the 'green' of the summer forest, and so on – are applied to the 'bad' Assyrians, and they are quickly swallowed up in images of horror, destruction and desolation – 'wither'd and strown', 'the eyes of the sleepers wax'd deadly and chill', 'cold as the spray of the rock-beating surf' – all of them the work of the Lord. The contrast between the stir of pride and vitality represented by the Assyrians, and the dead desolate landscape achieved by the Lord, together with the tug between our imaginative sympathies and our conventional reactions, creates, in other words, a genuine ironic tension – one which, as we have seen, underlies the whole of Byron's attitude towards the Almighty.

The surface movement of the poem is so rapid and dramatic that we are not always aware of these underlying tensions, but in fact they exist in nearly all of Byron's lyrics. Contrary to what many modern critics have concluded, in fact, they *will* stand up to the kind of analysis they advocate as the only worthwhile approach to poetry.

Conclusions

The picture of devastation in *The Destruction of Sennacherib* brings us back to Byron's essential greatness – his struggle, fierce, sometimes desperate but always courageous, to make some sort of sense out of a world which, it seemed to him, was utterly 'out of joint'. This attitude to the world is, of course, the exact opposite of that of Shelley and other Romantics, who believed passionately in the 'perfectibility' of mankind. In fact much of Byron's work can be seen not as anti-Romantic, but rather as the reverse side of the coin of Romanticism. He was not the only one, of course, to give expression to its negative aspects: 'diabolism', or the rejection of God and the elevation of evil, for example, became a popular fashion in the later stages of the Romantic Movement. The great difference between Byron and the poets of the Romantic decadence, however, is that in spite of his fondness for melodrama, Byron never surrendered to these negative elements or pretended that they were other than they are: on the contrary he made use of them in order to rise above them and to construct something that is ultimately vital and positive.

It is for this reason that Byron still has a tremendous relevance for the twentieth century. It is significant that James Joyce introduced Childe Harold, the Giaour, and other creations of the Byronic Byron into the complex network of *Finnegan's Wake*, itself a parable of a chaotic and disorientated world. For Joyce saw in these characters, and especially in Childe Harold (whom he more or less identifies with 'Everyman') prototypes of modern man, wandering exiled and lost in an anarchic universe. And Byron's world is that of Joyce, as it is that of the W. B. Yeats who wrote:

> Things fall apart; the centre cannot hold,
> Mere anarchy is loosed upon the world.

Or that of the T. S. Eliot who wrote in *The Waste Land*: 'These fragments I have shored against my ruin', and one of whose characters cries out in despair:

> I can connect
> Nothing with nothing.

Or that of the Samuel Beckett who pushes homelessness and exile to its farthest limits of deprivation and nullity.

The Byronic Byron is indeed relevant to all those writers of the modern waste land who struggle to give form and coherence to its apparent fragmentation and meaninglessness.

Damætas

In law an infant, and in years a boy,
In mind a slave to every vicious joy;
From every sense of shame and virtue wean'd;
In lies an adept, in deceit a fiend;
Versed in hypocrisy, while yet a child;
Fickle as wind, of inclinations wild;
Woman his dupe, his heedless friend a tool;
Old in the world, though scarcely broke from school;
Damætas ran through all the maze of sin,
10 And found the goal when others just begin:
Even still conflicting passions shake his soul,
And bid him drain the dregs of pleasure's bowl:
But, pall'd with vice, he breaks his former chain,
And what was once his bliss appears his bane.

I would I were a careless child

I would I were a careless child,
   Still dwelling in my Highland cave,
Or roaming through the dusky wild,
   Or bounding o'er the dark blue wave;
The cumbrous pomp of Saxon pride
   Accords not with the freeborn soul,
Which loves the mountain's craggy side,
   And seeks the rocks where billows roll.

Fortune! take back these cultured lands,
10   Take back this name of splendid sound!
I hate the touch of servile hands,
   I hate the slaves that cringe around.

Place me among the rocks I love,
    Which sound to Ocean's wildest roar;
I ask but this – again to rove
    Through scenes my youth hath known before.

Few are my years, and yet I feel
    The world was ne'er design'd for me:
Ah! why do dark'ning shades conceal
20   The hour when man must cease to be?
Once I beheld a splendid dream,
    A visionary scene of bliss:
Truth! – wherefore did thy hated beam
    Awake me to a world like this?

I loved – but those I loved are gone;
    Had friends – my early friends are fled:
How cheerless feels the heart alone,
    When all its former hopes are dead!
Though gay companions o'er the bowl
30   Dispel awhile the sense of ill;
Though pleasure stirs the maddening soul,
    The heart – the heart – is lonely still.

How dull! to hear the voice of those
    Whom rank or chance, whom wealth or power,
Have made, though neither friends nor foes,
    Associates of the festive hour.
Give me again a faithful few,
    In years and feelings still the same,
And I will fly the midnight crew,
40   Where boist'rous joy is but a name.

And woman, lovely woman! thou,
My hope, my comforter, my all!
How cold must be my bosom now,
When e'en thy smiles begin to pall!
Without a sigh would I resign
This busy scene of splendid woe,
To make that calm contentment mine,
Which virtue knows, or seems to know.

Fain would I fly the haunts of men –
50   I seek to shun, not hate mankind;
My breast requires the sullen glen,
Whose gloom may suit a darken'd mind.
Oh! that to me the wings were given
Which bear the turtle to her nest!
Then would I cleave the vault of heaven,
To flee away, and be at rest.

Childe Harold's Pilgrimage

from CANTO THE FIRST

[Farewell to England]

I

Oh, thou! in Hellas deem'd of heavenly birth,
Muse! form'd or fabled at the minstrel's will!
Since shamed full oft by later lyres on earth,
Mine dares not call thee from thy sacred hill:
Yet there I've wander'd by thy vaunted rill;
Yes! sigh'd o'er Delphi's long deserted shrine,
Where, save that feeble fountain, all is still;
Nor mote my shell awake the weary Nine
To grace so plain a tale – this lowly lay of mine.

II

10   Whilome in Albion's isle there dwelt a youth,
Who ne in virtue's ways did take delight;
But spent his days in riot most uncouth,
And vex'd with mirth the drowsy ear of Night.
Ah me! in sooth he was a shameless wight,
Sore given to revel and ungodly glee;
Few earthly things found favour in his sight
Save concubines and carnal companie,
And flaunting wassailers of high and low degree.

III

Childe Harold was he hight: – but whence his name
20   And lineage long, it suits me not to say;
Suffice it, that perchance they were of fame,
And had been glorious in another day:

But one sad losel soils a name for aye,
However mighty in the olden time;
Nor all that heralds rake from coffin'd clay,
Nor florid prose, nor honeyed lies of rhyme,
Can blazon evil deeds, or consescrate a crime.

IV

Childe Harold bask'd him in the noontide sun,
Disporting there like any other fly;
30 Nor deem'd before his little day was done
One blast might chill him into misery.
But long ere scarce a third of his pass'd by,
Worse than adversity the Childe befell;
He felt the fulness of satiety:
Then loathed he in his native land to dwell,
Which seem'd to him more lone than Eremite's sad cell.

V

For he through Sin's long labyrinth had run,
Nor made atonement when he did amiss,
Had sigh'd to many though he loved but one,
40 And that loved one, alas! could ne'er be his.
Ah, happy she! to 'scape from him whose kiss
Had been pollution unto aught so chaste;
Who soon had left her charms for vulgar bliss,
And spoil'd her goodly lands to gild his waste,
Nor calm domestic peace had ever deign'd to taste.

VI

And now Childe Harold was sore sick at heart,
And from his fellow bacchanals would flee;
'Tis said, at times the sullen tear would start,
But Pride congeal'd the drop within his ee:
50 Apart he stalk'd in joyless reverie,

43

And from his native land resolved to go,
And visit scorching climes beyond the sea;
With pleasure drugg'd, he almost long'd for woe,
And e'en for change of scene would seek the shades
    below.

VII

The Childe departed from his father's hall:
It was a vast and venerable pile;
So old, it seemed only not to fall,
Yet strength was pillar'd in each massy aisle.
Monastic dome! condemn'd to uses vile!
60   Where Superstition once had made her den
Now Paphian girls were known to sing and smile;
And monks might deem their time was come agen,
If ancient tales say true, nor wrong these holy men.

VIII

Yet oft-times in his maddest mirthful mood
Strange pangs would flash along Childe Harold's brow,
As if the memory of some deadly feud
Or disappointed passion lurk'd below:
But this none knew, nor haply cared to know;
For his was not that open, artless soul
70   That feels relief by bidding sorrow flow,
Nor sought he friend to counsel or condole,
Whate'er this grief mote be, which he could not control.

IX

And none did love him: though to hall and bower
He gather'd revellers from far and near,
He knew them flatt'rers of the festal hour;
The heartless parasites of present cheer.
Yea! none did love him – not his lemans dear –

But pomp and power alone are woman's care,
And where these are light Eros finds a feere;
80   Maidens, like moths, are ever caught by glare,
And Mammon wins his way where Seraphs might
     despair.

X

Childe Harold had a mother – not forgot,
Though parting from that mother he did shun;
A sister whom he loved, but saw her not
Before his weary pilgrimage begun:
If friends he had, he bade adieu to none.
Yet deem not thence his breast a breast of steel:
Ye, who have known what 'tis to dote upon
A few dear objects, will in sadness feel
90 Such partings break the heart they fondly hope to heal.

XI

His house, his home, his heritage, his lands,
The laughing dames in whom he did delight,
Whose large blue eyes, fair locks, and snowy hands,
Might shake the saintship of an anchorite,
And long had fed his youthful appetite;
His goblets brimm'd with every costly wine,
And all that mote to luxury invite,
Without a sigh he left, to cross the brine,
And traverse Paynim shores, and pass Earth's central
     line.

XII

100 The sails were fill'd, and fair the light winds blew,
As glad to waft him from his native home;
And fast the white rocks faded from his view,
And soon were lost in circumambient foam:
And then, it may be, of his wish to roam

45

Repented he, but in his bosom slept
The silent thought, nor from his lips did come
One word of wail, whilst others sate and wept,
And to the reckless gales unmanly moaning kept.

XIII

But when the sun was sinking in the sea
110   He seized his harp, which he at times could string,
And strike, albeit with untaught melody,
When deem'd he no strange ear was listening:
And now his fingers o'er it he did fling,
And tuned his farewell in the dim twilight.
While flew the vessel on her snowy wing,
And fleeting shores receded from his sight,
Thus to the elements he pour'd his last 'Good Night.'

I

Adieu, adieu! my native shore
   Fades o'er the waters blue;
120   The night-winds sigh, the breakers roar,
   And shrieks the wild sea-mew.
Yon sun that sets upon the sea
   We follow in his flight;
Farewell awhile to him and thee,
   My native Land – Good Night!

2

A few short hours and he will rise
   To give the morrow birth;
And I shall hail the main and skies,
   But not my mother earth.
130   Deserted is my own good hall,
   Its hearth is desolate;
Wild weeds are gathering on the wall;
   My dog howls at the gate.

46

3

'Come hither, hither, my little page!
   Why dost thou weep and wail?
Or dost thou dread the billows' rage,
   Or tremble at the gale?
But dash the tear-drop from thine eye;
   Our ship is swift and strong:
140 Our fleetest falcon scarce can fly
   More merrily along.'

4

'Let winds be shrill, let waves roll high,
   I fear not wave nor wind:
Yet marvel not, Sir Childe, that I
   Am sorrowful in mind;
For I have from my father gone,
   A mother whom I love,
And have no friend, save these alone,
   But thee – and one above.

5
150 'My father bless'd me fervently,
   Yet did not much complain;
But sorely will my mother sigh
   Till I come back again.' –
'Enough, enough, my little lad!
   Such tears become thine eye;
If I thy guileless bosom had,
   Mine own would not be dry.

6

'Come hither, hither, my staunch yeoman,
   Why dost thou look so pale?
160 Or dost thou dread a French foeman?
   Or shiver at the gale?' –

'Deem'st thou I tremble for my life?
    Sir Childe, I'm not so weak;
But thinking on an absent wife
    Will blanch a faithful cheek.

7

'My spouse and boys dwell near thy hall,
    Along the bordering lake,
And when they on their father call,
    What answer shall she make?' –
170   'Enough, enough, my yeoman good,
    Thy grief let none gainsay;
But I, who am of lighter mood,
    Will laugh to flee away.'

8

For who would trust the seeming sighs
    Of wife or paramour?
Fresh feeres will dry the bright blue eyes
    We late saw streaming o'er.
For pleasures past I do not grieve,
    Nor perils gathering near;
180   My greatest grief is that I leave
    No thing that claims a tear.

9

And now I'm in the world alone,
    Upon the wide, wide sea:
But why should I for others groan,
    When none will sigh for me?
Perchance my dog will whine in vain,
    Till fed by stranger hands;
But long ere I come back again
    He'd tear me where he stands.

48

10

190 With thee, my bark, I'll swiftly go
    Athwart the foaming brine;
Nor care what land thou bear'st me to,
    So not again to mine.
Welcome, welcome, ye dark-blue waves!
    And when you fail my sight,
Welcome, ye deserts and ye caves!
    My native Land – Good Night!

[Greeks Arise!]

from CANTO THE SECOND

LXXIII

Fair Greece! sad relic of departed worth!
Immortal, though no more; though fallen, great!
Who now shall lead thy scatter'd children forth,
And long accustom'd bondage uncreate?
Not such thy sons who whilome did await,
The hopeless warriors of a willing doom,
In bleak Thermopylæ's sepulchral strait –
Oh! who that gallant spirit shall resume,
Leap from Eurota's banks, and call thee from the tomb?

LXXIV

10 Spirit of freedom! when on Phyle's brow
Thou sat'st with Thrasybulus and his train,
Couldst thou forebode the dismal hour which now
Dims the green beauties of thine Attic plain?
Not thirty tyrants now enforce the chain,

But every carle can lord it o'er thy land;
Nor rise thy sons, but idly rail in vain,
Trembling beneath the scourge of Turkish hand;
From birth till death enslaved; in word, in deed,
    unmann'd.

LXXV

In all save form alone, how changed! and who
20   That marks the fire still sparkling in each eye,
Who would but deem their bosoms burn'd anew
With thy unquenched beam, lost Liberty!
And many dream withal the hour is nigh
That gives them back their fathers' heritage:
For foreign arms and aid they fondly sigh,
Nor solely dare encounter hostile rage,
Or tear their name defiled from Slavery's mournful page.

LXXVI

Hereditary bondsmen! know ye not
Who would be free themselves must strike the blow?
30   By their right arms the conquest must be wrought?
Will Gaul or Muscovite redress ye? no!
True, they may lay your proud despoilers low,
But not for you will Freedom's altars flame.
Shades of the Helots! triumph o'er your foe!
Greece! change thy lords, thy state is still the same;
Thy glorious day is o'er, but not thy years of shame.

[Lament for Greece – and Youth]

LXXXVIII

Where'er we tread 't is haunted, holy ground;
No earth of thine is lost in vulgar mould,
But one vast realm of wonder spreads around,
And all the Muse's tales seem truly told,

Till the sense aches with gazing to behold
The scenes our earliest dreams have dwelt upon;
Each hill and dale, each deepening glen and wold
Defies the power which crush'd thy temples gone:
Age shakes Athena's tower, but spares gray Marathon.

LXXXIX

10 The sun, the soil, but not the slave, the same;
Unchanged in all except its foreign lord;
Preserves alike its bounds and boundless fame
The Battle-field, where Persia's victim horde
First bow'd beneath the brunt of Hellas' sword,
As on the morn to distant Glory dear,
When Marathon became a magic word;
Which utter'd, to the hearer's eye appear
The camp, the host, the fight, the conqueror's career,

XC

The flying Mede, his shaftless broken bow;
20 The fiery Greek, his red pursuing spear;
Mountains above, Earth's, Ocean's plain below;
Death in the front, Destruction in the rear!
Such was the scene – what now remaineth here?
What sacred trophy marks the hallow'd ground,
Recording Freedom's smile and Asia's tear?
The rifled urn, the violated mound,
The dust thy courser's hoof, rude stranger! spurns around.

XCI

Yet to the remnants of thy splendour past
Shall pilgrims, pensive, but unwearied, throng;
30 Long shall the voyager, with th' Ionian blast,
Hail the bright clime of battle and of song;
Long shall thine annals and immortal tongue

Fill with thy fame the youth of many a shore;
Boast of the aged! lesson of the young!
Which sages venerate and bards adore,
As Pallas and the Muse unveil their awful lore.

XCII

The parted bosom clings to wonted home,
If aught that's kindred cheer the welcome hearth;
He that is lonely, hither let him roam,
40   And gaze complacent on congenial earth.
Greece is no lightsome land of social mirth:
But he whom Sadness sootheth may abide,
And scarce regret the region of his birth,
When wandering slow by Delphi's sacred side,
Or gazing o'er the plains where Greek and Persian died.

XCIII

Let such approach this consecrated land,
And pass in peace along the magic waste;
But spare its relics – let no busy hand
Deface the scenes, already how defaced!
50   Not for such purpose were these altars placed:
Revere the remnants nations once revered:
So may our country's name be undisgraced,
So may'st thou prosper where thy youth was rear'd,
By every honest joy of love and life endear'd!

XCIV

For thee, who thus in too protracted song
Hast soothed thine idlesse with inglorious lays,
Soon shall thy voice be lost amid the throng
Of louder minstrels in these later days:
To such resign the strife for fading bays –

52

60   Ill may such contests now the spirit move
       Which heeds nor keen reproach nor partial praise,
       Since cold each kinder heart that might approve,
And none are left to please when none are left to love.

XCV

     Thou too art gone, thou loved and lovely one!
       Whom youth and youth's affections bound to me;
       Who did for me what none beside have done,
       Nor shrank from one albeit unworthy thee.
       What is my being? thou hast ceased to be!
       Nor staid to welcome here thy wanderer home,
70   Who mourns o'er hours which we no more shall see –
       Would they had never been, or were to come!
Would he had ne'er return'd to find fresh cause to roam!

XCVI

     Oh! ever loving, lovely, and beloved!
       How selfish Sorrow ponders on the past,
       And clings to thoughts now better far removed!
       But Time shall tear thy shadow from me last.
       All thou couldst have of mine, stern Death! thou
         hast;
       The parent, friend, and now the more than friend;
       Ne'er yet for one thine arrows flew so fast,
80   And grief with grief continuing still to blend,
Hath snatch'd the little joy that life had yet to lend.

XCVII

     Then must I plunge again in to the crowd,
       And follow all that Peace disdains to seek?
       Where Revel calls, and Laughter, vainly loud,
       False to the heart, distorts the hollow cheek,
       To leave the flagging spirit doubly weak;

Still o'er the features, which perforce they cheer,
To feign the pleasure or conceal the pique?
Smiles form the channel of a future tear,
90   Or raise the writhing lip with ill-dissembled sneer.

XCVIII

What is the worst of woes that wait on age?
What stamps the wrinkle deeper on the brow?
To view each loved one blotted from life's page,
And be alone on earth, as I am now.
Before the Chastener humbly let me bow,
O'er hearts divided and o'er hopes destroy'd:
Roll on, vain days! full reckless may ye flow,
Since Time hath reft whate'er my soul enjoy'd,
And with the ills of Eld mine earlier years alloy'd.

from The Giaour:

A Fragment of a Turkish Tale

[Hymn to Liberty]

Clime of the unforgotten brave!
Whose land from plain to mountain-cave
Was Freedom's home or Glory's grave!
Shrine of the mighty! can it be,
That this is all remains of thee?
Approach, thou craven crouching slave:
   Say, is not this Thermopylæ?
These waters blue that round you lave, –
   Oh servile offspring of the free,
Pronounce what sea, what shore is this?
   The gulf, the rock of Salamis!
These scenes, their story not unknown,
Arise, and make again your own;
Snatch from the ashes of your sires
The embers of their former fires;
And he who in the strife expires
Will add to theirs a name of fear
That Tyranny shall quake to hear,
And leave his sons a hope, a fame,
They too will rather die than shame:
For Freedom's battle once begun,
Bequeath'd by bleeding Sire to Son,
Though baffled oft is ever won.
Bear witness, Greece, thy living page!
Attest it many a deathless age!
While kings, in dusty darkness hid,
Have left a nameless pyramid,

Thy heroes, though the general doom
Hath swept the column from their tomb,
A mightier monument command,
The mountains of their native land!
There points thy Muse to stranger's eye
The graves of those that cannot die!
'T were long to tell, and sad to trace,
Each step from splendour to disgrace;
Enough – no foreign foe could quell
Thy soul, till from itself it fell;
Yes! Self-abasement paved the way
To villain-bonds and despot sway.

['Who thundering comes']

Who thundering comes on blackest steed,
With slacken'd bit and hoof of speed?
Beneath the clattering iron's sound
The cavern'd echoes wake around
In lash for lash, and bound for bound;
The foam that streaks the courser's side
Seems gather'd from the ocean-tide:
Though weary waves are sunk to rest,
There's none within his rider's breast;
And though to-morrow's tempest lower,
'T is calmer than thy heart, young Giaour!
I know thee not, I loathe thy race,
But in thy lineaments I trace
What time shall strengthen, not efface:
Though young and pale, that sallow front

Is scathed by fiery passion's brunt;
Though bent on earth thine evil eye,
As meteor-like thou glidest by,
Right well I view and deem thee one
20 Whom Othman's sons should slay or shun.
  On – on he hasten'd, and he drew
My gaze of wonder as he flew:
Though like a demon of the night
He pass'd, and vanish'd from my sight,
His aspect and his air impress'd
A troubled memory on my breast,
And long upon my startled ear
Rung his dark courser's hoofs of fear.
He spurs his steed; he nears the steep,
30 That, jutting, shadows o'er the deep;
He winds around; he hurries by;
The rock relieves him from mine eye;
For well I ween unwelcome he
Whose glance is fix'd on those that flee;
And not a star but shines too bright
On him who takes such timeless flight.
He wound along; but ere he pass'd,
One glance he snatch'd, as if his last,
A moment check'd his wheeling steed,
40 A moment breathed him from his speed,
A moment on his stirrup stood –
Why looks he o'er the olive wood?
The crescent glimmers on the hill,
The Mosque's high lamps are quivering still;
Though too remote for sound to wake
In echoes of the far tophaike,
The flashes of each joyous peal
Are seen to prove the Moslem's zeal.
To-night, set Rhamazani's sun;
50 To-night, the Bairam feast's begun;

To-night – but who and what art thou
Of foreign garb and fearful brow?
And what are these to thine or thee,
That thou shouldst either pause or flee?

He stood – some dread was on his face,
Soon Hatred settled in its place:
It rose not with the reddening flush
Of transient Anger's hasty blush,
But pale as marble o'er the tomb,
60   Whose ghastly whiteness aids its gloom.
His brow was bent, his eye was glazed;
He raised his arm, and fiercely raised,
And sternly shook his hand on high,
As doubting to return or fly;
Impatient of his flight delay'd,
Here loud his raven charger neigh'd –
Down glanced that hand, and grasp'd his blade;
That sound had burst his waking dream,
As Slumber starts at owlet's scream,
70   The spur hath lanced his courser's sides;
Away, away, for life he rides:
Swift as the hurl'd on high jerreed
Springs to the touch his startled steed:
The rock is doubled, and the shore
Shakes with the clattering tramp no more;
The crag is won, no more is seen
His Christian crest and haughty mien.
'Twas but an instant he restrain'd
That fiery barb so sternly rein'd;
80   'Twas but a moment that he stood,
Then sped as if by death pursued;
But in that instant o'er his soul
Winters of Memory seem'd to roll,
And gather in that drop of time

A life of pain, an age of crime.
O'er him who loves, or hates, or fears,
Such moment pours the grief of years:
What felt _he_ then, at once opprest
By all that most distracts the breast?
90 That pause, which ponder'd o'er his fate,
Oh, who its dreary length shall date!
Though in Time's record nearly nought,
It was Eternity to Thought!
For infinite as boundless space
The thought that Conscience must embrace,
Which in itself can comprehend
Woe without name, or hope, or end.

The Corsair

from CANTO THE FIRST

[Pirates' Song]

I

'O'er the glad waters of the dark blue sea,
Our thoughts as boundless, and our souls as free,
Far as the breeze can bear, the billows foam,
Survey our empire, and behold our home!
These are our realms, no limits to their sway –
Our flag the sceptre all who meet obey.
Ours the wild life in tumult still to range
From toil to rest, and joy in every change.
Oh, who can tell? not thou, luxurious slave!
Whose soul would sicken o'er the heaving wave;
Not thou, vain lord of wantonness and ease!
Whom slumber soothes not – pleasure cannot please –
Oh, who can tell, save he whose heart hath tried,
And danced in triumph o'er the waters wide,
The exulting sense – the pulse's maddening play,
That thrills the wanderer of that trackless way?
That for itself can woo the approaching fight,
And turn what some deem danger to delight;
That seeks what cravens shun with more than zeal,
And where the feebler faint can only feel –
Feel – to the rising bosom's inmost core,
It's hope awaken and its spirit soar?
No dread of death if with us die our foes –
Save that it seems even duller than repose:
Come when it will – we snatch the life of life –
When lost – what recks it but disease or strife?

Let him who crawls enamour'd of decay,
Cling to his couch, and sicken years away:
Heave his thick breath, and shake his palsied head;
Ours – the fresh turf, and not the feverish bed.
While gasp by gasp he falters forth his soul,
Ours with one pang – one bound – escapes control.
His corse may boast its urn and narrow cave,
And they who loath'd his life may gild his grave:
Ours are the tears, though few, sincerely shed,
When Ocean shrouds and sepulchres our dead.
For us, even banquets fond regret supply
In the red cup that crowns our memory;
And the brief epitaph in danger's day,
When those who win at length divide the prey,
And cry, Remembrance saddening o'er each brow,
How had the brave who fell exulted *now!*'

[Portrait of Conrad]

IX

Unlike the heroes of each ancient race,
Demons in act, but Gods at least in face,
In Conrad's form seems little to admire,
Though his dark eyebrow shades a glance of fire:
Robust but not Herculean – to the sight
No giant frame sets forth his common height;
Yet, in the whole, who paused to look again,
Saw more than marks the crowd of vulgar men;
They gaze and marvel how – and still confess
That thus it is, but why they cannot guess.
Sun-burnt his cheek, his forehead high and pale
The sable curls in wild profusion veil;

And oft perforce his rising lip reveals
The haughtier thought it curbs, but scarce conceals.
Though smooth his voice, and calm his general mien,
Still seems there something he would not have seen:
His features' deepening lines and varying hue
At times attracted, yet perplex'd the view,
As if within that murkiness of mind
20   Work'd feelings fearful, and yet undefined;
Such might it be – that none could truly tell –
Too close inquiry his stern glance would quell.
There breathe but few whose aspect might defy
The full encounter of his searching eye;
He had the skill, when Cunning's gaze would seek
To probe his heart and watch his changing cheek,
At once the observer's purpose to espy,
And on himself roll back his scrutiny,
Lest he to Conrad rather should betray
30   Some secret thought, than drag that chief's to day.
There was a laughing Devil in his sneer,
That raised emotions both of rage and fear;
And where his frown of hatred darkly fell,
Hope withering fled, and Mercy sigh'd farewell!

X

Slight are the outward signs of evil thought,
Within – within – 'twas there the spirit wrought!
Love shows all changes – Hate, Ambition, Guile,
Betray no further than the bitter smile;
The lip's least curl, the lightest paleness thrown
40   Along the govern'd aspect, speak alone
Of deeper passions; and to judge their mien,
He, who would see, must be himself unseen.
Then – with the hurried tread, the upward eye,
The clenched hand, the pause of agony,
That listens, starting, lest the step too near

Approach intrusive on that mood of fear;
Then – with each feature working from the heart,
With feelings, loosed to strengthen – not depart,
That rise, convulse, contend – that freeze, or glow,
Flush in the cheek, or damp upon the brow;
Then, Stranger! If thou canst, and tremblest not,
Behold his soul – the rest that soothes his lot!
Mark how that lone and blighted bosom sears
The scathing thought of execrated years!
Behold – but who hath seen, or e'er shall see,
Man as himself – the secret spirit free?

XI

Yet was not Conrad thus by Nature sent
To lead the guilty – guilt's worse instrument –
His soul was changed, before his deeds had driven
Him forth to war with man and forfeit heaven.
Warp'd by the world in Disappointment's school,
In words too wise, in conduct *there* a fool;
Too firm to yield, and far too proud to stoop,
Doom'd by his very virtues for a dupe,
He cursed those virtues as the cause of ill,
And not the traitors who betray'd him still;
Nor deem'd that gifts bestow'd on better men
Had left him joy, and means to give again.
Fear'd, shunn'd, belied, ere youth had lost her force,
He hated man too much to feel remorse,
And thought the voice of wrath a sacred call,
To pay the injuries of some on all.
He knew himself a villain – but he deem'd
The rest no better than the thing he seem'd;
And scorn'd the best as hypocrites who hid
Those deeds the bolder spirit plainly did.
He knew himself detested, but he knew
The hearts that loath'd him, crouch'd and dreaded too.

Lone, wild, and strange, he stood alike exempt
From all affection and from all contempt:
His name could sadden, and his acts surprise;
But they that fear'd him dared not to despise:
Man spurns the worm, but pauses ere he wake
The slumbering venom of the folded snake:
The first may turn, but not avenge the blow;
The last expires, but leaves no living foe;
Fast to the doom'd offender's form it clings,
And he may crush – not conquer – still it stings!

XII

None are all evil – quickening round his heart
One softer feeling would not yet depart;
Oft could he sneer at others as beguiled
By passions worthy of a fool or child;
Yet 'gainst that passion vainly still he strove,
And even in him it asks the name of Love!
Yes, it was love – unchangeable – unchanged,
Felt but for one from whom he never ranged;
Though fairest captives daily met his eye,
He shunn'd, nor sought, but coldly pass'd them by;
Though many a beauty droop'd in prison'd bower,
None ever sooth'd his most unguarded hour.
Yes – it was Love – if thoughts of tenderness
Tried in temptation, strengthen'd by distress,
Unmoved by absence, firm in every clime,
And yet – oh more than all! untired by time;
Which nor defeated hope, nor baffled wile,
Could render sullen were she near to smile,
Nor rage could fire, nor sickness fret to vent
On her one murmur of his discontent;
Which still would meet with joy, with calmness part,
Lest that his look of grief should reach her heart;
Which naught removed, nor menaced to remove –

If there be love in mortals – this was love!
He was a villain – ay, reproaches shower
On him – but not the passion, nor its power,
Which only proved, all other virtues gone,
Not guilt itself could quench this loveliest one!

Stanzas for Music

I speak not, I trace not, I breathe not thy name,
There is grief in the sound, there is guilt in the fame:
But the tear which now burns on my cheek may impart
The deep thoughts that dwell in that silence of heart.

Too brief for our passion, too long for our peace,
Were those hours – can their joy or their bitterness cease?
We repent, we abjure, we will break from our chain, –
We will part, we will fly to – unite it again!

Oh! thine be the gladness, and mine be the guilt!
10   Forgive me, adored one! – forsake, if thou wilt; –
But the heart which is thine shall expire undebased,
And *man* shall not break it – whatever *thou* mayst.

And stern to the haughty, but humble to thee,
This soul, in its bitterest blackness, shall be;
And our days seem as swift, and our moments more sweet,
With thee by my side, than with worlds at our feet,
One sigh of thy sorrow, one look of thy love,
Shall turn me or fix, shall reward or reprove;
And the heartless may wonder at all I resign –
20   Thy lip shall reply, not to them, but to *mine*.

May 1814

Lara

from CANTO THE FIRST

[Lara's Homecoming]

I

The Serfs are glad through Lara's wide domain,
And slavery half forgets her feudal chain;
He, their unhoped, but unforgotten lord,
The long self-exiled chieftain, is restored:
There be bright faces in the busy hall,
Bowls on the board, and banners on the wall;
Far checkering o'er the pictured window, plays
The unwonted faggot's hospitable blaze;
And gay retainers gather round the hearth,
10 With tongues all loudness, and with eyes all mirth.

II

The chief of Lara is returned again:
And why had Lara cross'd the bounding main?
Left by his sire, too young such loss to know,
Lord of himself, – that heritage of woe,
That fearful empire which the human breast
But holds to rob the heart within of rest! –
With none to check, and few to point in time
The thousand paths that slope the way to crime;
Then, when he most required commandment, then
20 Had Lara's daring boyhood govern'd men.
It skills not, boots not step by step to trace
His youth through all the mazes of its race;
Short was the course his restlessness had run,
But long enough to leave him half undone.

And Lara left in youth his father-land;
But from the hour he waved his parting hand
Each trace wax'd fainter of his course, till all
Had nearly ceased his memory to recall.
His sire was dust, his vassals could declare,
30   'Twas all they knew, that Lara was not there;
Nor sent, nor came he, till conjecture grew
Cold in the many, anxious in the few.
His hall scarce echoes with his wonted name,
His portrait darkens in its fading frame,
Another chief consoled his destined bride,
The young forgot him, and the old had died;
'Yet doth he live!' exclaims the impatient heir,
And sighs for sables which he must not wear.
A hundred scutcheons deck with gloomy grace
40   The Lara's' last and longest dwelling-place;
But one is absent from the mouldering file,
That now were welcome in that Gothic pile.

IV

He comes at last in sudden loneliness,
And whence they know not, why they need not guess;
They more might marvel, when the greeting's o'er,
Not that he came, but came not long before:
No train is his beyond a single page,
Of foreign aspect, and of tender age.
Years had roll'd on, and fast they speed away
50   To those that wander as to those that stay;
But lack of tidings from another clime
Had lent a flagging wing to weary Time.
They see, they recognise, yet almost deem
The present dubious, or the past a dream.
He lives, nor yet is past his manhood's prime,
Though sear'd by toil, and something touch'd by time;

His faults, whate'er they were, if scarce forgot,
Might be untaught him by his varied lot;
Nor good nor ill of late were known, his name
60 Might yet uphold his patrimonial fame:
His soul in youth was haughty, but his sins
No more than pleasure from the stripling wins;
And such, if not yet harden'd in their course,
Might be redeem'd, nor ask a long remorse.

V

And they indeed were changed – 'tis quickly seen,
Whate'er he be, 'twas not what he had been:
That brow in furrow'd lines had fix'd at last,
And spake of passions, but of passion past:
The pride, but not the fire, of early days,
70 Coldness of mien, and carelessness of praise;
A high demeanour, and a glance that took
Their thoughts from others by a single look;
And that sarcastic levity of tongue,
The stinging of a heart the world hath stung.
That darts in seeming playfulness around,
And makes those feel that will not own the wound;
All these seem'd his, and something more beneath
Than glance could well reveal, or accent breathe
Ambition, glory, love, the common aim,
80 That some can conquer, and that all would claim,
Within his breast appear'd no more to strive,
Yet seem'd as lately they had been alive;
And some deep feeling it were vain to trace
At moments lighten'd o'er his livid face.

VI

Not much he loved long question of the past,
Nor told of wondrous wilds, and deserts vast,
In those far lands where he had wander'd lone,

And – as himself would have it seem – unknown;
Yet these in vain his eye could scarcely scan,
90   Nor glean experience from his fellow man;
But what he had beheld he shunn'd to show,
As hardly worth a stranger's care to know;
If still more prying such inquiry grew,
His brow felt darker, and his words more few.

VII

Not unrejoiced to see him once again,
Warm was his welcome to the haunts of men;
Born of high lineage, link'd in high command,
He mingled with the magnates of his land;
Join'd the carousals of the great and gay,
100   And saw them smile or sigh their hours away;
But still he only saw, and did not share,
The common pleasure or the general care;
He did not follow what they all pursued
With hope still baffled, still to be renew'd;
Nor shadowy honour, nor substantial gain,
Nor beauty'd preference, and the rival's pain:
Around him some mysterious circle thrown
Repell'd approach, and show'd him still alone;
Upon his eye sat something of reproof,
110   That kept at least frivolity aloof;
And things more timid that beheld him near
In silence gazed, or whisper'd mutual fear;
And they the wiser, friendlier few confess'd
They deem'd him better than his air express'd.

VIII

'Twas strange – in youth all action and all life,
Burning for pleasure, not averse from strife;
Woman, the field, the ocean, all that gave
Promise of gladness, peril of a grave,

In turn he tried – he ransack'd all below,
120   And found his recompense in joy or woe,
No tame, trite medium; for his feelings sought
In that intenseness an escape from thought:
The tempest of his heart in scorn had gazed
On that the feebler elements had raised;
The rapture of his heart had look'd on high,
And ask'd if greater dwelt beyond the sky:
Chain'd to excess, the slave of each extreme,
How woke he from the wildness of that dream?
Alas! he told not – but he did awake
130   To curse the wither'd heart that would not break.

The Wild Gazelle

I

The wild gazelle on Judah's hills
    Exulting yet may bound,
    And drink from all the living rills
    That gush on holy ground:
Its airy step and glorious eye
May glance in tameless transport by:–

II

A step as fleet, an eye more bright,
    Hath Judah witness'd there:
And o'er her scenes of lost delight
10   Inhabitants more fair.
The cedars wave on Lebanon,
But Judah's statelier maids are gone!

III

More blest each palm that shades those plains
    Than Israel's scatter'd race;
For, taking root, it there remains
    In solitary grace:
It cannot quit its place of birth,
It will not live in other earth.

IV

But we must wander witheringly,
    In other lands to die;
And where our fathers' ashes be,
    Our own may never lie:
Our temple hath not left a stone,
And Mockery sits of Salem's throne.

The Destruction of Sennacherib

I

The Assyrian came down like the wolf on the fold,
And his cohorts were gleaming in purple and gold;
And the sheen of their spears was like stars on the sea,
When the blue wave rolls nightly on deep Galilee.

II

Like the leaves of the forest when Summer is green,
That host with their banners at sunset were seen:
Like the leaves of the forest when Autumn hath blown,
That host on the morrow lay wither'd and strown.

For the Angel of Death spread his wings on the blast,
10 And breathed in the face of the foe as he pass'd;
And the eyes of the sleepers wax'd deadly and chill
And their hearts but once heaved, and for ever grew still!

IV

And there lay the steed with his nostril all wide,
But through it there roll'd not the breath of his pride;
And the foam of his gasping lay white on the turf,
And cold as the spray of the rock-beating surf.

V

And there lay the rider distorted and pale,
With the dew on his brow, and the rust on his mail:
And the tents were all silent, the banners alone,
20 The lances unlifted, the trumpet unblown.

VI

And the widows of Ashur are loud in their wail,
And the idols are broke in the temple of Baal;
And the might of the Gentile, unsmote by the sword,
Hath melted like snow in the glance of the Lord!

Stanzas for Music

There's not a joy the world can give like that it takes away,
When the glow of early thought declines in feeling's dull
decay;
'Tis not on youth's smooth cheek the blush alone, which
fades so fast,
But the tender bloom of heart is gone, ere youth itself be
past.

Then the few whose spirits float above the wreck of
    happiness
Are driven o'er the shoals of guilt or ocean of excess:
The magnet of their course is gone, or only points in vain
The shore to which their shiver'd sail shall never stretch
    again.

Then the mortal coldness of the soul like death itself
    comes down;
10 It cannot feel for others' woes, it dare not dream its own;
That heavy chill has frozen o'er the fountain of our tears,
And though the eye may sparkle still, 'tis where the ice
    appears.

Though wit may flash from fluent lips, and mirth distract
    the breast,
Through midnight hours that yield no more their former
    hope of rest;
'Tis but as ivy-leaves around the ruin'd turret wreath,
All green and wildly fresh without, but worn and grey
    beneath.

Oh could I feel as I have felt, – or be what I have been,
Or weep as I could once have wept o'er many a vanish'd
    scene;
As springs in deserts found seem sweet, all brackish
    though they be,
20 So, midst the wither'd waste of life, those tears would
    flow to me.

                          March 1815.

73

When We Two Parted

When we two parted
  In silence and tears,
Half broken-hearted
  To sever for years,
Pale grew thy cheek and cold,
  Colder thy kiss;
Truly that hour foretold
  Sorrow to this.

The dew of the morning
  Sunk chill on my brow –
It felt like the warning
  Of what I feel now.
Thy vows are all broken,
  And light is thy fame:
I hear thy name spoken,
  And share in its shame.

They name thee before me,
  A knell to mine ear;
A shudder comes o'er me –
  Why wert thou so dear?
They know not I knew thee,
  Who knew thee too well:–
Long, long shall I rue thee,
  Too deeply to tell.

In secret we met –
  In silence I grieve,
That thy heart could forget,
  Thy spirit deceive.

If I should meet thee
    After long years,
How should I greet thee? –
    With silence and tears.

1816.

Stanzas for Music

There be none of Beauty's daughters
    With a magic like thee;
And like music on the waters
    Is thy sweet voice to me:
When, as if its sound were causing
The charmed ocean's pausing,
The waves lie still and gleaming,
And the lull'd winds seem dreaming:

And the midnight moon is weaving
    Her bright chain o'er the deep;
Whose breast is gently heaving,
    As an infant's asleep:
So the spirit bows before thee,
To listen and adore thee;
With a full but soft emotion,
Like the swell of Summer's ocean.

Stanzas to Augusta

I

When all around grew drear and dark,
    And reason half withheld her ray –
And hope but shed a dying spark
    Which more misled my lonely way;

In that deep midnight of the mind,
   And that internal strife of heart,
When dreading to be deem'd too kind,
   The weak despair – the cold depart;

III

When fortune changed – and love fled far,
   And hatred's shafts flew thick and fast,
Thou wert the solitary star
   Which rose and set not to the last.

IV

Oh! blest be thine unbroken light!
   That watch'd me as a seraph's eye,
And stood between me and the night,
   For ever shining sweetly nigh.

V

And when the cloud upon us came,
   Which strove to blacken o'er thy ray –
Then purer spread its gentle flame,
   And dash'd the darkness all away.

VI

Still may thy spirit dwell on mine,
   And teach it what to brave or brook –
There's more in one soft word of thine
   Than in the world's defied rebuke.

VII

Thou stood'st, as stands a lovely tree,
   That still unbroke, though gently bent,
Still waves with fond fidelity
   Its boughs above a monument.

The winds might rend – the skies might pour,
 But there thou wert – and still wouldst be
Devoted in the stormiest hour
 To shed thy weeping leaves o'er me.

IX

But thou and thine shall know no blight,
 Whatever fate on me may fall;
For heaven in sunshine will requite
 The kind – and thee the most of all.

X

Then let the ties of baffled love
 Be broken – thine will never break;
Thy heart can feel – but will not move;
 Thy soul, though soft, will never shake.

XI

And these, when all was lost beside,
 Were found and still are fix'd in thee; –
And bearing still a breast so tried,
 Earth is no desert – ev'n to me.

Darkness

I had a dream, which was not all a dream.
The bright sun was extinguish'd, and the stars
Did wander darkling in the eternal space,
Rayless, and pathless, and the icy earth
Swung blind and blackening in the moonless air;
Morn came and went – and came, and brought no day,

And men forgot their passions in the dread
Of this their desolation; and all hearts
Were chill'd into a selfish prayer for light:
10 And they did live by watchfires – and the thrones,
The palaces of crowned kings – the huts,
The habitations of all things which dwell,
Were burnt for beacons; cities were consumed,
And men were gather'd round their blazing homes
To look once more into each other's face:
Happy were those who dwelt within the eye
Of the volcanos, and their mountain-torch:
A fearful hope was all the world contain'd;
Forests were set on fire – but hour by hour
20 They fell and faded – and the crackling trunks
Extinguish'd with a crash – and all was black.
The brows of men by the despairing light
Wore an unearthly aspect, as by fits
The flashes fell upon them; some lay down
And hid their eyes and wept; and some did rest
Their chins upon their clenched hands, and smiled;
And others hurried to and fro, and fed
Their funeral piles with fuel, and look'd up
With mad disquietude on the dull sky,
30 The pall of a past world; and then again
With curses cast them down upon the dust,
And gnash'd their teeth and howl'd: the wild birds shriek'd
And, terrified, did flutter on the ground,
And flap their useless wings; the wildest brutes
Came tame and tremulous; and vipers crawl'd
And twined themselves among the multitude,
Hissing, but stingless – they were slain for food
And War, which for a moment was no more,
Did glut himself again: – a meal was bought
40 With blood, and each sate sullenly apart

Gorging himself in gloom: no love was left;
All earth was but one thought – and that was death
Immediate and inglorious; and the pang
Of famine fed upon all entrails – men
Died, and their bones were tombless as their flesh;
The meagre by the meagre were devour'd,
Even dogs assail'd their masters, all save one,
And he was faithful to a corse, and kept
The birds and beasts and famish'd men at bay,
50 Till hunger clung them, or the dropping dead
Lured their lank jaws; himself sought out no food,
But with a piteous and perpetual moan,
And a quick desolate cry, licking the hand
Which answer'd not with a caress – he died.
The crowd was famish'd by degrees; but two
Of an enormous city did survive,
And they were enemies: they met beside
The dying embers of an altar-place
Where had been heap'd a mass of holy things
60 For an unholy usage; they raked up,
And shivering scraped with their cold skeleton hands
The feeble ashes, and their feeble breath
Blew for a little life, and made a flame
Which was a mockery; then they lifted up
Their eyes as it grew lighter, and beheld
Each other's aspects – saw, and shriek'd, and died –
Even of their mutual hideousness they died,
Unknowing who he was upon whose brow
Famine had written Fiend. The world was void,
70 The populous and the powerful was a lump
Seasonless, herbless, treeless, manless, lifeless,
A lump of death – a chaos of hard clay.
The rivers, lakes, and ocean all stood still,
And nothing stirr'd within their silent depths;
Ships sailorless lay rotting on the sea,

And their masts fell down piecemeal: as they dropp'd
They slept on the abyss without a surge –
The waves were dead; the tides were in their grave,
The moon, their mistress, had expired before;
80 The winds were wither'd in the stagnant air,
And the clouds perish'd; Darkness had no need
Of aid from them – She was the Universe.

Diodati, July 1816.

Prometheus

I

Titan! to whose immortal eyes
   The sufferings of mortality,
   Seen in their sad reality,
Were not as things that gods despise;
What was thy pity's recompense?
A silent suffering, and intense;
The rock, the vulture, and the chain,
All that the proud can feel of pain,
The agony they do not show,
10 The suffocating sense of woe,
   Which speaks but in its loneliness,
And then is jealous lest the sky
Should have a listener, nor will sigh
   Until its voice is echoless.

II

Titan! to thee the strife was given
   Between the suffering and the will,
   Which torture where they cannot kill;
And the inexorable Heaven,
And the deaf tyranny of fate,

The ruling principle of Hate,
Which for its pleasure doth create
The things it may annihilate,
Refused thee even the boon to die:
The wretched gift eternity
Was thine – and thou hast borne it well.
All that the Thunderer wrung from thee
Was but the menace which flung back
On him the torments of thy rack;
The fate thou didst so well foresee,
But would not to appease him tell;
And in thy Silence was his Sentence,
And in his Soul a vain repentance,
And evil dread so ill dissembled,
That in his hand the lightnings trembled.

III

Thy Godlike crime was to be kind,
   To render with thy precepts less
The sum of human wretchedness,
And strengthen Man with his own mind;
But baffled as thou wert from high,
Still in thy patient energy,
In the endurance, and repulse
   Of thine impenetrable Spirit,
Which Earth and Heaven could not convulse,
   A mighty lesson we inherit:
Thou art a symbol and a sign
   To Mortals of their fate and force;
Like thee, Man is in part divine,
   A troubled stream from a pure source;
And Man in portions can foresee
His own funereal destiny;
His wretchedness, and his resistance,
And his sad unallied existence:

To which his Spirit may oppose
Itself – and equal to all woes,
   And a firm will, and a deep sense,
Which even in torture can descry
   Its own concenter'd recompense,
Triumphant where it dares defy,
And making Death a Victory.

Diodati, July 1816.

A Fragment

Could I remount the river of my years
To the first fountain of our smiles and tears,
I would not trace again the stream of hours
Between their outworn banks of wither'd flowers,
But bid it flow as now – until it glides
Into the number of the nameless tides.

What is this Death? – a quiet of the heart?
The whole of that of which we are a part?
For life is but a vision – what I see
Of all which lives alone is life to me,
And being so – the absent are the dead,
Who haunt us from tranquility, and spread
A dreary shroud around us, and invest
With sad remembrances our hours of rest.
   The absent are the dead – for they are cold,
And ne'er can be what once we did behold;
And they are changed, and cheerless, – or if yet
The unforgotten do not all forget
Since thus divided – equal must it be
If the deep barrier be of earth, or sea;
It may be both – but one day end it must

In the dark union of insensate dust.
    The under-earth inhabitants – are they
But mingled millions decomposed to clay?
The ashes of a thousand ages spread
Wherever man has trodden or shall tread?
Or do they in their silent cities dwell
Each in his incommunicative cell?
Or have they their own language? and a sense
30   Of breathless being? – darken'd and intense
As midnight in her solitude? – Oh Earth!
Where are the past? – and wherefore had they birth?
The dead are thy inheritors – and we
But bubbles on thy surface; and the key
Of thy profundity is in the grave,
The ebon portal of thy peopled cave,
Where I would walk in spirit, and behold
Our elements resolved to things untold,
And fathom hidden wonders, and explore
40   The essence of great bosoms now no more.

                                    Diodati July, 1816.

Lines on Hearing that Lady Byron was Ill

And thou wert sad – yet I was not with thee;
    And thou wert sick, and yet I was not near;
Methought that joy and health alone could be
    Where I was *not* – and pain and sorrow here!
And it is thus? – is it as I foretold,
    And shall be more so; for the mind recoils
Upon itself, and the wreck'd heart lies cold,
    While heaviness collects the shatter'd spoils.

It is not in the storm nor in the strife
10   We feel benumb'd, and wish to be no more,
    But in the after-silence on the shore,
When all is lost, except a little life.

I am too well avenged! – but 'twas my right;
    Whate'er my sins might be, *thou* wert not sent
To be the Nemesis who should requite –
    Nor did Heaven choose so near an instrument.
Mercy is for the merciful! – if thou
Hast been of such, 'twill be accorded now.
Thy nights are banish'd from the realms of sleep! –
20   Yes! they may flatter thee, but thou shalt feel
    A hollow agony which will not heal,
For thou art pillow'd on a curse too deep;
Thou hast sown in my sorrow, and must reap
    The bitter harvest in a woe as real!
I have had many foes, but none like thee;
    For 'gainst the rest myself I could defend,
    And be avenged, or turn them into friend;
But thou in safe implacability
Hadst nought to dread – in thy own weakness shielded,
30   And in my love, which hath but too much yielded,
    And spared, for thy sake, some I should not spare;
And thus upon the world – trust in thy truth,
And the wild fame of my ungovern'd youth –
    On things that were not, and on things that are –
Even upon such a basis hast thou built
A monument, whose cement hath been guilt!
    The moral Clytemnestra of thy lord,
    And hew'd down, with an unsuspected sword,
Fame, peace, and hope – and all the better life,
40   Which, but for this cold treason of thy heart,
    Might still have risen from out the grave of strife,
    And found a nobler duty than to part.

But of thy virtues didst thou make a vice,
　　Trafficking with them in a purpose cold,
　　For present anger, and for future gold –
And buying other's grief at any price.
And thus once enter'd into crooked ways,
The early truth, which was thy proper praise,
Did not still walk beside thee – but at times,
50　And with a breast unknowing its own crimes,
Deceit, averments incompatible,
Equivocations, and the thoughts which dwell
　　In Janus-spirits – the significant eye
Which learns to lie with silence – the pretext
Of prudence, with advantages annex'd –
The acquiescence in all things which tend,
No matter how, to the desired end –
　　All found a place in thy philosophy.
The means were worthy, and the end is won –
60　I would not do by thee as thou hast done!

September 1816.

Childe Harold's Pilgrimage

from CANTO THE THIRD

[Exiles]

I

Is thy face like thy mother's, my fair child!
ADA! sole daughter of my house and heart?
When last I saw thy young blue eyes they smiled,
And then we parted, – not as now we part,
But with a hope. –
         Awaking with a start,
The waters heave around me; and on high
The winds lift up their voices: I depart,
Whither I know not; but the hour's gone by,
When Albion's lessening shores could grieve or glad mine
    eye.

II

10   Once more upon the waters! yet once more!
And the waves bound beneath me as a steed
That knows his rider. Welcome to their roar!
Swift be their guidance, wheresoe'er it lead!
Though the strain'd mast should quiver as a reed,
And the rent canvas fluttering strew the gale,
Still must I on; for I am as a weed,
Flung from the rock, on Ocean's foam to sail
Where'er the surge may sweep, the tempest's breath
    prevail.

III

In my youth's summer I did sing of One,
20   The wandering outlaw of his own dark mind;
Again I seize the theme, then but begun,
And bear it with me, as the rushing wind

Bears the cloud onwards: in that Tale I find
The furrows of long thought, and dried-up tears,
Which, ebbing, leave a sterile track behind,
O'er which all heavily the journeying years
Plod the last sands of life, – where not a flower appears.

IV

Since my young days of passion – joy, or pain,
Perchance my heart and harp have lost a string,
And both may jar: it may be, that in vain
I would essay as I have sung to sing.
Yet, though a dreary strain, to this I cling;
So that it wean me from the weary dream
Of selfish grief or gladness – so it fling
Forgetfulness around me – it shall seem
To me, though to none else, a not ungrateful theme.

V

He, who grown aged in this world of woe,
In deeds, not years, piercing the depths of life,
So that no wonder waits him; nor below
Can love or sorrow, fame, ambition, strife,
Cut to his heart again with the keen knife
Of silent, sharp endurance: he can tell
Why thought seeks refuge in lone caves, yet rife
With airy images, and shapes which dwell
Still unimpair'd, though old, in the soul's haunted cell.

VI

'T is to create, and in creating live
A being more intense that we endow
With form our fancy, gaining as we give
The life we image, even as I do now.

87

50   What am I? Nothing: but not so art thou,
    Soul of my thought! with whom I traverse earth,
    Invisible but gazing, as I glow
    Mix'd with thy spirit, blended with thy birth,
And feeling still with thee in my crush'd feelings' dearth.

VII

    Yet must I think less wildly: – I *have* thought
    Too long and darkly, till my brain became,
    In its own eddy boiling and o'erwrought,
    A whirling gulf of phantasy and flame:
    And thus, untaught in youth my heart to tame,
60   My springs of life were poison'd. 'Tis too late!
    Yet am I changed; though still enough the same
    In strength to bear what time cannot abate,
And feed on bitter fruits without accusing Fate.

VIII

    Something too much of this: – but now 't is past,
    And the spell closes with its silent seal.
    Long absent HAROLD re-appears at last;
    He of the breast which fain no more would feel,
    Wrung with the wounds which kill not, but ne'er heal:
    Yet Time, who changes all, had alter'd him
70   In soul and aspect as in age: years steal
    Fire from the mind as vigour from the limb;
And life's enchanted cup but sparkles near the brim.

IX

    His had been quaff'd too quickly, and he found
    The dregs were wormwood; but he fill'd again,
    And from a purer fount, on holier ground,
    And deem'd its spring perpetual; but in vain!

Still round him clung invisibly a chain
Which gall'd for ever, fettering though unseen,
And heavy though it clank'd not; worn with pain,
80   Which pined although it spoke not, and grew keen,
Entering with every step he took through many a scene.

X

Secure in guarded coldness, he had mix'd
Again in fancied safety with his kind,
And deem'd his spirit now so firmly fix'd
And sheath'd with an invulnerable mind,
That, if no joy, no sorrow lurk'd behind;
And he, as one, might 'midst the many stand
Unheeded, searching through the crowd to find
Fit speculation; such as in strange land
90 He found in wonder-works of God and Nature's hand.

XI

But who can view the ripen'd rose, nor seek
To wear it? who can curiously behold
The smoothness and the sheen of beauty's cheek,
Nor feel the heart can never all grow old?
Who can contemplate Fame through clouds unfold
The star which rises o'er her steep, nor climb?
Harold, once more within the vortex, roll'd
On with the giddy circle, chasing Time,
Yet with a nobler aim than in his youth's fond prime.

XII

100 But soon he knew himself the most unfit
Of men to herd with Man; with whom he held
Little in common; untaught to submit
His thoughts to others, though his soul was quell'd
In youth by his own thoughts; still uncompell'd,

He would not yield dominion of his mind
To spirits against whom his own rebell'd;
Proud though in desolation; which could find
A life within itself, to breathe without mankind.

XIII

Where rose the mountains, there to him were friends;
Where roll'd the ocean, thereon was his home;
Where a blue sky, and glowing clime, extends,
He had the passion and the power to roam;
The desert, forest, cavern, breaker's foam,
Were unto him companionship; they spake
A mutual language, clearer than the tome
Of his land's tongue, which he would oft forsake
For Nature's pages glass'd by sunbeams on the lake.

XIV

Like the Chaldean, he could watch the stars,
Till he had peopled them with beings bright
As their own beams; and earth, and earth-born jars,
And human frailties, were forgotten quite:
Could he have kept his spirit to that flight
He had been happy; but this clay will sink
Its spark immortal, envying it the light
To which it mounts, as if to break the link
That keeps us from yon heaven which woos us to its brink.

XV

But in Man's dwellings he became a thing
Restless and worn, and stern and wearisome,
Droop'd as a wild-born falcon with clipt wing,
To whom the boundless air alone were home:

Then came his fit again, which to o'ercome,
As eagerly the barr'd-up bird will beat
His breast and beak against his wiry dome
Till the blood tinge his plumage, so the heat
Of his impeded soul would through his bosom eat.

XVI

Self-exiled Harold wanders forth again,
With nought of hope left, but with less of gloom;
The very knowledge that he lived in vain,
That all was over on this side the tomb,
140 Had made Despair a smilingness assume,
Which, though 'twere wild, – as on the plunder'd wreck
When mariners would madly meet their doom
With draughts intemperate on the sinking deck, –
Did yet inspire a cheer, which he forbore to check.

[Waterloo]

XVII

Stop! – for thy tread is on an Empire's dust!
An Earthquake's spoil is sepulchred below!
Is the spot mark'd with no colossal bust?
Nor column trophied for triumphal show?
None; but the moral's truth tells simpler so,
As the ground was before, thus let it be; –
How that red rain hath made the harvest grow!
And is this all the world has gain'd by thee,
Thou first and last of fields! king-making Victory?

XVIII

10 And Harold stands upon this place of skulls,
The grave of France, the deadly Waterloo!
How in an hour the power which gave annuls
Its gifts, transferring fame as fleeting too!

In 'pride of place' here last the eagle flew,
Then tore with bloody talon the rent plain,
Pierced by the shaft of banded nations through;
Ambition's life and labours all were vain;
He wears the shatter'd links of the world's broken chain.

XIX

Fit retribution! Gaul may champ the bit
And foam in fetters; – but is Earth more free?
Did nations combat to make *One* submit;
Or league to teach all kings true sovereignty?
What! shall reviving Thraldom again be
The patch'd-up idol of enlighten'd days?
Shall we, who struck the Lion down, shall we
Pay the Wolf homage? proffering lowly gaze
And servile knees to thrones? No; *prove* before ye praise!

XX

If not, o'er one fallen despot boast no more!
In vain fair cheeks were furrow'd with hot tears
For Europe's flowers long rooted up before
The trampler of her vineyards; in vain years
Of death, depopulation, bondage, fears,
Have all been borne, and broken by the accord
Of roused-up millions; all that most endears
Glory, is when the myrtle wreathes a sword
Such as Harmodius drew on Athens' tyrant lord.

XXI

There was a sound of revelry by night,
And Belgium's capital had gather'd then
Her Beauty and her Chivalry, and bright
The lamps shone o'er fair women and brave men;
A thousand hearts beat happily; and when

92

Music arose with its voluptuous swell,
　Soft eyes look'd love to eyes which spake again,
　And all went merry as a marriage bell;
But hush! hark! a deep sound strikes like a rising knell!

XXII

Did ye not hear it? – No; 'twas but the wind,
　Or the car rattling o'er the stony street;
　On with the dance! let joy be unconfined;
　No sleep till morn, when Youth and Pleasure meet
50　To chase the glowing Hours with flying feet –
　But hark! – that heavy sound breaks in once more,
　As if the clouds its echo would repeat;
　And nearer, clearer, deadlier than before!
Arm! Arm! it is – it is – the cannon's opening roar!

XXIII

Within a window'd niche of that high hall
　Sate Brunswick's fated chieftain; he did hear
　That sound the first amidst the festival,
　And caught its tone with Death's prophetic ear;
　And when they smiled because he deem'd it near,
60　His heart more truly knew that peal too well
　Which stretch'd his father on a bloody bier,
　And roused the vengeance blood alone could quell;
He rush'd into the field, and, foremost fighting, fell.

XXIV

Ah! then and there was hurrying to and fro,
　And gathering tears, and tremblings of distress,
　And cheeks all pale, which but an hour ago
　Blush'd at the praise of their own loveliness;
　And there were sudden partings, such as press

The life from out young hearts, and choking sighs
70   Which ne'er might be repeated; who could guess
If ever more should meet those mutual eyes,
Since upon night so sweet such awful morn could rise!

XXV

And there was mounting in hot haste: the steed,
The mustering squadron, and the clattering car,
Went pouring forward with impetuous speed,
And swiftly forming in the ranks of war;
And the deep thunder peal on peal afar;
And near, the beat of the alarming drum
Roused up the soldier ere the morning star;
80   While throng'd the citizens with terror dumb,
Or whispering, with white lips – 'The foe! they come!
    they come!'

XXVI

And wild and high the 'Cameron's gathering' rose!
The war-note of Lochiel, which Albyn's hills
Have heard, and heard, too, have her Saxon foes: –
How in the noon of night that pibroch thrills,
Savage and shrill! But with the breath which fills
Their mountain-pipe, so fill the mountaineers
With the fierce native daring which instils
The stirring memory of a thousand years,
90 And Evan's, Donald's fame rings in each clansman's ears!

XXVII

And Ardennes waves above them her green leaves,
Dewy with nature's tear-drops as they pass,
Grieving, if aught inanimate e'er grieves,
Over the unreturning brave, – alas!
Ere evening to be trodden like the grass

Which now beneath them, but above shall grow
In its next verdure, when this fiery mass
Of living valour, rolling on the foe
And burning with high hope shall moulder cold and low.

XXVIII

100 Last noon beheld them full of lusty life,
Last eve in Beauty's circle proudly gay,
The midnight brought the signal-sound of strife,
The morn the marshalling in arms, – the day
Battle's magnificently stern array!
The thunder-clouds close o'er it, which when rent
The earth is cover'd thick with other clay,
Which her own clay shall cover, heap'd and pent,
Rider and horse, – friend, foe, – in one red burial blent!

[On the Rhine]

LI

A thousand battles have assail'd thy banks,
But these and half their fame have pass'd away,
And Slaughter heap'd on high his weltering ranks;
Their very graves are gone, and what are they?
Thy tide wash'd down the blood of yesterday,
And all was stainless, and on thy clear stream
Glass'd with its dancing light, the sunny ray;
But o'er the blacken'd memory's blighting dream
Thy waves would vainly roll, all sweeping as they seem.

LII

10 Thus Harold inly said, and pass'd along,
Yet not insensible to all which here
Awoke the jocund birds to early song
In glens which might have made even exile dear:

Though on his brow were graven lines austere,
And tranquil sternness, which had ta'en the place
Of feelings fierier far but less severe,
Joy was not always absent from his face,
But o'er it in such scenes would steal with transient trace.

LIII

Nor was all love shut from him, though his days
20   Of passion had consumed themselves to dust.
It is in vain that we would coldly gaze
On such as smile upon us; the heart must
Leap kindly back to kindness, though disgust
Hath wean'd it from all worldlings: thus he felt,
For there was soft remembrance, and sweet trust
In one fond breast, to which he own would melt,
And in its tenderer hour on that his bosom dwelt.

LIV

And he had learn'd to love, – I know not why,
For this in such as him seems strange of mood, –
30   The helpless looks of blooming infancy,
Even in its earliest nurture; what subdued,
To change like this, a mind so far imbued
With scorn of man, it little boots to know;
But thus it was; and though in solitude
Small power the nipp'd affections have to grow,
In him this glow'd when all beside had ceased to glow.

LV

And there was one soft breast, as hath been said,
Which unto his was bound by stronger ties
Than the church links withal; and, though unwed,
40   *That* love was pure, and, far above disguise,
Had stood the test of mortal enmities

96

Still undivided, and cemented more
By peril, dreaded most in female eyes;
But this was firm, and from a foreign shore
Well to that heart might his these absent greetings pour!

1

The castled crag of Drachenfels
Frowns o'er the wide and winding Rhine,
Whose breast of waters broadly swells
Between the banks which bear the vine,
And hills all rich with blossom'd trees,
And fields which promise corn and wine,
And scatter'd cities crowning these,
Whose far white walls along them shine,
Have strew'd a scene, which I should see
With double joy wert *thou* with me.

2

And peasant girls, with deep blue eyes,
And hands which offer early flowers,
Walk smiling o'er this paradise;
Above, the frequent feudal towers
Through green leaves lift their walls of gray;
And many a rock which steeply lowers,
And noble arch in proud decay,
Look o'er this vale of vintage-bowers;
But one thing want these banks of Rhine, –
Thy gentle hand to clasp in mine!

3

I send the lilies given to me;
Though long before thy hand they touch,
I know that they must wither'd be,
But yet reject them not as such;

97

70 For I have cherish'd them as dear,
Because they yet may meet thine eye,
And guide thy soul to mine even here,
When thou behold'st them drooping nigh,
And know'st them gather'd by the Rhine,
And offer'd from my heart to thine!

4

The river nobly foams and flows,
The charm of this enchanted ground,
And all its thousand turns disclose
Some fresher beauty varying round:
80 The haughtiest breast its wish might bound
Through life to dwell delighted here;
Nor could on earth a spot be found
To nature and to me so dear,
Could thy dear eyes in following mine
Still sweeten more these banks of Rhine!

[Escape into Nature]

LXVIII

Lake Leman woos me with its crystal face,
The mirror where the stars and mountains view
The stillness of their aspect in each trace
Its clear depth yields of their far height and hue:
There is too much of man here, to look through
With a fit mind the might which I behold;
But soon in me shall Loneliness renew
Thoughts hid, but not less cherish'd than of old,
Ere mingling with the herd had penn'd me in their fold.

10 To fly from, need not be to hate, mankind:
    All are not fit with them to stir and toil,
    Nor is it discontent to keep the mind
    Deep in its fountain, lest it overboil
    In the hot throng, where we become the spoil
    Of our infection, till too late and long
    We may deplore and struggle with the coil,
    In wretched interchange of wrong for wrong
Midst a contentious world, striving where none are strong.

    There, in a moment we may plunge our years
20 In fatal penitence, and in the blight
    Of our own soul turn all our blood to tears,
    And colour things to come with hues of Night;
    The race of life becomes a hopeless flight
    To those that walk in darkness: on the sea
    The boldest steer but where their ports invite;
    But there are wanderers o'er Eternity
Whose bark drives on and on, and anchor'd ne'er shall be.

    Is it not better, then, to be alone,
    And love Earth only for its earthly sake?
30 By the blue rushing of the arrowy Rhone,
    Or the pure bosom of its nursing lake,
    Which feeds it as a mother who doth make
    A fair but froward infant her own care,
    Kissing its cries away as these awake; –
    Is not better thus our lives to wear,
Than join the crushing crowd, doom'd to inflict or bear?

99

LXXII

I live not in myself, but I become
Portion of that around me; and to me
High mountains are a feeling, but the hum
Of human cities torture: I can see
Nothing to loathe in nature, save to be
A link reluctant in a fleshly chain,
Class'd among creatures, when the soul can flee
And with the sky, the peak, the heaving plain
Of ocean, or the stars, mingle, and not in vain.

LXXIII

And thus I am absorb'd, and this is life:
I look upon the peopled desert past,
As on a place of agony and strife,
Where, for some sin, to sorrow I was cast,
To act and suffer, but remount at last
With a fresh pinion; which I feel to spring,
Though young, yet waxing vigorous as the blast
Which it would cope with, on delighted wing,
Spurning the clay-cold bonds which round our being cling.

LXXIV

And when, at length, the mind shall be all free
From what it hates in this degraded form,
Reft of its carnal life, save what shall be
Existent happier in the fly and worm, –
When elements to elements conform,
And dust is as it should be, shall I not
Feel all I see, less dazzling, but more warm?
The bodiless thought? the Spirit of each spot?
Of which, even now, I share at times the immortal lot?

Are not the mountains, waves, and skies, a part
Of me and of my soul, as I of them?
Is not the love of these deep in my heart
With a pure passion? should I not contemn
All objects, if compared with these? and stem
A tide of suffering, rather than forego
70   Such feelings for the hard and wordly phlegm
Of those whose eyes are only turn'd below,
Gazing upon the ground, with thoughts which dare not
    glow?

[A Truce with the World]

CXIII

I have not loved the world, nor the world me;
I have not flatter'd its rank breath, nor bow'd
To its idolatories a patient knee,
Nor coin'd my cheek to smiles, nor cried aloud
In worship of an echo; in the crowd
They could not deem me one of such; I stood
Among them, but not of them; in a shroud
Of thoughts which were not their thoughts, and still
    could,
Had I not filed my mind, which thus itself subdued.

CXIV

10   I have not loved the world, nor the world me, –
But let us part fair foes; I do believe,
Though I have found them not, that there may be
Words which are things, hopes which will not deceive
And virtues which are merciful, nor weave

Snares for the failing; I would also deem
O'er others' griefs that some sincerely grieve;
That two, or one, are almost what they seem,
That goodness is no name, and happiness no dream.

CXV

My daughter! with thy name this song begun;
20   My daughter! with thy name thus much shall end;
I see thee not, I hear thee not, but none
Can be so wrapt in thee; thou art the friend
To whom the shadows of far years extend:
Albeit my brow thou never shouldst behold,
My voice shall with thy future visions blend,
And reach into thy heart, when mine is cold,
A token and a tone, even from thy father's mould.

CXVI

To aid thy mind's development, to watch
Thy dawn of little joys, to sit and see
30   Almost thy very growth, to view thee catch
Knowledge of objects, – wonders yet to thee!
To hold thee lightly on a gentle knee,
And print on thy soft cheek a parent's kiss, –
This, it should seem, was not reserved for me;
Yet this was in my nature: as it is,
I know not what is there, yet something like to this.

CXVII

Yet, though dull Hate as duty should be taught,
I know that thou wilt love me; though my name
Should be shut from thee, as a spell still fraught
40   With desolation, and a broken claim:
Though the grave closed between us, – 'twere the same,

I know that thou wilt love me; thou to drain
My blood from out thy being were an aim,
And an attainment, – all would be in vain, –
Still thou wouldst love me, still that more than life retain.

CXVIII

The child of love, though born in bitterness,
And nurtured in convulsion. Of thy sire
These were the elements, and thine no less.
As yet such are around thee, but thy fire
Shall be more temper'd, and thy hope far higher.
Sweet be thy cradled slumbers! O'er the sea
And from the mountains where I now respire,
Fain would I waft such blessing upon thee,
As, with a sigh, I deem thou might'st have been to me.

The Prisoner of Chillon

I

My hair is grey, but not with years,
   Nor grew it white
   In a single night,
As men's have grown from sudden fears:
My limb's are bow'd, though not with toil,
But rusted with a vile repose,
For they have been a dungeon's spoil,
   And mine has been the fate of those
To whom the goodly earth and air
Are bann'd, and barr'd – forbidden fare:
But this was for my father's faith
I suffer'd chains and courted death;
That father perish'd at the stake
For tenets he would not forsake;
And for the same his lineal race
In darkness found a dwelling-place;
We were seven – who now are one,
   Six in youth, and one in age,
Finish'd as they had begun,
   Proud of Persecution's rage;
One in fire, and two in field,
Their belief with blood have seal'd,
Dying as their father died,
For the God their foes denied;
Three were in a dungeon cast,
Of whom this wreck is left the last.

II

There are seven pillars of Gothic mould,
In Chillon's dungeons deep and old
There are seven columns, massy and grey,

Dim with a dull imprison'd ray,
A sunbeam which hath lost its way,
And through the crevice and the cleft
Of the thick wall is fallen and left;
Creeping o'er the floor so damp,
Like a marsh's meteor lamp:
And in each pillar there is a ring,
   And in each ring there is a chain;
That iron is a cankering thing,
For in these limbs its teeth remain,
With marks that will not wear away,
Till I have done with this new day,
Which now is painful to these eyes,
Which have not seen the sun so rise
For years – I cannot count them o'er,
I lost their long and heavy score,
When my last brother droop'd and died,
And I lay living by his side.

III

They chain'd us each to a column stone,
And we were three – yet, each alone;
We could not move a single pace,
We could not see each other's face,
But with that pale and livid light
That made us strangers in our sight:
And thus together – yet apart,
Fetter'd in hand, but join'd in heart,
'Twas still some solace, in the dearth
Of the pure elements of earth,
To hearken to each other's speech,
And each turn comforter to each
With some new hope, or legend old,
Or song heroically bold;
But even these at length grew cold.

Our voices took a dreary tone,
An echo of the dungeon stone,
  A grating sound, not full and free,
  As they of yore were wont to be:
  It might be fancy, but to me
They never sounded like our own.

IV

I was the eldest of the three,
  And to uphold and cheer the rest
  I ought to do – and did my best –
And each did well in his degree.
  The youngest, whom my father loved,
Because our mother's brow was given
To him, with eyes as blue as heaven –
  For him my soul was sorely moved;
And truly might it be distress'd
To see such bird in such a nest;
For he was beautiful as day –
  (When day was beautiful to me
As to young eagles, being free) –
  A polar day, which will not see
A sunset till its summer's gone,
  Its sleepless summer of long light,
The snow-clad offspring of the sun:
  And thus he was as pure and bright,
And in his natural spirit gay,
With tears for nought but others' ills,
And then they flow'd like mountain rills,
Unless he could assuage the woe
Which he abhorr'd to view below.

V

The other was as pure of mind,
But form'd to combat with his kind;

70

80

90

Strong in his frame, and of a mood
Which 'gainst the world in war had stood,
And perish'd in the foremost rank
    With joy: – but not in chains to pine:
His spirit wither'd with their clank,
    I saw it silently decline –
    And so perchance in sooth did mine:
But yet I forced it on to cheer
Those relics of a home so dear.
He was a hunter of the hills,
    Had follow'd there the deer and wolf;
To him his dungeon was a gulf,
And fetter'd feet the worst of ills.

VI

Lake Leman lies by Chillon's walls:
A thousand feet in depth below
Its massy waters meet and flow;
Thus much the fathom-line was sent
From Chillon's snow-white battlement,
    Which round about the wave inthrals:
A double dungeon walls and wave
Have made – and like a living grave
Below the surface of the lake
The dark vault lies wherein we lay,
We heard it ripple night and day;
    Sounding o'er our heads it knock'd;
And I have felt the winter's spray
Wash through the bars when winds were high
And wanton in the happy sky;
    And then the very rock hath rock'd,
    And I have felt it shake, unshock'd,
Because I could have smiled to see
The death that would have set me free.

VII

I said my nearer brother pined,
I said his mighty heart declined,
He loathed and put away his food;
It was not that 'twas coarse and rude,
For we were used to hunter's fare,
And for the like had little care:
The milk drawn from the mountain goat
Was changed for water from the moat,
Our bread was such as captives' tears
Have moisten'd many a thousand years,
Since man first pent his fellow men
Like brutes within an iron den;
But what were these to us or him?
These wasted not his heart or limb;
My brother's soul was of that mould
Which in a palace has grown cold,
Had his free breathing been denied
The range of the steep mountain's side;
But why delay the truth? – he died.
I saw, and could not hold his head,
Nor reach his dying hand – nor dead, –
Though hard I strove, but strove in vain,
To rend and gnash my bonds in twain.
He died, and they unlock'd his chain,
And scoop'd for him a shallow grave
Even from the cold earth of our cave,
I begg'd them as a boon to lay
His corse in dust whereon the day
Might shine – it was a foolish thought,
But then within my brain it wrought,
That even in death his freeborn breast
In such a dungeon could not rest.
I might have spared my idle prayer –
They coldly laugh'd, and laid him there:

The flat and turfless earth above
The being we so much did love;
His empty chain above it leant,
Such murder's fitting monument!

VIII

But he, the favourite and the flower,
Most cherish'd since his natal hour,
His mother's image in fair face,
The infant love of all his race,
His martyr'd father's dearest thought,
My latest care, for whom I sought
To hoard my life, that his might be
Less wretched now, and one day free;
He, too, who yet had held untired
A spirit natural or inspired –
He, too, was struck, and day by day
Was wither'd on the stalk away.
Oh, God! it is a fearful thing
To see the human soul take wing
In any shape, in any mood:
I've seen it rushing forth in blood,
I've seen it on the breaking ocean
Strive with a swoln convulsive motion,
I've seen the sick and ghastly bed
Of Sin delirious with its dread;
But these were horrors – this was woe
Unmix'd with such – but sure and slow:
He faded, and so calm and meek,
So softly worn, so sweetly weak,
So tearless, yet so tender, kind,
And grieved for those he left behind;
With all the while a cheek whose bloom
Was as a mockery of the tomb,

Whose tints as gently sunk away
As a departing rainbow's ray;
An eye of most transparent light,
That almost made the dungeon bright,
And not a word of murmur, not
A groan o'er his untimely lot, –
A little talk of better days,
A little hope my own to raise,
200 For I was sunk in silence – lost
In this last loss, of all the most;
And then the sighs he would suppress
Of fainting nature's feebleness,
More slowly drawn, grew less and less:
I listen'd, but I could not hear;
I call'd, for I was wild with fear;
I knew 'twas hopeless, but my dread
Would not be thus admonished;
I call'd, and thought I heard a sound –
210 I burst my chain with one strong bound,
And rush'd to him: – I found him not,
I only stirr'd in this black spot,
I only lived, *I* only drew
The accursed breath of dungeon-dew;
The last, the sole, the dearest link
Between me and the eternal brink,
Which bound me to my failing race,
Was broken in this fatal place.
One on the earth, and one beneath –
220 My brothers – both had ceased to breathe:
I took that hand which lay so still,
Alas! my own was full as chill;
I had not strength to stir, or strive,
But felt that I was still alive –
A frantic feeling, when we know
That what we love shall ne'er be so.

        I know not why
        I could not die,
    I had no earthly hope but faith,
    And that forbade a selfish death.

IX

What next befell me then and there
    I know not well – I never knew –
First came the loss of light, and air,
    And then of darkness too:
I had no thought, no feeling – none –
Among the stones I stood a stone,
And was, scarce conscious what I wist,
As shrubless crags within the mist;
For all was blank, and bleak, and grey;
It was not night, it was not day;
It was not even the dungeon-light,
So hateful to my heavy sight,
But vacancy absorbing space,
And fixedness without a place;
There were no stars, no earth, no time,
No check, no change, no good, no crime,
But silence, and a stirless breath
Which neither was of life nor death;
A sea of stagnant idleness,
Blind, boundless, mute, and motionless!

X

A light broke in upon my brain, –
    It was the carol of a bird;
It ceased, and then it came again,
    The sweetest song ear ever heard,
And mine was thankful till my eyes
Ran over with the glad surprise,

And they that moment could not see
I was the mate of misery;
But then by dull degrees came back
My senses to their wonted track;
I saw the dungeon walls and floor
Close slowly round me as before,
I saw the glimmer of the sun
Creeping as it before had done,
But through the crevice where it came
That bird was perch'd, as fond and tame,
    And tamer than upon the tree;
A lovely bird, with azure wings,
And song that said a thousand things,
    And seem'd to say them all for me!
I never saw its like before,
I ne'er shall see its likeness more:
It seem'd like me to want a mate,
But was not half so desolate,
And it was come to love me when
None lived to love me so again,
And cheering from my dungeon's brink,
Had brought me back to feel and think.
I know not if it late were free,
    Or broke its cage to perch on mine,
But knowing well captivity,
    Sweet bird! I could not wish for thine!
Or if it were, in winged guise,
A visitant from Paradise;
For – Heaven forgive that thought! the while
Which made me both to weep and smile –
I sometimes deem'd that it might be
My brother's soul come down to me;
But then at last away it flew,
    And then 'twas mortal well I knew,
For he would never thus have flown,

And left me twice so doubly lone,
Lone as the corse within its shroud,
Lone as a solitary cloud, –
    A single cloud on a sunny day,
While all the rest of heaven is clear,
A frown upon the atmosphere,
That hath no business to appear
    When skies are blue, and earth is gay.

XI

₃₀₀   A kind of change came in my fate,
My keepers grew compassionate;
I know not what had made them so,
They were inured to sights of woe,
But so it was: – my broken chain
With links unfasten'd did remain,
And it was liberty to stride
Along my cell from side to side,
And up and down, and then athwart,
And tread it over every part;
₃₁₀   And round the pillars one by one,
Returning where my walk begun,
Avoiding only, as I trod,
My brothers' graves without a sod;
For if I thought with heedless tread
My step profaned their lowly bed,
My breath came gaspingly and thick,
And my crush'd heart fell blind and sick.

XII

I made a footing in the wall,
    It was not therefrom to escape,
₃₂₀   For I had buried one and all
        Who loved me in a human shape;

And the whole earth would henceforth be
A wider prison unto me:
No child, no sire, no kin had I,
No partner in my misery;
I thought of this, and I was glad,
For thought of them had made me mad;
But I was curious to ascend
To my barr'd windows, and to bend
330 Once more, upon the mountains high,
The quiet of a loving eye.

XIII

I saw them, and they were the same,
They were not changed like me in frame;
I saw their thousand years of snow
On high – their wide long lake below,
And the blue Rhone in fullest flow;
I heard the torrents leap and gush
O'er channell'd rock and broken bush;
I saw the white-wall'd distant town,
340 And whiter sails go skimming down;
And then there was a little isle,
Which in my very face did smile,
  The only one in view;
A small green isle, it seem'd no more,
Scarce broader than my dungeon floor,
But in it there were three tall trees,
And o'er it blew the mountain breeze,
And by it there were waters flowing,
And on it there were young flowers growing
350 Of gentle breath and hue.
The fish swam by the castle wall,
And they seem'd joyous each and all;
The eagle rode the rising blast,
Methought he never flew so fast

114

As then to me he seem'd to fly;
And then new tears came in my eye,
And I felt troubled – and would fain
I had not left my recent chain;
And when I did descend again,
The darkness of my dim abode
Fell on me as a heavy load;
It was as is a new-dug grave,
Closing o'er one we sought to save, –
And yet my glance, too much opprest,
Had almost need of such a rest.

XIV

It might be months, or years, or days,
    I kept no count, I took no note,
I had no hope my eyes to raise,
    And clear them of their dreary mote;
At last men came to set me free;
    I ask'd not why, and reck'd not where;
It was at length the same to me,
Fetter'd or fetterless to be,
    I learn'd to love despair.
And thus when they appear'd at last,
And all my bonds aside were cast,
These heavy walls to me had grown
A hermitage – and all my own!
And half I felt as they were come
To tear me from a second home:
With spiders I had friendship made,
And watch'd them in their sullen trade,
Had seen the mice by moonlight play,
And why should I feel less than they?
We were all inmates of one place,
And I, the monarch of each race,

Had power to kill – yet, strange to tell!
In quiet we had learn'd to dwell;
My very chains and I grew friends,
390   So much a long communion tends
To make us what we are: – even I
Regain'd my freedom with a sigh.

Song for the Luddites

I

As the Liberty lads o'er the sea
Bought their freedom, and cheaply, with blood,
        So we, boys, we
    Will *die* fighting, or *live* free,
And down with all kings but King Ludd!

II

When the web that we weave is complete,
And the shuttle exchanged for the sword,
        We will fling the winding sheet
        O'er the despot at our feet,
10   And dye it deep in the gore he has pour'd.

III

Though black as his heart its hue,
Since his veins are corrupted to mud,
        Yet this is the dew
        Which the tree shall renew
Of Liberty, planted by Ludd!

December 1816.

Manfred: A Dramatic Poem

from ACT II, SCENE IV

*The Hall of Arimanes – Arimanes on his
Throne, a Globe of Fire, surrounded by
the Spirits.*
Hymn of the SPIRITS.

Hail to our Master! – Prince of Earth and Air!
  Who walks the clouds and waters – in his hand
The sceptre of the elements, which tear
  Themselves to chaos at his high command!
He breatheth – and a tempest shakes the sea;
  He speaketh – and the clouds reply in thunder;
He gazeth – from his glance the sunbeams flee;
  He moveth – earthquakes rend the world asunder.
Beneath his footsteps the volcanoes rise;
10   His shadow is the Pestilence; his path
The comets herald through the crackling skies;
  And planets turn to ashes at his wrath.
To him War offers daily sacrifice;
  To him Death pays its tribute; Life is his,
With all its infinite of agonies –
  And his the spirit of whatever is!

Enter the DESTINIES *and* NEMESIS.

First Des. Glory to Arimanes! on the earth
His power increaseth – both my sisters did
His bidding, nor did I neglect my duty!
20   *Second Des.* Glory to Arimanes! we who bow
The necks of men, bow down before his throne!

117

Third Des. Glory to Arimanes! we await his nod!

Nem. Sovereign of Sovereigns! we are thine,
And all that liveth, more or less, is ours,
And most things wholly so; still to increase
Our power, increasing thine, demands our care,
And we are vigilant. Thy late commands
Have been fulfill'd to the utmost.

Enter MANFRED.

A Spirit.   What is here?
A mortal! – Thou most rash and fatal wretch,
30 Bow down and worship!

Second Spirit.   I do know the man –
A Magian of great power, and fearful skill!

Third Spirit. Bow down and worship, slave! –
    What, know'st thou not
Thine and our Sovereign? – Tremble, and obey!

All the Spirits. Prostrate thyself, and thy condemned
    clay,
Child of the Earth! or dread the worst.

Man.   I know it;
And yet ye see I kneel not.

Fourth Spirit.   'T will be taught thee.

Man. 'Tis taught already; – many a night on the earth,
On the bare ground, have I bow'd down my face,
And strew'd my head with ashes; I have known
40 The fulness of humiliation, for
I sunk before my vain despair, and knelt
To my own desolation.

Fifth Spirit.   Dost thou dare
Refuse to Arimanes on his throne
What the whole earth accords, beholding not
The terror of his glory? – Crouch, I say.

Man. Bid *him* bow down to that which is above him,
The overruling Infinite – the Maker

Who made him not for worship – let him kneel,
And we will kneel together.
    The Spirits.   Crush the worm!
50 Tear him in pieces! –
    First Des.   Hence! avaunt! – he's mine.
Prince of the Powers invisible! This man
Is of no common order, as his port
And presence here denote; his sufferings
Have been of an immortal nature, like
Our own; his knowledge, and his powers and will,
As far as is compatible with clay,
Which clogs the ethereal essence, have been such
As clay hath seldom borne; his aspirations
Have been beyond the dwellers of the earth,
60 And they have only taught him what we know –
That knowledge is not happiness, and science
But an exchange of ignorance for that
Which is another kind of ignorance.
This is not all – the passions, attributes
Of earth and heaven, from which no power, nor being,
Nor breath from the worm upwards is exempt,
Have pierced his heart, and in their consequence
Made him a thing which I, who pity not,
Yet pardon those who pity. He is mine,
70 And thine, it may be; be it so, or not,
No other Spirit in this region hath
A soul like his – or power upon his soul.
    Nem. What doth he here then?
    First Des.   Let him answer that.
    Man. Ye know what I have known; without power
I could not be amongst ye: but there are
Powers deeper still beyond – I come in quest
Of such, to answer unto what I seek.
    Nem. What wouldst thou?
    Man.   Thou canst not reply to me.

Call up the dead – my question is for them

80   *Nem.* Great Arimanes, doth thy will avouch
The wishes of this mortal?

    Ari.   Yea.

    Nem.   Whom wouldst thou
Uncharnel?

    Man.   One without a tomb – call up
Astarte.

NEMESIS

        Shadow or Spirit!
          Whatever thou art,
        Which still doth inherit
          The whole or a part
        Of the form of thy birth,
          Of the mould of thy clay,
90   Which return'd to the earth,
          Re-appear to the day!
        Bear what thou borest,
          The heart and the form,
        And the aspect thou worest
          Redeem from the worm.
    Appear! – Appear! – Appear!
    Who sent thee there requires thee here!

    [*The Phantom of* ASTARTE *rises and stands in the midst.*

Man. Can this be death? there's bloom upon her cheek;
But now I see it is no living hue,
100 But a strange hectic – like the unnatural red
Which Autumn plants upon the perish'd leaf.
It is the same! Oh, God! that I should dread
To look upon the same – Astarte! – No,
I cannot speak to her – but bid her speak –
Forgive me or condemn me.

    By the power which hath broken
      The grave which enthrall'd thee,
    Speak to him who hath spoken,
      Or those who have call'd thee!

110   *Man.*   She is silent,
And in that silence I am more than answer'd.
    Nem. My power extends no further. Prince of Air!
It rests with thee alone – command her voice.
    Ari. Spirit – obey this sceptre!
    Nem.   Silent still!
She is not of our order, but belongs
To the other powers. Mortal! Thy quest is vain,
And we are baffled also.
    Man.   Hear me, hear me –
Astarte! my beloved! speak to me:
I have so much endured – so much endure –
120 Look on me! the grave hath not changed thee more
Than I am changed for thee. Thou lovedst me
Too much, as I loved thee: we were not made
To torture thus each other, though it were
The deadliest sin to love as we have loved.
Say that thou loath'st me not – that I do bear
This punishment for both – that thou wilt be
One of the blessed – and that I shall die;
For hitherto all hateful things conspire
To bind me in existence – in a life
130 Which makes me shrink from immortality –
A future like the past. I cannot rest.
I know not what I ask, nor what I seek:
I feel but what thou art, and what I am;
And I would hear yet once before I perish
The voice which was my music – Speak to me!
For I have call'd on thee in the still night,
Startled the slumbering birds from the hush'd boughs,

And woke the mountain wolves, and made the caves
Acquainted with thy vainly echoed name,
140 Which answer'd me – many things answer'd me –
Spirits and men – but thou wert silent all.
Yet speak to me! I have outwatch'd the stars,
And gazed o'er heaven in vain in search of thee.
Speak to me! I have wander'd o'er the earth,
And never found thy likeness – Speak to me!
Look on the fiends around – they feel for me:
I fear them not, and feel for thee alone –
Speak to me! though it be in wrath; – but say –
I reck not what – but let me hear thee once –
150 This once – once more!

    Phantom of Astarte. Manfred!

    Man.   Say on, say on –
I live but in the sound – it is thy voice!

    Phan. Manfred! Tomorrow ends thine earthly ills.
Farewell!

    Man. Yet one word more – am I forgiven?

    Phan. Farewell!

    Man.   Say, shall we meet again?

    Phan. Farewell!

    Man. One word for mercy! Say, thou lovest me.

    Phan. Manfred!

                    [*The Spirit of* Astarte *disappears.*

    Nem. She's gone, and will not be recall'd;
Her words will be fulfill'd. Return to the earth.

    A Spirit. He is convulsed. – This is to be a mortal
And seek the things beyond mortality.

160   *Another Spirit.* Yet, see, he mastereth himself, and makes
His torture tributary to his will.
Had he been one of us, he would have made
An awful spirit.

    Nem.   Hast thou further question
Of our great sovereign, or his worshippers?

Man. None.

Nem.   Then for a time farewell.

Man. We meet then! Where? On the earth? –
Even as thou wilt: and for the grace accorded
I now depart a debtor. Fare ye well!

                                        [*Exit* MANFRED.

          (*Scene closes.*)

ACT III, SCENE I

A Hall in the Castle of Manfred.

MANFRED *and* HERMAN.

Man. What is the hour?

Her.   It wants but one till sunset,
And promises a lovely twilight.

Man.   Say,
Are all things so disposed of in the tower
As I directed?

Her.   All, my lord, are ready:
Here is the key and casket.

Man.   It is well:
Thou may'st retire.   [*Exit* HERMAN.

Man (*alone*). There is a calm upon me –
Inexplicable stillness! which till now
Did not belong to what I knew of life.
If that I did not know philosophy

10 To be of our vanities the motliest,
The merest word that ever fool'd the ear
From out the schoolman's jargon, I should deem
The golden secret, the sought 'Kalon,' found,
And seated in my soul. It will not last,
But it is well to have known it, though but once:

123

It hath enlarged my thoughts with a new sense,
And I within my tablets would note down
That there is such a feeling. Who is there?

Re-enter HERMAN

   Her. My lord, the abbot of St Maurice craves
20 To greet your presence.

Enter the ABBOT OF ST MAURICE

   Abbot.   Peace be with Count Manfred!
   Man. Thanks, holy father! welcome to these walls;
Thy presence honours them, and blesseth those
Who dwell within them.
   Abbot.   Would it were so, Count! –
But I would fain confer with thee alone.
   Man. Herman, retire. – What would my reverend guest?
   Abbot. Thus, without prelude: – Age and zeal, my
       office,
And good intent, must plead my privilege;
Our near, though not acquainted neighbourhood,
May also be my herald. Rumours strange,
30 And of unholy nature, are abroad,
And busy with thy name; a noble name
For centuries: may he who bears it now
Transmit it unimpair'd!
   Man.   Proceed, – I listen.
   Abbot. 'Tis said thou holdest converse with the things
Which are forbidden to the search of man;
That with the dwellers of the dark abodes,
The many evil and unheavenly spirits
Which walk the valley of the shade of death,
Thou communest. I know that with mankind,
40 Thy fellows in creation, thou dost rarely
Exchange thy thoughts, and that thy solitude
Is as an anchorite's, were it but holy.

Man. And what are they who do avouch these things?

Abbot. My pious brethren – the sacred peasantry –
Even thy own vassals – who do look on thee
With most unquiet eyes. Thy life's in peril.

Man. Take it.

Abbot.   I come to save, and not destroy:
I would not pry into thy secret soul;
But if these things be sooth, there still is time
50 For penitence and pity: reconcile thee
With the true church, and through the church to heaven.

Man. I hear thee. This is my reply: whate'er
I may have been, or am, doth rest between
Heaven and myself. I shall not choose a mortal
To be my mediator. Have I sinn'd
Against your ordinances? prove and punish!

Abbot. My son! I did not speak of punishment,
But penitence and pardon; – with thyself
The choice of such remains – and for the last,
60 Our institutions and our strong belief
Have given me power to smooth the path from sin
To higher hope and better thoughts; the first
I leave to heaven, – 'Vengeance is mine alone!'
So saith the Lord, and with all humbleness
His servant echoes back the awful word.

Man. Old man! there is no power in holy men,
Nor charm in prayer, nor purifying form
Of penitence, nor outward look, nor fast,
Nor agony – nor, greater than all these,
70 The innate tortures of that deep despair,
Which is remorse without the fear of hell,
But all in all sufficient to itself
Would make a hell of heaven – can exorcise
From out the unbounded spirit the quick sense
Of its own sins, wrongs, sufferance, and revenge
Upon itself; there is no future pang

Can deal that justice on the self-condemn'd
He deals on his own soul.

    Abbot   All this is well;
For this will pass away, and be succeeded
80 By an auspicious hope, which shall look up
With calm assurance to that blessed place,
Which all who seek may win, whatever be
Their earthly errors, so they be atoned:
And the commencement of atonement is
The sense of its necessity. Say on –
And all our church can teach thee shall be taught;
And all we can absolve thee shall be pardon'd.

    Man. When Rome's sixth emperor was near his last,
The victim of a self-inflicted wound,
90 To shun the torments of a public death
From senates once his slaves, a certain soldier
With show of loyal pity, would have stanch'd
The gushing throat with his officious robe;
The dying Roman thrust him back, and said –
Some empire still in his expiring glance –
'It is too late – is this fidelity?'

    Abbot. And what of this?

    Man.   I answer with the Roman –
'It is too late!'

    Abbot.   It never can be so,
To reconcile thyself with thy own soul,
100 And thy own soul with heaven. Hast thou no hope?
'T is strange – even those who do despair above,
Yet shape themselves some fantasy on earth.
To which frail twig they cling, like drowning men.

    Man. Ay – father! I have had those earthly visions,
And noble aspirations in my youth,
To make my own the mind of other men,
The enlightener of nations; and to rise
I knew not whither – it might be to fall;

But fall, even as the mountain-cataract,
110 Which having leapt from its more dazzling height,
Even in the foaming strength of its abyss,
Which casts up misty columns that become
Clouds raining from the re-ascended skies,)
Lies low but mighty still. – But this is past,
My thoughts mistook themselves.

    Abbot.   And wherefore so?
    Man. I could not tame my nature down; for he
Must serve who fain would sway; and soothe, and sue,
And watch all time, and pry into all place,
And be a living lie, who would become
120 A mighty thing amongst the mean, and such
The mass are; I disdain'd to mingle with
A herd, though to be leader – and of wolves.
The lion is alone, and so am I.

    Abbot. And why not live and act with other men?
    Man. Because my nature was averse from life;
And yet not cruel; for I would not make,
But find a desolation. Like the wind,
The red-hot breath of the most lone simoom,
Which dwells but in the desert, and sweeps o'er
130 The barren sands which bear no shrubs to blast,
And revels o'er their wild and arid waves,
And seeketh not, so that it is not sought,
But being met is deadly, – such hath been
The course of my existence; but there came
Things in my path which are no more.

    Abbot.   Alas!
I 'gin to fear that thou art past all aid
From me and from my calling; yet so young,
I still would –

    Man.   Look on me! there is an order
Of mortals on the earth, who do become
140 Old in their youth, and die ere middle age,

Without the violence of warlike death;
Some perishing of pleasure, some of study,
Some worn with toil, some of mere weariness,
Some of disease, and some insanity,
And some of wither'd or of broken hearts;
For this last is a malady which slays
More than are number'd in the lists of Fate,
Taking all shapes, and bearing many names.
Look upon me! for even of all these things
150 Have I partaken; and of all these things,
One were enough; then wonder not that I
Am what I am, but that I ever was,
Or having been, that I am still on earth.
    Abbot. Yet, hear me still –
    Man.   Old man! I do respect
Thine order, and revere thine years; I deem
Thy purpose pious, but it is in vain:
Think me not churlish; I would spare thyself,
Far more than me, in shunning at this time
All further colloquy – and so – farewell.
                                  [*Exit* MANFRED
    Abbot. This should have been a noble creature: he
160 Hath all the energy which would have made
A goodly frame of glorious elements,
Had they been wisely mingled; as it is,
It is an awful chaos – light and darkness,
And mind and dust, and passions and pure thoughts
Mix'd, and contending without end or order, –
All dormant or destructive: he will perish,
And yet he must not; I will try once more.
For such are worth redemption; and my duty
170 Is to dare all things for a righteous end.
I'll follow him – but cautiously, though surely.
                                  [*Exit* ABBOT

Another Chamber

MANFRED *and* HERMAN

Her. My lord, you bade me wait on you at sunset:
He sinks behind the mountain.
    Man.   Doth he so?
I will look on him.   [MANFRED *advances to the*
                              Window of the Hall.
                Glorious Orb! the idol
Of early nature, and the vigorous race
Of undiseased mankind, the giant sons
Of the embrace of angels, with a sex
More beautiful than they, which did draw down
The erring spirits who can ne'er return. –
Most glorious orb! that wert a worship, ere
10 The mystery of thy making was reveal'd!
Thou earliest minister of the Almighty,
Which gladden'd, on their mountain tops, the hearts
Of the Chaldean shepherds, till they pour'd
Themselves in orisons! Thou material God!
And representative of the Unknown –
Who chose thee for his shadow! Thou chief star!
Centre of many stars! which mak'st our earth
Endurable, and temperest the hues
And hearts of all who walk within thy rays!
20 Sire of the seasons! Monarch of the climes,
And those who dwell in them! for near or far,
Our inborn spirits have a tint of thee
Even as our outward aspects; – thou dost rise,
And shine, and set in glory. Fare thee well!
I ne'er shall see thee more. As my first glance
Of love and wonder was for thee, then take
My latest look; thou wilt not beam on one

129

To whom the gifts of life and warmth have been
Of a more fatal nature. He is gone:
30   I follow.   [*Exit* MANFRED.

from ACT III, SCENE IV

Man. Pronounce – what is thy mission?
Spirit.   Come!
Abbot. What art thou, unknown being? answer! – speak!
Spirit. The genius of this mortal. – Come! 'tis time.
Man. I am prepared for all things, but deny
The power which summons me. Who sent thee here?
Spirit. Thou'lt know anon – Come! come!
Man.   I have commanded
Things of an essence greater far than thine,
And striven with thy masters. Get thee hence!
Spirit. Mortal! thine hour is come – Away! I say.
10   *Man.* I knew, and know my hour is come but not
To render up my soul to such as thee:
Away! I'll die as I have lived – alone.
Spirit. Then I must summon up my brethren. – Rise!
                                    [*Other Spirits rise up.*
Abbot. Avaunt! ye evil ones! – Avaunt! I say;
Ye have no power where piety hath power,
And I do charge ye in the name –
Spirit.   Old man!
We know ourselves, our mission, and thine order:
Waste not thy holy words on idle uses,
It were in vain: this man is forfeited.
20   Once more I summon him – Away! Away!
Man. I do defy ye, – though I feel my soul
Is ebbing from me, yet I do defy ye;
Nor will I hence, while I have earthly breath

130

To breathe my scorn upon ye – earthly strength
To wrestle, though with spirits; what ye take
Shall be ta'en limb by limb.

  Spirit   Reluctant mortal!
Is this the Magian who would so pervade
The world invisible, and make himself
Almost our equal? Can it be that thou
30 Art thus in love with life? the very life
Which made thee wretched!

  Man.   Thou false fiend, thou liest!
My life is in its last hour, – *that* I know,
Nor would redeem a moment of that hour;
I do not combat against death, but thee
And thy surrounding angels; my past power,
Was purchased by no compact with thy crew,
But by superior science – penance, daring,
And length of watching, strength of mind, and skill
In knowledge of our fathers – when the earth
40 Saw men and spirits walking side by side,
And gave ye no supremacy: I stand
Upon my strength – I do defy – deny –
Spurn back, and scorn ye! –

  Spirit.   But thy many crimes
Have made thee –

  Man.   What are they to such as thee?
Must crimes be punish'd but by other crimes,
And greater criminals? – Back to thy hell!
Thou hast no power upon me, that I feel;
Thou never shalt possess me, *that* I know:
What I have done is done; I bear within
50 A torture which could nothing gain from thine:
The mind which is immortal makes itself
Requital for its good or evil thoughts, –
Is its own origin of ill and end
And its own place and time: its innate sense,

When stripp'd of this mortality, derives
No colour from the fleeting things without,
But is absorb'd in sufferance or in joy,
Born from the knowledge of its own desert.
Thou didst not tempt me, and thou couldst not tempt me;
60 I have not been thy dupe, nor am thy prey –
But was my own destroyer, and will be
My own hereafter. – Back, ye baffled fiends! –
The hand of death is on me – but not yours!
                                        [*The Demons disappear*
   Abbot. Alas! how pale thou art – thy lips are white –
And thy breast heaves – and in thy gasping throat
The accents rattle: Give thy prayers to heaven –
Pray – albeit but in thought, – but die not thus.
   Man. 'Tis over – my dull eyes can fix thee not;
But all things swim around me, and the earth
70 Heaves as it were beneath me. Fare thee well!
Give me thy hand.
   Abbot.   Cold – cold – even to the heart –
But yet one prayer – Alas! how fares it with thee?
   Man. Old man! 'tis not so difficult to die.
                                        [MANFRED *expires*
   Abbot. He's gone – his soul hath ta'en its earthless
       flight;
Whither? I dread to think – but he is gone.

───────────

So, we'll go no more a roving

I

So, we'll go no more a roving
    So late into the night,
Though the heart be still as loving,
    And the moon be still as bright.

II

For the sword outwears its sheath,
    And the soul wears out the breast,
And the heart must pause to breathe,
    And love itself have rest.

III

Though the night was made for loving,
    And the day returns too soon,
Yet we'll go no more a roving
    By the light of the moon.

1817

To Thomas Moore

I

My boat is on the shore,
    And my bark is on the sea;
But, before I go, Tom Moore,
    Here's a double health to thee!

II

Here's a sigh to those who love me,
    And a smile to those who hate;
And, whatever sky's above me,
    Here'a heart for every fate.

III

Though the ocean roar around me,
    Yet it still shall bear me on;
Though a desert should surround me,
    It hath springs that may be won.

Were't the last drop in the well,
   As I gasp'd upon the brink,
Ere my fainting spirit fell,
   'Tis to thee that I would drink.

V

With that water, as this wine,
   The libation I would pour
Should be – peace with thine and mine,
   And a health to thee, Tom Moore.

July 1817

Childe Harold's Pilgrimage

[Venice]

I

I stood in Venice, on the Bridge of Sighs;
A palace and a prison on each hand:
I saw from out the wave her structures rise
As from the stroke of the enchanter's wand:
A thousand years their cloudy wings expand
Around me, and a dying Glory smiles
O'er the far times, when many a subject land
Look'd to the winged Lion's marble piles,
Where Venice sate in state, throned on her hundred isles!

II

10 She looks a sea Cybele, fresh from ocean,
Rising with her tiara of proud towers
At airy distance, with majestic motion,
A ruler of the waters and their powers:
And such she was; – her daughters had their dowers
From spoils of nations, and the exhaustless East
Pour'd in her lap all gems in sparkling showers.
In purple was she robed, and of her feast
Monarchs partook, and deem'd their dignity increased.

III

In Venice Tasso's echoes are no more,
20 And silent rows the songless gondolier;
Her palaces are crumbling to the shore,

135

And music meets not always now the ear:
Those days are gone – but Beauty still is here.
States fall, arts fade – but Nature doth not die,
Nor yet forget how Venice once was dear,
The pleasant place of all festivity,
The revel of the earth, the masque of Italy!

IV

But unto us she hath a spell beyond
Her name in story, and her long array
Of mighty shadows, whose dim forms despond
Above the dogeless city's vanish'd sway;
Ours is a trophy which will not decay
With the Rialto; Shylock and the Moor,
And Pierre, cannot be swept or worn away –
The keystones of the arch! though all were o'er,
For us repeopled were the solitary shore.

V

The beings of the mind are not of clay;
Essentially immortal, they create
And multiply in us a brighter ray
And more beloved existence: that which Fate
Prohibits to dull life, in this our state
Of mortal bondage, by these spirits supplied,
First exiles, then replaces what we hate;
Watering the heart whose early flowers have died,
And with a fresher growth replenishing the void.

VI

Such is the refuge of our youth and age,
The first from Hope, the last from Vacancy;
And this worn feeling peoples many a page,
And, may be, that which grows beneath mine eye:
Yet there are things whose strong reality

Outshines our fairy-land; in shape and hues
More beautiful than our fantastic sky,
And the strange constellations which the Muse
O'er her wild universe is skilful to diffuse:

VII

I saw or dream'd of such, – but let them go, –
They came like truth, and disappear'd like dreams;
And whatsoe'er they were – are now but so:
I could replace them if I would; still teems
My mind with many a form which aptly seems
60   Such as I sought for, and at moments found;
Let these too go – for waking Reason deems
Such overweening phantasies unsound,
And other voices speak, and other sights surround.

VIII

I've taught me other tongues, and in strange eyes
Have made me not a stranger; to the mind
Which is itself, no changes bring surprise;
Nor is it harsh to make, nor hard to find
A country with – ay, or without mankind;
Yet was I born where men are proud to be, –
70   Not without cause, and should I leave behind
The inviolate island of the sage and free,
And seek me out a home by a remoter sea,

IX

Perhaps I loved it well: and should I lay
My ashes in a soil which is not mine,
My spirit shall resume it – if we may
Unbodied choose a sanctuary. I twine
My hopes of being remember'd in my line

With my land's language: if too fond and far
These aspirations in their scope incline, –
80   If my fame should be, as my fortunes are,
Of hasty growth and blight, and dull Oblivion bar

X

My name from out the temple where the dead
Are honour'd by the nations – let it be –
And light the laurels on a loftier head!
And be the Spartan's epitaph on me –
'Sparta hath many a worthier son than he,'
Meantime I seek no sympathies, nor need;
The thorns which I have reap'd are of the tree
I planted: they have torn me, and I bleed:
90   I should have known what fruit would spring from such a
        seed.

XI

The spouseless Adriatic mourns her lord;
And, annual marriage now no more renew'd.
The Bucentaur lies rotting unrestored,
Neglected garment of her widowhood!
St Mark yet sees his lion where he stood
Stand, but in mockery of his wither'd power,
Over the proud Place where an Emperor sued,
And monarchs gazed and envied in the hour
When Venice was a queen with an unequall'd dower.

XII

100   The Suabian sued, and now the Austrian reigns –
An Emperor tramples where an Emperor knelt;
Kingdoms are shrunk to provinces, and chains
Clank over sceptred cities; nations melt
From power's high pinnacle, when they have felt

The sunshine for a while, and downward go
Like lauwine loosen'd from the mountain's belt;
Oh for one hour of blind old Dandolo!
Th' octogenarian chief, Byzantium's conquering foe.

XIII

Before St Mark still glow his steeds of brass,
Their gilded collars glittering in the sun;
But is not Doria's menace come to pass?
Are they not *bridled*? – Venice, lost and won,
Her thirteen hundred years of freedom done,
Sinks, like a seaweed, into whence she rose!
Better be whelm'd beneath the waves, and shun,
Even in destruction's depth's her foreign foes,
From whom submission wrings an infamous repose.

XIV

In youth she was all glory, – a new Tyre;
Her very by-word sprung from victory,
The 'Planter of the Lion,' which through fire
And blood she bore o'er subject earth and sea;
Though making many slaves, herself still free,
And Europe's bulwark 'gainst the Ottomite;
Witness Troy's rival, Candia! Vouch it, ye
Immortal waves that saw Lepanto's fight!
For ye are names no time nor tyranny can blight.

XV

Statues of glass – all shiver'd – the long file
Of her dead Doges are declined to dust;
But where they dwelt, the vast and sumptuous pile
Bespeaks the pageant of their splendid trust;
Their sceptre broken, and their sword in rust,

Have yielded to the stranger: empty halls,
Thin streets, and foreign aspects, such as must
Too oft remind her who and what inthrals,
Have flung a desolate cloud o'er Venice' lovely walls.

XVI

When Athens' armies fell at Syracuse,
And fetter'd thousands bore the yoke of war,
Redemption rose up in the Attic Muse,
Her voice their only ransom from afar:
140 See! as they chant the tragic hymn, the car
Of the o'ermaster'd victor stops, the reins
Fall from his hands, his idle scimitar
Starts from its belt – he rends his captive's chains,
And bids him thank the bard for freedom and his strains.

XVII

Thus Venice, if no stronger claim were thine,
Were all thy proud historic deeds forgot,
Thy choral memory of the Bard divine,
Thy love of Tasso, should have cut the knot
Which ties thee to thy tyrants; and thy lot
150 Is shameful to the nations, – most of all,
Albion! to thee: the Ocean queen should not
Abandon Ocean's children; in the fall
Of Venice think of thine, despite thy watery wall.

XVIII

I loved her from my boyhood; she to me
Was as a fairy city of the heart,
Rising like water-columns from the sea,

140

Of joy the sojourn, and of wealth the mart;
And Otway, Radcliffe, Schiller, Shakespeare's art,
Had stamp'd her image in me, and even so,
60   Although I found her thus, we did not part;
Perchance even dearer in her day of woe,
Than when she was a boast, a marvel, and a show.

[Suffering and Ruin]

XXI

Existence may be borne, and the deep root
Of life and sufferance make its firm abode
The bare and desolated bosoms: mute
The camel labours with the heaviest load,
And the wolf dies in silence, – not bestow'd
In vain should such example be; if they,
Things of ignoble or of savage mood,
Endure and shrink not, we of nobler clay
May temper it to bear, – it is but for a day.

XXII

10   All suffering doth destroy, or is destroy'd,
Even by the sufferer; and, in each event,
Ends: Some, with hope replenish'd and rebuoy'd,
Return to whence they came – with like intent,
And weave their web again; some, bow'd and bent,
Wax gray and ghastly, withering ere their time,
And perish with the reed on which they leant;
Some seek devotion, toil, war, good or crime,
According as their souls were form'd to sink or climb.

XXIII

But ever and anon of griefs subdued
20   There comes a token like a scorpion's sting,
Scarce seen, but with fresh bitterness imbued;
And slight withal may be the things which bring
Back on the heart the weight which it would fling
Aside for ever: it may be a sound –
A tone of music – summer's eve – or spring –
A flower – the wind – the ocean – which shall wound,
Striking the electric chain wherewith we are darkly bound;

XXIV

And how and why we know not, nor can trace
Home to its cloud this lightning of the mind,
30   But feel the shock renew'd, nor can efface
The blight and blackening which it leaves behind,
Which out of things familiar, undesign'd,
When least we deem of such, calls up to view
The spectres whom no exorcism can bind, –
The cold, the changed, perchance the dead – anew,
The mourn'd, the loved, the lost – too many! yet how few!

XXV

But my soul wanders; I demand it back
To meditate amongst decay, and stand
A ruin amidst ruins; there to track
40   Fall'n states and buried greatness, o'er a land
Which *was* the mightiest in its old command,
And *is* the loveliest, and must ever be
The master-mould of Nature's heavenly hand;
Wherein were cast the heroic and the free,
The beautiful, the brave, the lords of earth and sea,

[Thoughts on Italy]

Italia! oh Italia! thou who hast
The fatal gift of beauty, which became
A funeral dower of present woes and past,
On thy sweet brow is sorrow plough'd by shame,
And annals graved in characters of flame.
Oh, God! that thou wert in thy nakedness
Less lovely or more powerful, and couldst claim
Thy right, and awe the robbers back, who press
To shed thy blood, and drink the tears of thy distress;

10 Then might'st thou more appal; or, less desired,
Be homely and be peaceful, undeplored
For thy destructive charms; then, still untired,
Would not be seen the armed torrents pour'd
Down the deep Alps; nor would the hostile horde
Of many-nation'd spoilers from the Po
Quaff blood and water; nor the stranger's sword
Be thy sad weapon of defence, and so,
Victor or vanquish'd, thou the slave of friend or foe.

 Wandering in youth, I traced the path of him,
20 The Roman friend of Rome's least-mortal mind,
The friend of Tully: as my bark did skim
The bright blue waters with a fanning wind,
Came Megara before me, and behind
Ægina lay, Piræus on the right,
And Corinth on the left; I lay reclined
Along the prow, and saw all these unite
In ruin, even as he had seen the desolate sight;

For Time hath not rebuilt them, but uprear'd
Barbaric dwellings on their shatter'd site,
30   Which only make more mourn'd and more endear'd
The few last rays of their far-scatter'd light,
And the crush'd relics of their vanish'd might.
The Roman saw these tombs in his own age,
These sepulchres of cities, which excite
Sad wonder, and his yet surviving page
The moral lesson bears, drawn from such pilgrimage.

XLVI

That page is now before me, and on mine
His country's ruin added to the mass
Of perish'd states he mourn'd in their decline,
40   And I in desolation: all that *was*
Of then destruction *is*; and now, alas!
Rome – Rome imperial, bows her to the storm,
In the same dust and blackness, and we pass
The skeleton of her Titanic form,
Wrecks of another world, whose ashes still are warm.

XLVII

Yet, Italy! through every other land
Thy wrongs should ring, and shall, from side to side;
Mother of Arts! as once of arms; thy hand
Was then our guardian, and is still our guide;
50   Parent of our religion! whom the wide
Nations have knelt to for the keys of heaven!
Europe, repentant of her parricide,
Shall yet redeem thee, and, all backward driven,
Roll the barbarian tide, and sue to be forgiven.

[Rome]

Oh Rome! my country! city of the soul!
The orphans of the heart must turn to thee,
Lone mother of dead empires! and control
In their shut breasts their petty misery.
What are our woes and sufferance? Come and see
The cypress, hear the owl, and plod your way,
O'er steps of broken thrones and temples, Ye!
Whose agonies are evils of a day –
A world is at our feet as fragile as our clay.

10 The Niobe of nations! there she stands,
Childless and crownless, in her voiceless woe;
An empty urn within her wither'd hands,
Whose holy dust was scatter'd long ago;
The Scipios' tomb contains no ashes now;
The very sepulchres lie tenantless
Of their heroic dwellers: dost thou flow,
Old Tiber! through a marble wilderness?
Rise, with thy yellow waves, and mantle her distress.

The Goth, the Christian, Time, War, Flood, and Fire,
20 Have dealt upon the seven-hill'd city's pride;
She saw her glories star by star expire,
And up the steep barbarian monarchs ride,
Where the car climb'd the Capitol; far and wide
Temple and tower went down, nor left a site:
Chaos of ruins! who shall trace the void,
O'er the dim fragments cast a lunar light,
And say, 'here was, or is,' where all is doubly night?

The double night of ages, and of her,
Night's daughter, Ignorance, hath wrapt and wrap
30 All round us: we but feel our way to err:
The ocean hath its chart, the stars their map,
And Knowledge spreads them on her ample lap;
But Rome is as the desert, where we steer
Stumbling o'er recollections; now we clap
Our hands, and cry 'Eureka!' it is clear –
When but some false mirage of ruin rises near.

LXXXII

Alas! the lofty city! and alas!
The trebly hundred triumphs! and the day
When Brutus made the dagger's edge surpass
40 The conqueror's sword in bearing fame away!
Alas, for Tully's voice, and Virgil's lay,
And Livy's pictured page! – but these shall be
Her resurrection; all beside – decay.
Alas, for Earth, for never shall we see
That brightness in her eye she bore when Rome was free!

[Freedom for Italy]

XCVI

Can tyrants but by tyrants conquer'd be,
And Freedom find no champion and no child
Such as Columbia saw arise when she
Sprung forth a Pallas, arm'd and undefiled?
Or must such minds be nourish'd in the wild,
Deep in the unpruned forest, 'midst the roar
Of cataracts, where nursing Nature smiled
On infant Washington? Has Earth no more
Such seeds within her breast, or Europe no such shore?

10 But France got drunk with blood to vomit crime,
And fatal have her Saturnalia been
To Freedom's cause, in every age and clime;
Because the deadly days which we have seen,
And vile Ambition, and built up between
Man and his hopes an adamantine wall,
And the base pageant last upon the scene,
Are grown the pretext for the eternal thrall
  Which nips life's tree, and dooms man's worst – his second
    fall.

XCVIII

Yet, Freedom! yet thy banner, torn, but flying,
20 Streams like the thunder-storm *against* the wind;
Thy trumpet voice, though broken now and dying,
The loudest still the tempest leaves behind;
Thy tree hath lost its blossoms, and the rind,
Chopp'd by the axe, looks rough and little worth,
But the sap lasts, – and still the seed we find
Sown deep, even in the bosom of the North;
So shall a better spring less bitter fruit bring forth.

[Egeria—and Human Love]

CXV

Egeria! sweet creation of some heart
Which found no mortal resting-place so fair
As thine ideal breast; whate'er thou art
Or wert, – a young Aurora of the air,
The nympholepsy of some fond despair;

Or, it might be, a beauty of the earth,
Who found a more than common votary there
Too much adoring; whatsoe'er thy birth,
Thou wert a beautiful thought, and softly bodied forth.

CXVI

10 The mosses of thy fountain still are sprinkled
With thine Elysian water-drops; the face
Of thy cave-guarded spring with years unwrinkled,
Reflects the meek-eyed genius of the place,
Whose green, wild margin now no more erase
Art's works; nor must the delicate waters sleep,
Prison'd in marble, bubbling from the base
Of the cleft statue, with a gentle leap
The rill runs o'er, and round fern, flowers, and ivy creep,

CXVII

Fantastically tangled: the green hills
20 Are clothed with early blossoms, through the grass
The quick-eyed lizard rustles, and the bills
Of summer-birds sing welcome as ye pass;
Flowers fresh in hue, and many in their class,
Implore the pausing step, and with their dyes,
Dance in the soft breeze in a fairy mass;
The sweetness of the violet's deep blue eyes,
Kiss'd by the breath of heaven seems colour'd by its skies.

CXVIII

Here didst thou dwell, in this enchanted cover,
Egeria! thy all heavenly bosom beating
30 For the far footsteps of thy mortal lover;
The purple Midnight veil'd that mystic meeting
With her most starry canopy, and seating

Thyself by thine adorer, what befell?
This cave was surely shaped out for the greeting
Of an enamour'd Goddess, and the cell
Haunted by holy Love – the earliest oracle!

CXIX

And didst thou not, thy breast to his replying,
Blend a celestial with a human heart;
And Love, which dies as it was born, in sighing,
Share with immortal transports? could thine art
Make them indeed immortal, and impart
The purity of heaven to earthly joys,
Expel the venom and not blunt the dart –
The dull satiety which all destroys –
And root from out the soul the deadly weed which cloys?

CXX

Alas! our young affections run to waste,
Or water but the desert; whence arise
But weeds of dark luxuriance, tares of haste,
Rank at the core, though tempting to the eyes,
Flowers whose wild odours breathe but agonies,
And trees whose gums are poisons; such the plants
Which spring beneath her steps as Passion flies
O'er the world's wilderness, and vainly pants
For some celestial fruit forbidden to our wants

CXXI

Oh Love! no habitant of earth thou art –
An unseen seraph, we believe in thee, –
A faith whose martyrs are the broken heart, –
But never yet hath seen, nor e'er shall see
The naked eye, thy form, as it should be;

149

The mind hath made thee, as it peopled heaven,
Even with its own desiring phantasy,
And to a thought such shape and image given,
As haunts the unquench'd soul – parch'd, wearied, wrung,
        and riven.

CXXII

Of its own beauty is the mind diseased,
And fevers into false creation: – where,
Where are the forms the sculptor's soul hath seiz'd?
In him alone. Can Nature show so fair?
Where are the charms and virtues which we dare
Conceive in boyhood and pursue as men,
70 The unreach'd Paradise of our despair,
Which o'er-informs the pencil and the pen,
And overpowers the page where it would bloom again?

CXXIII

Who loves, raves – 't is youth's frenzy – but the cure
Is bitterer still, as charm by charm unwinds
Which robed our idols, and we see too sure
Nor worth nor beauty dwells from out the mind's
Ideal shape of such; yet still it binds
The fatal spell, and still it draws us on,
Reaping the whirlwind from the oft-sown winds;
80 The stubborn heart, its alchemy begun,
Seems ever near the prize – wealthiest when most undone.

CXXIV

We wither from our youth, we gasp away –
Sick – sick; unfound the boon, unslaked the thirst,
Though to the last, in verge of our decay,
Some phantom lures, such as we sought at first –
But all too late, – so are we doubly curst.

Love, fame, ambition, avarice – 'tis the same,
Each idle, and all ill, and none the worst –
For all are meteors with a different name,
90 And Death the sable smoke where vanishes the flame.

CXXV

Few – none – find what they love or could have loved,
Though accident, blind contact, and the strong
Necessity of loving, have removed
Antipathies – but to recur, ere long,
Envenom'd with irrevocable wrong;
And Circumstance, that unspiritual god
And miscreator, makes and helps along
Our coming evils with a crutch-like rod,
Whose touch turns Hope to dust, – the dust we all have
    trod.

CXXVI

100 Our life is a false nature: 'tis not in
The harmony of things, – this hard decree,
This uneradicable taint of sin,
This boundless upas, this all-blasting tree,
Whose root is earth, whose leaves and branches be
The skies which rain their plagues on men like dew –
Disease, death, bondage – all the woes we see,
And worse, the woes we see not – which throb through
The immedicable soul, with heart-aches ever new.

CXXVII

Yet let us ponder boldly – 'tis a base
110 Abandonment of reason to resign
Our right of thought – our last and only place
Of refuge; this, at least, shall still be mine:

151

Though from our birth the faculty divine
Is chain'd and tortured – cabin'd, cribb'd, confined,
And bred in darkness, lest the truth should shine
Too brightly on the unprepared mind,
The beam pours in, for time and skill will couch the blind.

[Vengeance—or Forgiveness?]

CXXX

Oh Time! the beautifier of the dead,
Adorner of the ruin, comforter
And only healer when the heart hath bled;
Time! the corrector where our judgments err,
The test of truth, love – sole philosopher,
For all beside are sophists – from thy thrift,
Which never loses though it doth defer –
Time, the avenger! unto thee I lift
My hands, and eyes, and heart, and crave of thee a gift:

CXXXI

10   Amidst this wreck, where thou hast made a shrine
And temple more divinely desolate,
Among thy mightier offerings here are mine,
Ruins of years, though few, yet full of fate:
If thou hast ever seen me too elate,
Hear me not; but if calmly I have borne
Good, and reserved my pride against the hate
Which shall not whelm me, let me not have worn
This iron in my soul in vain – shall *they* not mourn?

And thou, who never yet of human wrong
20   Left the unbalanced scale, great Nemesis!
Here, where the ancient paid thee homage long –
Thou who didst call the Furies from the abyss,
And round Orestes bade them howl and hiss
For that unnatural retribution – just,
Had it been from hands less near – in this
Thy former realm, I call thee from the dust!
Dost thou not hear my heart? – Awake! thou shalt, and
      must.

It is not that I may not have incurr'd
For my ancestral faults or mine the wound
30   I bleed withal, and, had it been conferr'd
With a just weapon, it had flow'd unbound;
But now my blood shall not sink in the ground;
To thee I do devote it – *thou* shalt take
The vengeance, which shall yet be sought and found,
Which if *I* have not taken for the sake –
But let that pass – I sleep, but thou shalt yet awake.

And if my voice break forth, 'tis not that now
I shrink from what is suffer'd: let him speak
Who hath beheld decline upon my brow,
40   Or seen my mind's convulsion leave it weak;
But in this page a record will I seek.
Not in the air shall these my words disperse,
Though I be ashes; a far hour shall wreak
The deep prophetic fulness of this verse,
And pile on human heads the mountain of my curse!

That curse shall be Forgiveness. – Have I not –
Hear me, my mother Earth! behold it, Heaven!
Have I not had to wrestle with my lot?
Have I not suffer'd things to be forgiven?
50   Have I not had my brain sear'd, my heart riven,
Hopes sapp'd, name blighted, Life's life lied away?
And only not to desperation driven,
Because not altogether of such clay
As rots into the souls of those whom I survey.

CXXXVI

From mighty wrongs to petty perfidy
Have I not seen what human things could do?
From the load roar of foaming calumny
To the small whisper of the as paltry few,
And subtler venom of the reptile crew,
60   The Janus glance of whose significant eye.
Learning to lie with silence, would *seem* true,
And without utterance, save the shrug or sigh,
Deal round to happy fools its speechless obloquy.

CXXXVII

But I have lived, and have not lived in vain:
My mind may lose its force, my blood its fire,
And my frame perish even in conquering pain;
But there is that within me which shall tire
Torture and Time, and breathe when I expire;
Something unearthly, which they deem not of,
70   Like the remember'd tone of a mute lyre,
Shall on their soften'd spirits sink, and move
In hearts all rocky now the late remorse of love.

[The Last of Childe Harold]

But where is he, the Pilgrim of my song,
The being who upheld it through the past?
Methinks he cometh late and tarries long.
He is no more – these breathings are his last;
His wanderings done, his visions ebbing fast,
And he himself as nothing: – if he was
Aught but a phantasy, and could be class'd
With forms which live and suffer – let that pass –
His shadow fades away into Destruction's mass.

10   Which gathers shadow, substance, life, and all
That we inherit in its mortal shroud,
And spreads the dim and universal pall
Through which all things grow phantoms; and the cloud
Between us sinks and all which ever glow'd,
Till Glory's self is twilight, and displays
A melancholy halo scarce allow'd
To hover on the verge of darkness; rays
Sadder than saddest night, for they distract the gaze,

And send us prying into the abyss,
20   To gather what we shall be when the frame
Shall be resolved to something less than this
Its wretched essence; and to dream of fame,
And wipe the dust from off the idle name
We never more shall hear, – but never more,
Oh, happier thought! can we be made the same:
It is enough in sooth that *once* we bore
These fardels of the heart – the heart whose sweat was
    gore.

[Nature, Ocean—and Farewell]

CLXXVII

Oh! that the Desert were my dwelling-place,
With one fair Spirit for my minister,
That I might all forget the human race,
And, hating no one, love but only her!
Ye elements! – in whose ennobling stir
I feel myself exalted – Can ye not
Accord me such a being? Do I err
In deeming such inhabit many a spot?
Though with them to converse can rarely be our lot.

CLXXVIII

10 There is a pleasure in the pathless woods,
There is a rapture on the lonely shore,
There is society, where none intrudes,
By the deep Sea, and music in its roar:
I love not Man the less, but Nature more,
From these our interviews, in which I steal
From all I may be, or have been before,
To mingle with the Universe, and feel
What I can ne'er express, yet cannot all conceal.

CLXXIX

20 Roll on, thou deep and dark blue Ocean – roll!
Ten thousand fleets sweep over thee in vain;
Man marks the earth with ruin – his control
Stops with the shore; upon the watery plain
The wrecks are all thy deed, nor doth remain
A shadow of man's ravage, save his own,
When, for a moment, like a drop of rain,
He sinks into thy depths with bubbling groan,
Without a grave, unknell'd, uncoffin'd, and unknown.

His steps are not upon thy paths, – thy fields
Are not a spoil for him, – thou dost arise
30   And shake him from thee; the vile strength he wields
For earth's destruction thou dost all despise,
Spurning him from thy bosom to the skies,
And send'st him, shivering in thy playful spray
And howling, to his Gods, where haply lies
His petty hope in some near port or bay,
And dashest him again to earth: – there let him lay.

CLXXXI

The armaments which thunderstrike the walls
Of rock-built cities, bidding nations quake,
And monarchs tremble in their capitals,
40   The oak leviathans, whose huge ribs make
Their clay creator the vain title take
Of lord of thee, and arbiter of war –
These are thy toys, and, as the snowy flake,
They melt into thy yeast of waves, which mar
Alike the Armada's pride or spoils of Trafalgar.

CLXXXII

Thy shores are empires, changed in all save thee –
Assyria, Greece, Rome, Carthage, what are they?
Thy waters wash'd them power while they were free,
And many a tyrant since; their shores obey
50   The stranger, slave, or savage; their decay
Has dried up realms to deserts: – not so thou; –
Unchangeable, save to thy wild waves' play,
Time writes no wrinkle on thine azure brow:
Such as creation's dawn beheld, thou rollest now.

CLXXXIII

Thou glorious mirror, where the Almighty's form
Glasses itself in tempests; in all time, –
Calm or convulsed, in breeze, or gale, or storm,
Icing the pole, or in the torrid clime
Dark-heaving – boundless, endless, and sublime,
60   The image of eternity, the throne
Of the Invisible; even from out thy slime
The monsters of the deep are made; each zone
Obeys thee; thou goest forth, dread, fathomless, alone.

CLXXXIV

And I have loved thee, Ocean! and my joy
Of youthful sports was on thy breast to be
Borne, like thy bubbles, onward: from a boy
I wanton'd with thy breakers – they to me
Were a delight; and if the freshening sea
Made them a terror – 'twas a pleasing fear,
70   For I was as it were a child of thee,
And trusted to thy billows far and near,
And laid my hand upon thy name – as I do here.

CLXXXV

My task is done, my song hath ceased, my theme
Has died into an echo; it is fit
The spell should break of this protracted dream.
The torch shall be extinguish'd which hath lit
My midnight lamp – and what is writ, is writ;
Would it were worthier! but I am not now
That which I have been – and my visions flit
80   Less palpably before me – and the glow
Which in my spirit dwelt is fluttering, faint, and low.

Farewell! a word that must be, and hath been –
A sound which makes us linger; – yet – farewell!
Ye! who have traced the Pilgrim to the scene
Which is his last, if in your memories dwell
A thought which once was his, if on ye swell
A single recollection, not in vain
He wore his sandal-shoon and scallop-shell;
Farewell! with *him* alone may rest the pain,
90   If such there were – with *you*, the moral of his strain.

from Mazeppa

[Mazeppa's Ride]

IX

' "Bring forth the horse!" – the horse was brought;
  In truth, he was a noble steed,
  A Tartar of the Ukraine breed,
Who look'd as though the speed of thought
Were in his limbs; but he was wild,
  Wild as the wild deer, and untaught,
With spur and bridle undefiled –
  'Twas but a day he had been caught;
And snorting, with erected mane,
And struggling fiercely, but in vain,
In the full foam of wrath and dread
To me the desert-born was led:
They bound me on, that menial throng;
Upon his back with many a throng;
Then loosed him with a sudden lash –
Away! – away! – and on we dash!
Torrents less rapid and less rash.

X

'Away! – away! My breath was gone,
I saw not where he hurried on:
'Twas scarcely yet the break of day,
And on he foam'd – away! – away!
The last of human sounds which rose,
As I was darted from my foes,

160

Was the wild shout of savage laughter,
Which on the wind came roaring after
A moment from that rabble rout:
With sudden wrath I wrench'd my head,
   And snapp'd the cord, which to the mane
   Had bound my neck in lieu of rein,
30 And, writhing half my form about,
Howl'd back my curse; but 'midst the tread,
The thunder of my courser's speed,
Perchance they did not hear nor heed:
It vexes me – for I would fain
Have paid their insult back again.
I paid it well in after days:
There is not of that castle gate,
Its drawbridge and portcullis' weight,
Stone, bar, moat, bridge, or barrier left;
40 Nor of its fields a blade of grass,
   Save what grows on a ridge of wall,
   Where stood the hearth-stone of the hall;
And many a time ye there might pass,
Nor dream that e'er that fortress was.
I saw its turrets in a blaze,
Their crackling battlements all cleft,
   And the hot lead pour down like rain
From off the scorch'd and blackening roof,
Whose thickness was not vengeance-proof.
50   They little thought that day of pain,
When launch'd, as on the lightning's flash,
They bade me to destruction dash,
   That one day I should come again,
With twice five thousand horse, to thank
   The Count for his uncourteous ride.
They play'd me then a bitter prank,
   When, with the wild horse for my guide,
They bound me to his foaming flank:

At length I play'd them one as frank
For time at last sets all things even –
    And if we do but watch the hour,
There never yet was human power
Which could evade, if unforgiven,
The patient search and vigil long
Of him who treasures up a wrong.

XI

'Away, away, my steed and I,
    Upon the pinions of the wind,
    All human dwellings left behind;
We sped like meteors through the sky,
When with its crackling sound the night
Is chequer'd with the northern light:
Town – village – none were on our track,
    But a wild plain of far extent,
And bounded by a forest black;
    And, save the scarce seen battlement
On distant heights of some strong hold,
Against the Tartars built of old,
No trace of man. The year before
A Turkish army had march'd o'er;
And where the Spahi's hood hath trod,
The verdure flies the bloody sod:
The sky was dull, and dim, and gray,
    And a low breeze crept moaning by –
    I could have answer'd with a sigh –
But fast we fled, away, away,
And I could neither sigh nor pray;
And my cold sweat-drops fell like rain
Upon the courser's bristling mane;
But, snorting still with rage and fear,
He flew upon his far career:
At times I almost thought, indeed,

162

He must have slacken'd in his speed;
But no – my bound and slender frame
　　Was nothing to his angry might,
And merely like a spur became:
Each motion which I made to free
My swoln limbs from their agony
　　Increased his fury and affright:
I tried my voice, – 'twas faint and low,
But yet he swerved as from a blow;
And, starting to each accent, sprang
As from a sudden trumpet's clang:
Meantime my cords were wet with gore,
Which, oozing through my limbs, ran o'er;
And in my tongue the thirst became
A something fierier far than flame.

XII

'We near'd the wild wood – 'twas so wide,
I saw no bounds on either side;
'Twas studded with old sturdy trees,
That bent not to the roughest breeze
Which howls down from Siberia's waste,
And strips the forest in its haste, –
But these were few and far between,
Set thick with shrubs more young and green,
Luxuriant with their annual leaves,
Ere strown by those autumnal eyes
That nip the forest's foliage dead,
Discolour'd with a lifeless red,
Which stands thereon like stiffen'd gore
Upon the slain when battle's o'er,
And some long winter's night hath shed
Its frost o'er every tombless head,
So cold and stark the raven's beak
May peck unpierced each frozen cheek:

'Twas a wild waste of underwood,
And here and there a chestnut stood,
The strong oak, and the hardy pine;
　　But far apart – and well it were,
Or else a different lot were mine –
130　　The boughs gave way, and did not tear
My limbs; and I found strength to bear
My wounds, already scarr'd with cold;
My bonds forbade to loose my hold.
We rustled through the leaves like wind,
Left shrubs, and trees, and wolves behind;
By night I heard them on the track,
Their troop came hard upon our back,
With their long gallop, which can tire
The hound's deep hate, and hunter's fire:
140　　Where'er we flew they follow'd on,
Nor left us with the morning sun;
Behind I saw them, scarce a rood,
At day-break winding through the wood,
And through the night had heard their feet
Their stealing, rustling step repeat.
Oh! how I wish'd for spear or sword,
At least to die amidst the horde,
And perish – if it must be so –
At bay, destroying many a foe!
150　　When first my courser's race begun,
I wish'd the goal already won;
But now I doubted strength and speed.
Vain doubt! his swift and savage breed
Had nerved him like the mountain-roe;
Nor faster falls the blinding snow
Which whelms the peasant near the door
Whose threshold he shall cross no more,
Bewilder'd with the dazzling blast,
Than through the forest-paths he pass'd –

Untired, untamed, and worse than wild;
All furious as a favour'd child
Balk'd of its wish; or fiercer still –
A woman piqued – who has her will.

XIII

'The wood was past; 'twas more than noon,
But chill the air, although in June;
Or it might be my veins ran cold –
Prolong'd endurance tames the bold;
And I was then not what I seem,
But headlong as a wintry stream,
And wore my feeling out before
I well could count their causes o'er:
And what with fury, fear, and wrath,
The tortures which beset my path,
Cold, hunger, sorrow, shame, distress,
Thus bound in nature's nakedness;
Sprung from a race whose rising blood,
When stirr'd beyond its calmer mood,
And trodden hard upon, is like
The rattle-snake's, in act to strike,
What marvel if this worn-out trunk
Beneath its woes a moment sunk?
The earth gave way, the skies roll'd round,
I seem'd to sink upon the ground;
But err'd, for I was fastly bound.
My heart turn'd sick, my brain grew sore,
And throbb'd awhile, then beat no more:
The skies spun like a mighty wheel;
I saw the trees like drunkards reel,
And a slight flash sprang o'er my eyes,
Which saw no farther: he who dies
Can die no more than then I died.
O'ertortured by that ghastly ride,

I felt the blackness come and go,
    And strove to wake; but could not make
My senses climb up from below:
I felt as on a plank at sea,
When all the waves that dash o'er thee,
At the same time upheave and whelm,
And hurl thee towards a desert realm.
200 My undulating life was as
The fancied lights that flitting pass
Our shut eyes in deep midnight, when
Fever begins upon the brain;
But soon it pass'd, with little pain,
    But a confusion worse than such:
    I own that I should deem it much,
Dying, to feel the same again;
And yet I do suppose we must
Feel far more ere we turn to dust:
210 No matter; I have bared my brow
Full in Death's face – before – and now.

XIV

'My thoughts came back; where was I? Cold,
    And numb, and giddy: pulse by pulse
Life reassumed its lingering hold,
And throb by throb, – till grown a pang
    Which for a moment would convulse,
    My blood reflow'd, though thick and chill;
My ear with uncouth noises rang,
    My heart began once more to thrill;
220 My sight return'd, though dim; alas!
And thicken'd, as it were, with glass.
Methought the dash of waves was nigh;
There was a gleam too of the sky,
Studded with stars; – it is no dream;
The wild horse swims the wilder stream:

The bright broad river's gushing tide
Sweeps, winding onward, far and wide,
And we are half-way, struggling o'er
To yon unknown and silent shore.
230 The waters broke my hollow trance,
And with a temporary strength
　　My stiffen'd limbs were rebaptized.
My courser's broad breast proudly braves,
And dashes off the ascending waves,
And onward we advance!
We reach the slippery shore at length,
A haven I but little prized,
For all behind was dark and drear,
And all before was night and fear.
240 How many hours of night or day
In those suspended pangs I lay,
I could not tell; I scarcely knew
If this were human breath I drew.

XV

'With glossy skin, and dripping mane,
　　And reeling limbs, and reeking flank,
The wild steed's sinewy nerves still strain
　　Up the repelling bank.
We gain the top: a boundless plain
Spreads through the shadow of the night,
250 And onward, onward, onward, seems,
　　Like precipices in our dreams,
To stretch beyond the sight;
And here and there a speck of white,
Or scatter'd spot of dusky green,
In masses broke into the light,
As rose the moon upon my right:
　　But nought distinctly seen
In the dim waste would indicate

The omen of a cottage gate;
260　No twinkling taper from afar
Stood like a hospitable star;
Not even an ignis-fatuus rose
To make him merry with my woes:
　That very cheat had cheer'd me then!
Although detected, welcome still,
Reminding me, through every ill,
　Of the abodes of men.

XVI

'Onward we went – but slack and slow;
　His savage force at length o'erspent,
270　The drooping courser, faint and low,
　All feebly foaming went.
A sickly infant had had power
To guide him forward in that hour
　But useless all to me:
His new-born tameness nought avail'd –
My limbs were bound; my force had fail'd,
　Perchance, had they been free.
With feeble effort still I tried
To rend the bonds so starkly tied,
280　But still it was in vain;
My limbs were only wrung the more,
And soon the idle strife gave o'er,
　Which but prolong'd their pain:
The dizzy race seem'd almost done,
Although no goal was nearly won:
Some streaks announced the coming sun –
　How slow, alas! he came!
Methought that mist of dawning gray
Would never dapple into day;
290　How heavily it roll'd away –
　Before the eastern flame

168

Rose crimson, and deposed the stars,
And call'd the radiance from their cars,
And fill'd the earth, from his deep throne,
With lonely lustre, all his own.

XVII

'Up rose the sun; the mists were curl'd
Back from the solitary world
Which lay around, behind, before.
What booted it to traverse o'er
300   Plain, forest, river? Man nor brute,
Nor dint of hoof, nor print of foot,
Lay in the wild luxuriant soil;
No sign of travel, none of toil;
The very air was mute;
And not an insect's shrill small horn,
Nor matin bird's new voice was borne
From herb nor thicket. Many a werst,
Panting as if his heart would burst,
The weary brute still stagger'd on;
310   And still we were – or seem'd – alone.
At length, while reeling on our way,
Methought I heard a courser neigh,
From out yon tuft of blackening firs.
Is it the wind those branches stirs?
No, no! from out the forest prance
    A trampling troop; I see them come!
In one vast squadron they advance!
    I strove to cry – my lips were dumb.
The steeds rush on in plunging pride;
320   But where are they the reins to guide?
A thousand horse, and none to ride!
With flowing tail, and flying mane,
Wide nostrils never stretch'd by pain,
Mouths bloodless to the bit or rein,

And feet that iron never shod,
And flanks unscarr'd by spur or rod,
A thousand horse, the wild, the free,
Like waves that follow o'er the sea,
    Came thickly thundering on,
330   As if our faint approach to meet;
The sight re-nerved my courser's feet,
A moment staggering, feebly fleet,
A moment, with a faint low neigh,
    He answer'd, and then fell;
With gasps and glazing eyes he lay,
    And reeking limbs immoveable,
        His first and last career is done!
On came the troop – they saw him stoop,
    They saw me strangely bound along
340   His back with many a bloody thong:
They stop, they start, they snuff the air,
Gallop a moment here and there,
Approach, retire, wheel round and round,
Then plunging back with sudden bound,
Headed by one black mighty steed,
Who seem'd the patriarch of his breed,
    Without a single speck or hair
Of white upon his shaggy hide;
They snort, they foam, neigh, swerve aside,
350   And backward to the forest fly,
By instinct, from a human eye.
They left me there to my despair,
Link'd to the dead and stiffening wretch,
Whose lifeless limbs beneath me stretch,
Relieved from that unwonted weight,
From whence I could not extricate
Nor him nor me – and there we lay,
    The dying on the dead!
I little deem'd another day

Would see my houseless, helpless head.
And there from morn to twilight bound,
I felt the heavy hours toil round,
With just enough of life to see
My last of suns go down on me,
In hopeless certainty of mind,
That makes us feel at length resign'd
To that which our foreboding years
Present the worst and last of fears:
Inevitable — even a boon,
Nor more unkind for coming soon,
Yet shunn'd and dreaded with such care,
As if it only were a snare
   That prudence might escape:
At times both wish'd for and implored,
At times sought with self-pointed sword,
Yet still a dark and hideous close
To even intolerable woes,
   And welcome in no shape.
And, strange to say, the sons of pleasure,
They who have revell'd beyond measure
In beauty, wassail, wine, and treasure,
Die calm, or calmer, oft than he
Whose heritage was misery:
For he who hath in turn run through
All that was beautiful and new,
   Hath nought to hope, and nought to leave;
And, save the future, (which is view'd
Not quite as men are base or good,
But as their nerves may be endued,)
With nought perhaps to grieve:
The wretch still hopes his woes must end,
And Death, whom he should deem his friend,
Appears, to his distemper'd eyes,
Arrived to rob him of his prize,

The tree of his new Paradise.
To-morrow would have given him all,
Repaid his pangs, repair'd his fall;
To-morrow would have been the first
Of days no more deplored or curst,
But bright, and long, and beckoning years,
Seen dazzling through the mist of tears,
Guerdon of many a painful hour;
To-morrow would have given him power
To rule, to shine, to smite, to save –
And must it dawn upon his grave?

XVIII
'The sun was sinking – still I lay
    Chain'd to the chill and stiffening steed;
I thought to mingle there our clay,
    And my dim eyes of death had need;
    No hope arose of being freed:
I cast my last looks up the sky,
    And there between me and the sun
I saw the expecting raven fly,
Who scarce would wait till both should die,
    Ere his repast begun;
He flew, and perch'd, then flew once more,
And each time nearer than before;
I saw his wing through twilight flit,
And once so near me he alit
    I could have smote, but lack'd the strength;
But the slight motion of my hand,
And feeble scratching of the sand,
The exerted throat's faint struggling noise,
Which scarcely could be called a voice,
    Together scared him off at length.
I know no more – my latest dream
    Is something of a lovely star

Which fix'd my dull eyes from afar,
And went and came with wandering beam,
And of the cold, dull, swimming, dense
Sensation of recurring sense,
And then subsiding back to death,
And then again a little breath,
A little thrill, a short suspense,
    An icy sickness curdling o'er
My heart, and sparks that cross'd my brain –
A gasp, a throb, a start of pain,
    A sigh, and nothing more.

XIX

'I woke – where was I? – Do I see
A human face look down on me?
And doth a roof above me close?
Do these limbs on a couch repose?
Is this a chamber where I lie?
And is it mortal yon bright eye,
That watches me with gentle glance?
    I closed my own again once more,
As doubtful that my former trance
    Could not as yet be o'er.
A slender girl, long-hair'd, and tall,
Sate watching by the cottage wall;
The sparkle of her eye I caught,
Even with my first return of thought;
For ever and anon she threw
    A prying, pitying glance on me
    With her black eyes so wild and free:
I gazed, and gazed, until I knew
    No vision it could be, –
But that I lived, and was released
From adding to the vulture's feast:
And when the Cossack maid beheld

My heavy eyes at length unseal'd,
She smiled – and I essay'd to speak,
　　But fail'd – and she approach'd, and made
　　With lip and finger signs that said,
I must not strive as yet to break
The silence, till my strength should be
Enough to leave my accents free;
And then her hand on mine she laid,
And smooth'd the pillow for my head,
470　And stole along on tiptoe tread,
　　And gently oped the door, and spake
In whispers – ne'er was voice so sweet!
Even music follow'd her light feet:
　　But those she call'd were not awake,
And she went forth; but, ere she pass'd,
Another look on me she cast,
　　Another sign she made, to say,
That I had nought to fear, that all
Were near, at my command or call,
480　　And she would not delay
Her due return: – while she was gone,
Methought I felt too much alone.

XX

'She came with mother and with sire –
What need of more? – I will not tire
With long recital of the rest,
Since I became the Cossack's guest.
They found me senseless on the plain,
　　They bore me to the nearest hut,
They brought me into life again –
490　Me – one day o'er their realm to reign!
　　Thus the vain fool who strove to glut
His rage, refining on my pain,
　　Sent me forth to the wilderness,

174

Bound, naked, bleeding, and alone,
To pass the desert to a throne, –
  What mortal his own doom may guess?
  Let none despond, let none despair!
To-morrow the Borysthenes
May see our coursers graze at ease
Upon his Turkish bank, and never
Had I such welcome for a river
  As I shall yield when safely there.
Comrades, good night!' – The Hetman threw
  His length beneath the oak-tree shade,
  With leafy couch already made,
A bed nor comfortless nor new
To him, who took his rest whene'er
The hour arrived, no matter where:
  His eyes the hastening slumbers steep.
And if ye marvel Charles forgot
To thank his tale, *he* wonder'd not, –
  The kind had been an hour asleep.

500

510

Stanzas

When a man hath no freedom to fight for at home,
  Let him combat for that of his neighbours;
Let him think of the glories of Greece and of Rome,
  And get knock'd on the head for his labours.

To do good to mankind is the chivalrous plan,
  And is always as nobly requited;
Then battle for freedom wherever you can,
  And, if not shot or hang'd, you'll get knighted.

November 1820.

Stanzas Written on the Road
Between Florence and Pisa

Oh, talk not to me of a name great in story;
The days of our youth are the days of our glory;
And the myrtle and ivy of sweet two-and-twenty
Are worth all your laurels, though ever so plenty.

What are garlands and crowns to the brow that is wrinkled?
'T is but as a dead-flower with May-dew be-sprinkled.
Then away with all such from the head that is hoary!
What care I for the wreaths that can *only* give glory!

Oh Fame! – if I e'er took delight in thy praises,
10 'T was less for the sake of thy high-sounding phrases,
Than to see the bright eyes of the dear one discover,
She thought that I was not unworthy to love her.

There chiefly I sought thee, *there* only I found thee;
Her glance was the best of the rays that surround thee:
When is sparkled o'er aught that was bright in my story,
I knew it was love, and I felt it was glory.

November 1821.

Cain: A Mystery

The Land without Paradise
Time, Sunrise.

ADAM, EVE, CAIN, ABEL, ADAH, ZILLAH,
offering a sacrifice

Adam. God, the Eternal! Infinite! All-wise! –
Who out of darkness on the deep didst make
Light on the waters with a word – all hail!
Jehovah, with returning light, all hail!
Eve. God! who didst name the day, and separate
Morning from night, till then divided never –
Who didst divide the wave from wave, and call
Part of thy work the firmament – all hail!
Abel. God! who didst call the elements into
10 Earth, ocean, air, and fire, and with the day
And night, and worlds which these illuminate,
Or shadow, madest beings to enjoy them,
And love both them and thee – all hail! all hail!
Adah. God, the Eternal! Parent of all things!
Who didst create these best and beauteous beings,
To be beloved, more than all, save thee –
Let me love thee and them: – All hail! all hail!
Zillah. Oh, God! who loving, making, blessing all,
Yet didst permit the serpent to creep in,
20 And drive my father forth from Paradise,
Keep us from further evil: Hail! all Hail!
    Adam. Son Cain, my first-born, wherefore art thou
       silent?
    Cain. Why should I speak?

Adam. To pray.

Cain. Have ye not pray'd?

Adam. We have, most fervently.

Cain. And loudly: I
Have heard you.

Adam. So will God, I trust.

Abel. Amen!

Adam. But thou, my eldest born, art silent still.

Cain. 'T is better I should be so.

Adam. Wherefore so?

Cain. I have nought to ask.

Adam. Nor aught to thank for!

Cain. No.

Adam. Dost thou not live?

Cain. Must I not die?

Eve. Alas!
30 The fruit of our forbidden tree begins
To fall.

Adam. And we must gather it again.
Oh, God! why didst thou plant the tree of knowledge?

Cain. And wherefore pluck'd ye not the tree of life?
Ye might have then defied him.

Adam. Oh! my son,
Blaspheme not: these are serpent's words.

Cain Why not?
The snake spoke *truth*; it *was* the tree of knowledge;
It *was* the tree of life: knowledge is good,
And life is good; and how can both be evil?

Eve. My boy! thou speakest as I spoke, in sin,
40 Before thy birth: let me not see renew'd
My misery in thine. I have repented.
Let me not see my offspring fall into
The snares beyond the walls of Paradise,
Which e'en in Paradise destroy'd his parents.
Content thee with what *is*. Had we been so,

178

Thou now hadst been contented. – Oh, my son!

Adam. Our orisons completed, let us hence,
Each to his task of toil – not heavy, though
Needful: the earth is young, and yields us kindly
50 Her fruits with little labour.

Eve.   Cain, my son,
Behold thy father cheerful and resign'd,
And do as he doth.   [*Exeunt* ADAM *and* EVE.

Zillah.   Wilt thou not, my brother?

Abel. Why wilt thou wear this gloom upon thy brow,
Which can avail thee nothing, save to rouse
The Eternal anger?

Adah.   My beloved Cain,
Wilt thou frown even on me?

Cain.   No, Adah! no;
I fain would be alone a little while.
Abel, I'm sick at heart; but it will pass;
Precede me, brother – I will follow shortly.
60 And you, too, sisters, tarry not behind:
Your gentleness must not be harshly met;
I'll follow you anon.

Adah.   If not, I will
Return to seek you here.

Abel.   The peace of God
Be on your spirit, brother!

              [*Exeunt* ABEL, ZILLAH, *and* ADAH.

Cain (solus).   And this is
Life! – Toil! and wherefore should I toil? – because
My father could not keep his place in Eden.
What had *I* done in this? – I was unborn:
I sought not to be born; nor love the state
To which that birth has brought me. Why did he
Yield to the serpent and the woman? or,
70 Yielding, why suffer? What was there in this?
The tree was planted, and why not for him?

If not, why place him near it, where it grew,
The fairest in the centre? They have but
One answer to all questions, ' 'Twas *his* will,
And *he* is good,' How know I that? Because
He is all-powerful, must all-good, too, follow?
I judge but by the fruits – and they are bitter –
Which I must feed on for a fault not mine.
80 Whom have we here? – A shape like to the angels,
Yet of a sterner and a sadder aspect
Of spiritual essence: why do I quake?
Why should I fear him more than other spirits,
    Whom I see daily wave their fiery swords
Before the gates round which I linger oft,
In twilight's hour, to catch a glimpse of those
Gardens which are my just inheritance,
Ere the night closes o'er the inhibited walls
And the immortal trees which overtop
90 The cherubim-defended battlements?
If I shrink not from these, the fire-arm'd angels,
Why should I quail from him who now approaches?
Yet he seems mightier far than them, nor less
Beauteous, and yet not all as beautiful
As he hath been, and might be: sorrow seems
Half of his immortality. And is it
So? and can aught grieve save humanity?
He cometh.

                    Enter LUCIFER

    Lucifer   Mortal!
    Cain.   Spirit, who art thou?
    Lucifer. Master of Spirits.
    Cain.   And being so, canst thou
100 Leave them, and walk with dust?
        Lucifer.   I know the thoughts
    Of dust, and feel for it, and with you.
    Cain.   How!

You know my thoughts?

Lucifer.   They are the thoughts of all
Worthy of thought; – 'tis your immortal part
Which speaks within you.

Cain.   What immortal part?
This has not been reveal'd: the tree of life
Was withheld from us by my father's folly,
While that of knowledge, by my mother's haste,
Was pluck'd too soon; and all the fruit is death!

Lucifer. They have deceived thee; thou shalt live.

Cain.   I live,
110 But live to die, and, living, see no thing
To make death hateful, save an innate clinging,
A loathsome, and yet all invincible
Instinct of life, which I abhor, as I
Despise myself, yet cannot overcome –
And so I live. Would I had never lived!

Lucifer. Thou livest, and must live for ever: think not
The earth, which is thine outward cov'ring, is
Existence – it will cease, and thou wilt be
                    No less than thou art now.

Cain.   No *less!* and why
120 No more?

Lucifer. It may be thou shalt be as we.

Cain. And ye?

Lucifer   Are everlasting.

Cain   Are ye happy?

Lucifer. We are mighty.

Cain.   Are ye happy?

Lucifer.   No: art   thou?

Cain. How should I be so? Look on me!

Lucifer.   Poor clay!
And thou pretendest to be wretched! Thou!

Cain. I am: – and thou, with all thy might, what art
        thou?

181

Lucifer. One who aspired to be what made thee, and
Would not have made thee what thou art.
    Cain   Ah!
Thou look'st almost a god; and –
    Lucifer.   I am none:
And having fail'd to be one, would be nought
130 Save what I am. He conquer'd; let him reign!
    Cain. Who?
    Lucifer. Thy sire's Maker, and the earth's.
    Cain.   And heaven's,
And all that in them is. So I have heard
His seraphs sing; and so my father saith.
    Lucifer. They say – what they must sing and say, on pain
Of being that which I am – and thou art –
Of sprits and of men.
    Cain.   And what is that?
    Lucifer. Souls who dare use their immortality –
Souls who dare look the Omnipotent tyrant in
His everlasting face, and tell him that
140 His evil is not good! If he has made,
As he saith – which I know not, nor believe –
But, if he made us – he cannot unmake:
We are immortal! nay, he'd *have* us so,
That he may torture: – let him! He is great –
But, in his greatness, is no happier than
We in our conflict: Goodness would not make
Evil; and what else hath he made? But let him
Sit on his vast and solitary throne,
Creating worlds, to make eternity
150 Less burthensome to his immense existence
And unparticipated solitude;
Let him crowd orb on orb: he is alone
Indefinite, indissoluble tyrant;
Could he but brush himself, 't were the best boon
He ever granted: but let him reign on,

And multiply himself in misery!
Spirits and Men, at least we sympathise –
And, suffering in concert, make our pangs
Innumerable more endurable,
160 By the unbounded sympathy of all
With all! But *He!* so wretched in his height,
So restless in his wretchedness, must still
Create, and re-create –

    Cain. Thou speak'st to me of things which long have
      swum
In visions through my thought: I never could
Reconcile what I saw with what I heard.
My father and my mother talk to me
Of serpents, and of fruits and trees: I see
The gates of what they call their Paradise
170 Guarded by fiery-sworded cherubim,
Which shut them out and me: I feel the weight
Of daily toil, and constant thought: I look
Around a world where I seem nothing, with
Thoughts which arise within me, as if they
Could master all things – but I thought alone
This misery was *mine*. My father is
Tamed down; my mother has forgot the mind
Which made her thirst for knowledge at the risk,
Of an eternal curse; my brother is
180 A watching shepherd boy, who offers up
The firstlings of the flock to him who bids
The earth yield nothing to us without sweat;
My sister Zillah sings an earlier hymn
Than the birds' matins; and my Adah, my
Own and beloved, she, too, understands not
The mind which overwhelms me: never till
Now met I aught to sympathise with me.
'Tis well – I rather would consort with spirits.
    Lucifer. And hadst thou not been fit by thine own soul

190 For such companionship, I would not now
Have stood before thee as I am: a serpent
Had been enough to charm ye, as before.
    Cain. Ah! didst *thou* tempt my mother?
    Lucifer.   I tempt none,
Save with the truth: was not the tree the tree
Of knowledge? and was not the tree of life
Still fruitful? Did *I* bid her pluck them not?
Did *I* plant things prohibited within
The reach of beings innocent, and curious
By their own innocence? I would have made ye
200 Gods; and even He who thrust ye forth, so thrust ye
Because 'ye should not eat the fruits of life,
And become gods as we.' Were those his words?
    Cain. They were, as I have heard from those who heard
        them,
In thunder.
    Lucifer. Then who was the demon? He
Who would not let ye live, or he who would
Have made ye live for ever in the joy
And power of knowledge?
    Cain   Would they had snatch'd both
The fruits, or neither!
    Lucifer.   One is yours already,
The other may be still.
    Cain.   How so?
    Lucifer   by being
210 Yourselves, in your resistance. Nothing can
Quench the mind, if the mind will be itself
And centre of surrounding things – 'tis made
To sway.
    Cain. But didst thou tempt my parents?
    Lucifer.   I?
Poor clay! what should I tempt them for, or how?
    Cain. They say the serpent was a spirit.

    Lucifer.   Who
Saith that? It is not written so on high:
The proud One will not so far falsify,
Though man's vast fears and little vanity
Would make him cast upon the spiritual nature
220 His own low failing. The snake *was* the snake –
No more; and yet not less than those he tempted,
In nature being earth also – *more* in *wisdom*,
Since he could overcome them, and foreknew
The knowledge fatal to their narrow joys.
Think'st thou I'd take the shape of things that die?
    Cain. But the thing had a demon?
    Lucifer.   He but woke one
In those he spake to with his forky tongue.
I tell thee that the serpent was no more
Than a mere serpent: ask the cherubim
230 Who guard the tempting tree. When thousand ages
Have roll'd o'er your dead ashes, and your seed's,
The seed of the then world may thus array
Their earliest fault in fable, and attribute
To me a shape I scorn, as I scorn all
That bows to him, who made things but to bend
Before his sullen, sole eternity;
But we, who see the truth, must speak it. Thy
Fond parents listen'd to a creeping thing,
And fell. For what should spirits tempt them? What
240 Was there to envy in the narrow bounds
Of Paradise, that spirits who pervade
Space – but I speak to thee of what thou know'st not,
With all thy tree of knowledge.
    Cain.   But thou canst not
Speak aught of knowledge which I would not know,
And do no thirst to know, and bear a mind
To know.
    Lucifer. And heart to look on?

Cain   Be it proved.
Lucifer. Darest thou look on Death?
Cain.   He has not yet
Been seen.
Lucifer. But must be undergone.
Cain.   My father
Says he is something dreadful, and my mother
250 Weeps when he's named; and Abel lifts his eyes
To heaven, and Zillah casts hers to the earth,
And sighs a prayer; and Adah looks on me,
And speaks not.
Lucifer.   And thou?
Cain.   Thoughts unspeakable
Crowd in my breast to burning, when I hear
Of this almighty Death, who is, it seems,
Inevitable. Could I wrestle with him?
I wrestled with the lion, when a boy,
In play, till he ran roaring from my gripe.
Lucifer. It has no shape; but will absorb all things
260 That bear the form of earth-born being.
Cain.   Ah!
I thought it was a being: who could do
Such evil things to beings save a being?
Lucifer. Ask the Destroyer.
Cain.   Who?
Lucifer.   The Maker – call him
Which name thou wilt: he makes but to destroy.
Cain. I knew not that, yet thought it, since I heard
Of death: although I know not what it is,
Yet it seems horrible. I have look'd out
In the vast desolate night in search of him;
And when I saw gigantic shadows in
270 The umbrage of the walls of Eden, chequer'd
By the far-flashing of the cherubs' swords,
I watch'd for what I thought his coming: for

186

With fear rose longing in my heart to know
What 't was which shook us all – but nothing came.
And then I turn'd my weary eyes from off
Our native and forbidden Paradise,
Up to the lights above us, in the azure,
Which are so beautiful shall they, too, die?

  Lucifer. Perhaps – but long outlive both thine and thee.

280 *Cain.* I'm glad of that: I would not have them die –
They are so lovely. What is death? I fear,
I feel, it is a dreadful thing; but what,
I cannot compass: 'tis denounced against us,
Both them who sinn'd and sinn'd not, as an ill –
What ill?

  Lucifer. To be resolved into the earth.

  Cain. But shall I know it?

  Lucifer.   As I know not death,
I cannot answer.

  Cain.   Were I quiet earth,
That were no evil: would I ne'er had been
Aught else but dust!

  Lucifer.   That is a grovelling wish,

290 Less than thy father's, for he wish'd to know.

  Cain. But not to live, or wherefore pluck'd he not
The life-tree?

  Lucifer. He was hinder'd.

  Cain.   Deadly error!
Not to snatch first that fruit: – but ere he pluck'd
The knowledge, he was ignorant of death.
Alas! I scarcely now know what it is,
And yet I fear it – fear I know not what!

  Lucifer. And I, who know all things, fear nothing; see
What is true knowledge.

  Cain.   Wilt thou teach me all?

  Lucifer. Ay, upon one condition.

  Cain.   Name it.

187

Lucifer.   That
300 Thou dost fall down and worship me – thy Lord.
    Cain. Thou art not the Lord my father worships.
    Lucifer.   No.
    Cain. His equal?
    Lucifer. No; – I have nought in common with him!
Nor would: I would be aught above – beneath –
Aught save a sharer or a servant of
His power. I dwell apart; but I am great: –
Many there are who worship me, and more
Who shall – be thou amongst the first.
    Cain   I never
As yet have bow'd unto my father's God,
Although my brother Abel oft implores
310 That I would join with him in sacrifice: –
Why should I bow to thee?
    Lucifer.   Hast thou e'er bow'd
To him?
    Cain. Have I not said it? – need I say it?
Could not thy mighty knowledge teach thee that?
    Lucifer. He who bows not to him has bow'd to me.
    Cain. But I will bend to neither.
    Lucifer.   Ne'er the less,
Thou art my worshipper; not worshipping
Him makes thee mine the same.
    Cain.   And what is that?
    Lucifer. Thou'lt know here – and hereafter.
    Cain.   Let me but
Be taught the mystery of my being.
    Lucifer.   Follow
320 Where I will lead thee.
    Cain.   But I must retire
To till the earth – for I had promised –
    Lucifer.   What?
    Cain. To cull some first-fruits.

Lucifer.   Why?
Cain   To offer up
With Abel on an altar.
    Lucifer.   Said'st thou not
Thou ne'er hadst bent to him who made thee?
    Cain.   Yes –
But Abel's earnest prayer has wrought upon me.
The offering is more his than mine – and Adah –
    Lucifer.   Why dost thou hesitate?
    Cain.   She is my sister,
Born on the same day, of the same womb; and
She wrung from me, with tears, this promise; and
330 Rather than see her weep, I would, methinks,
Bear all – and worship aught.
    Lucifer.   Then follow me!
    Cain.   I will.

Enter ADAH

    Adah   My brother, I have come for thee;
It is our hour of rest and joy – and we
Have less without thee. Thou hast labour'd not
This morn; but I have done thy task: the fruits
Are ripe, and glowing as the light which ripens:
Come away.
    Cain.   Seest thou not?
    Adah.   I see an angel;
We have seen many: will he share our hour
Of rest? – he is welcome.
    Cain.   But he is not like
340 The angels we have seen.
    Adah.   Are there, then, others?
But he is welcome, as they were: they deign'd
To be our guests – will he?
    Cain (to Lucifer).   Wilt thou?
    Lucifer.   I ask
Thee to be mine.

Cain.　　　　I must away with him.

Adah. And leave us?

　Cain.　　　Ay.

　Adah.　　　　And *me?*

　Cain.　　　　　Beloved Adah!

　Adah. Let me go with thee.

　Lucifer.　　　No, she must not.

　Adah.　　　　　　Who
Art thou that steppest between heart and heart?

　Cain. He is a god.

　Adah.　　　How know'st thou?

　Cain.　　　　　　He speaks like
A god.

　Adah. So did the serpent, and it lied.

　Lucifer. Thou errest, Adah! – was not the tree that
350 Of knowledge?

　Adah.　　　Ay – to our eternal sorrow.

　Lucifer. And yet that grief is knowledge – so he lied not:
And if he did betray you, 't was with truth;
And truth in its own essence cannot be
But good.

　Adah. But all we know of it has gather'd
Evil on ill; expulsion from our home,
And dread, and toil, and sweat, and heaviness;
Remorse of that which was – and hope of that
Which cometh not. Cain! walk not with this spirit.
Bear with what we have borne, and love me – I
360 Love thee.

　Lucifer. More than thy mother, and thy sire?

　Adah. I do. Is that a sin, too?

　Lucifer.　　　　No, not yet;
It one day will be in your children.

　Adah.　　　　　　What!
Must not my daughter love her brother Enoch?

　Lucifer. Not as thou lovest Cain.

 Adah.   Oh, my God!
Shall they not love and bring forth things that love
Out of their love? have they not drawn their milk
Out of this bosom? was not he, their father,
Born of the same sole womb, in the same hour
With me? did we not love each other? and
370 In multiplying our being multiply
Things which will love each other as we love
Them? – And as I love thee, my Cain! go not
Forth with this spirit; he is not of ours.
 Lucifer. The sin I speak of is not of my making,
And cannot be a sin in you – whate'er
It seem in those who will replace ye in
Mortality.
 Adah.   What is the sin which is not
Sin in itself? Can circumstance make sin
Or virtue? – if it doth, we are the slaves
380 Of –
 Lucifer. Higher things than ye are slaves: and higher
Than them or ye would be so, did they not
Prefer an independency of torture
To the smooth agonies of adulation,
In hymns and harpings, and self-seeking prayers,
To that which is omnipotent, because
It is omnipotent, and not from love,
But terror and self-hope.
 Adah.   Omnipotence
Must be all goodness.
 Lucifer.   Was it so in Eden?
Adah. Fiend! Tempt me not with beauty; thou art fairer
390 Than was the serpent, and as false.
 Lucifer.   As true.
Ask Eve, your mother: bears she not the knowledge
Of good and evil?
 Adah.   Oh, my mother! thou

Hast pluck'd a fruit more fatal to thine offspring
Than to thyself; thou at the least hast pass'd
Thy youth in Paradise, in innocent
And happy intercourse with happy spirits:
But we, thy children, ignorant of Eden,
Are girt about by demons, who assume
The words of God, and tempt us with our own
400 Dissatisfied and curious thoughts – as thou
Wert work'd on by the snake, in thy most flush'd
And heedless, harmless wantonness of bliss.
I cannot answer this immortal thing
Which stands before me; I cannot abhor him;
I look upon him with a pleasing fear,
And yet I fly not from him: in his eye
There is a fastening attraction which
Fixes my fluttering eyes on his; my heart
Beats quick; he awes me, and yet draws me near,
410 Nearer and nearer: – Cain – Cain – save me from him!
   Cain. What dreads my Adah? This is no ill spirit.
   Adah. He is not God – nor God's: I have beheld
The cherubs and the seraphs; he looks not
Like them.
   Cain. But there are spirits loftier still –
The archangels.
   Lucifer.   And still loftier than the archangels.
   Adah. Ay – but not blessed.
   Lucifer.   If the blessedness
Consists in slavery – no.
   Adah.   I have heard it said,
The seraphs *love most* – cherubim *know most* –
And this should be a cherub – since he loves not.
420   *Lucifer.* And if the higher knowledge quenches love,
What must *he be* you cannot love when known?
Since the all-knowing cherubim love least,
The seraphs' love can be but ignorance:

That they are not compatible, the doom
Of thy fond parents, for their daring, proves.
Choose betwixt love and knowledge – since there is
No other choice: your sire hath chosen already:
His worship is but fear.

    Adah.   Oh, Cain! choose love.

    Cain. For thee, my Adah, I choose not – it was
Born with me – but I love nought else.

    Adah.   Our parents?

430   *Cain.* Did they love us when they snatch'd from the tree
That which hath driven us all from Paradise?

    Adah. We were not born then – and if we had been,
Should we not love them and our children, Cain?

    Cain. My little Enoch! and his lisping sister!
Could I but deem them happy, I would half
Forget – but it can never be forgotten
Through thrice a thousand generations! never
Shall men love the remembrance of the man
Who sow'd the seed of evil and mankind
440 In the same hour! They pluck'd the tree of science
And sin – and, not content with their own sorrow,
Begot *me* – *thee* – and all the few that are,
And all the unnumber'd and innumerable
Multitudes, millions, myriads, which may be,
To inherit agonies accumulated
By ages! – and *I* must be sire of such things!
Thy beauty and thy love – my love and joy,
The rapturous moment and the placid hour,
All we love in our children and each other,
450 But lead them and ourselves through many years
Of sin and pain – or few, but still of sorrow,
Intercheck'd with an instant of brief pleasure,
To Death – the unknown! Methinks the tree of knowledge
Hath not fulfill'd its promise: – if they sinn'd,
At least they ought to have known all things that are

Of knowledge – and the mystery of death.
What do they know? – that they are miserable.
What need of snakes and fruits to teach us that?

Adah. I am not wretched, Cain, and if thou
460 Wert happy –

Cain.   Be thou happy, then, alone –
I will have nought to do with happiness,
Which humbles me and mine.

Adah.   Alone I could not,
Nor *would* be happy; but with those around
I think I could be so, despite of death,
Which, as I know it not, I dread not, though
It seems an awful shadow – if I may
Judge from what I have heard.

Lucifer.   And thou couldst not
Alone, thou say'st, be happy?

Adah.   Alone! Oh, my God!
Who could be happy and alone, or good?
470 To me my solitude seems sin; unless
When I think how soon I shall see my brother,
His brother, and our children, and our parents.

Lucifer. Yet thy God is alone; and is he happy,
Lonely, and good?

Adah.   He is not so; he hath
The angels and the mortals to make happy.
And thus becomes so in diffusing joy.
What else can joy be, but the spreading joy!

Lucifer. Ask of your sire, the exile fresh from Eden;
Or of his first-born son: ask your own heart;
480 It is not tranquil.

Adah.   Alas! no! and you –
Are you of heaven?

Lucifer.   If I am not, inquire
The cause of this all-spreading happiness
(Which you proclaim) of the all-great and good

Maker of life and living things; it is
His secret, and he keeps it. *We* must bear,
And some of us resist, and both in vain,
His seraphs say: but it is worth the trial,
Since better may not be without: there is
A wisdom in the spirit, which directs
490 To right, as in the dim blue air the eye
Of you, young mortals, lights at once upon
The star which watches, welcoming the morn.
   Adah. It is a beautiful star; I love it for Its beauty.
   Lucifer. And why not adore?
   Adah.   Our father
Adores the Invisible only.
   Lucifer.   But the symbols
Of the Invisible are the loveliest
Of what is visible; and yon bright star
Is leader of the host of heaven.
   Adah.   Our father
Saith that he has beheld the God himself
Who made him and our mother.
500   *Lucifer.*   Hast *thou* seen him!
   Adah. Yes – in his works.
   Lucifer.   But in his being!
   Adah.   No -
Save in my father, who is God's own image;
Or in his angels, who are like to thee –
And brighter, yet less beautiful and powerful
In seeming: as the silent sunny noon,
All light, they look upon us; but thou seem'st
Like an ethereal night, where long white clouds
Streak the deep purple, and unnumber'd stars
Spangle the wonderful mysterious vault
510 With things that look as if they would be suns;
So beautiful, unnumber'd, and endearing,
Not dazzling, and yet drawing us to them,

195

They fill my eyes with tears, and so dost thou.
Thou seem'st unhappy: do not make us so,
And I will weep for thee.
  Lucifer.   Alas! those tears!
Couldst thou but know what oceans will be shed –
  Adah. By me?
  Lucifer.   By all.
  Adah.   What all?
  Lucifer.   The million millions –
The myriad myriads – the all-peopled earth –
The unpeopled earth – and the o'er-peopled hell,
520 Of which thy bosom is the germ.
  Adah.   O Cain!
This spirit curseth us.
  Cain.   Let him say on;
Him will I follow.
  Adah.   Whither?
  Lucifer.   To a place
Whence he shall come back to thee in an hour;
But in that hour see things of many days.
  Adah. How can that be?
  Lucifer.   Did not your Maker make
Out of old worlds this new one in few days?
And cannot I, who aided in this work,
Show in an hour what he hath made in many,
Or hath destroy'd in few?
  Cain.   Lead on.
  Adah.   Will he,
530 In sooth, return within an hour?
  Lucifer.   He shall.
With us acts are exempt from time, and we
Can crowd eternity into an hour,
Or stretch an hour into eternity:
We breathe not by a mortal measurement –
But that's a mystery. Cain, come on with me

Adah. Will he return?

Lucifer.   Ay, woman! he alone
Of mortals from that place (the first and last
Who shall return, save ONE), shall come back to thee,
To make that silent and expectant world
540 As populous as this: at present there
Are few inhabitants.

    Adah.   Where dwellest thou?

    Lucifer. Throughout all space. Where should I dwell?
      Where are
Thy Gods or Gods – there am I: all things are
Divided with me: life and death – and time –
Eternity – and heaven and earth – and that
Which is not heaven nor earth, but peopled with
Those who once peopled or shall people both –
These are my realms! So that I do divide
His, and possess a kingdom which is not
550 *His.* If I were not that which I have said,
Could I stand here? His angels are within
Your vision.

    Adah. So they were when the fair serpent
Spoke with our mother first.

    Lucifer.   Cain! thou hast heard.
If thou dost long for knowledge, I can satiate
That thirst; nor ask thee to partake of fruits
Which shall deprive thee of a single good
The conqueror has left thee. Follow me.

    Cain. Spirit, I have said it.

                       [*Exeunt* LUCIFER *and* CAIN.
    Adah (*follows exclaiming*). Cain! my brother! Cain!

Lucifer. Away, then! on our mighty wings.
    Cain. Oh! how we cleave the blue! The stars fade from
      us!
The earth! where is my earth? Let me look on it,
For I was made of it.
    Lucifer.   'Tis now beyond thee,
Less, in the universe, than thou in it;
Yet deem not that thou canst escape it; thou
Shalt soon return to earth, and all its dust:
'Tis part of thy eternity, and mine.
    Cain. Where dost thou lead me?
    Lucifer.   To what was before thee!
10 The phantasm of the world; of which thy world
Is but the wreck.
    Cain.   What! is it not then new?
    Lucifer. No more than life is; and that was ere thou
Or *I* were, or the things which seem to us
Greater than either: many things will have
No end; and some, which would pretend to have
Had no beginning, have had one as mean
As thou; and mightier things have been extinct
To make way for much meaner than we can
Surmise; for *moments* only and the *space*
20 Have been and must be all *unchangeable*.
But changes make not death, except to clay,
But thou art clay – and canst but comprehend
That which was clay, and such thou shalt behold.
    Cain. Clay, spirit! what thou wilt, I can survey.
    Lucifer. Away, then!
    Cain.   But the lights fade from me fast,
And some till now grew larger as we approach'd,
And wore the look of worlds.
    Lucifer.   And such they are.

Cain. And Edens in them?

Lucifer.   It may be.

Cain.   And men?

Lucifer. Yea, or things higher.

Cain.   Ay? and serpents too?

Lucifer. Wouldst thou have men without them? must no reptiles

Breathe, save the erect ones?

Cain.   How the lights recede!

Where fly we?

Lucifer. To the world of phantoms, which

Are beings past, and shadows still to come.

Cain. But it grows dark, and dark – the stars are gone!

Lucifer. And yet thou seest.

Cain.   'Tis a fearful light!

No sun, no moon, no lights innumerable.

The very blue of the empurpled night

Fades to a dreary twilight, yet I see

Huge dusky masses; but unlike the worlds

We were approaching, which, begirt with light,

Seem'd full of life even when their atmosphere

Of light gave way, and show'd them taking shapes

Unequal, of deep valleys and vast mountains;

And some emitting sparks, and some displaying

Enormous liquid plains, and some begirt

With luminous belts, and floating moons, which took,

Like them, the features of fair earth:– instead,

All here seems dark and dreadful.

Lucifer.   But distinct.

Thou seekest to behold death, and dead things?

Cain. I seek it not; but as I know there are

Such, and that my sire's sin makes him and me,

And all that we inherit, liable

To such, I would behold at once, what I

Must one day see perforce.

Lucifer.   Behold!
Cain.   'T is darkness.
Lucifer. And so it shall be ever; but we will
Unfold its gates!
Cain.   Enormous vapours roll
Apart – what's this?
Lucifer.   Enter!
Cain.   Can I return?
60   *Lucifer.* Return! be sure: how else should death be
            peopled?
Its present realm is thin to what it will be
Through thee and thine.
Cain.   The clouds still open wide
And wider, and make widening circles round us.
Lucifer. Advance!
Cain.   And thou!
Lucifer.   Fear not – without me thou
Couldst not have gone beyond thy world. On! on!
                    [*They disappear through the clouds.*

from ACT III, SCENE I

A voice from within exclaims, Cain! Cain!
Adah.   Hear'st thou that voice?
The Voice within. Cain! Cain!
Adah.   It soundeth like an angel's tone.

Enter the ANGEL *of the Lord.*

Angel. Where is thy brother Abel?
Cain.   Am I then
My brother's keeper?
Angel.   Cain! what hast thou done?
The voice of thy slain brother's blood cries out,
Even from the ground, unto the Lord! – Now art thou
Cursed from the earth, which open'd late her mouth

To drink thy brother's blood from thy rash hand.
Henceforth, when thou shalt till the ground, it shall not

10 Yield thee her strength; a fugitive shalt thou
Be from this day, and vagabond on earth!

    Adah. This punishment is more than he can bear.
Behold, thou driv'st him from the face of earth,
And from the face of God shall he be hid.
A fugitive and vagabond on earth,
'T will come to pass, that whoso findeth him
Shall slay him.

    Cain.   Would they could! but who are they
Shall slay me? Where are these on the lone earth
As yet unpeopled?

    Angel.   Thou hast slain thy brother,

20 And who shall warrant thee against thy son?

    Adah. Angel of Light! be merciful, nor say
That this poor aching breast now nourishes
A murderer in my boy, and of his father.

    Angel. Then he would but be what his father is.
Did not the milk of Eve give nutriment
To him thou now see'st so besmear'd with blood?
The fratricide might well engender parricides. –
But it shall not be so – the Lord thy God
And mine commandeth me to set his seal

30 On Cain, so that he may go forth in safety.
Who slayeth Cain, a sevenfold vengeance shall
Be taken on his head. Come hither!

    Cain.   What
Wouldst thou with me?

    Angel.   To mark upon thy brow
Exemption from such deeds as thou hast done.

    Cain. No, let me die!

    Angel.   It must not be.

               [*The* ANGEL *sets the mark on* CAIN'S *brow.*

    Cain.   It burns

My brow, but nought to that which is within it.
Is there more? let me meet it as I may.

    Angel.   Stern hast thou been and stubborn from the
        womb,
As the ground thou must henceforth till; but he
40 Thou slew'st was gentle as the flocks he tended.

    Cain. After the fall too soon was I begotten;
Ere yet my mother's mind subsided from
The serpent, and my sire still mourn'd for Eden.
That which I am, I am; I did not seek
For life, nor did I make myself; but could I
With my own death redeem him from the dust –
And why not so? let him return to day,
And I lie ghastly! so shall be restored
By God the life to him he loved; and taken
50 From me a being I ne'er loved to bear.

    Angel. Who shall heal murder? what is done, is done;
Go forth! fulfil thy days! and be thy deeds
Unlike the last!   [*The* ANGEL *disappears.*

    Adah.   He's gone, let us go forth;
I hear our little Enoch cry within
Our bower.

    Cain.   Ah! little knows he what he weeps for!
And I who have shed blood cannot shed tears!
But the four rivers would not cleanse my soul.
Think'st thou my boy will bear to look on me?

    Adah. If I thought that he would not, I would –
    Cain (*interrupting her*). No.
60 No more of threats: we have had too many of them:
Go to our children; I will follow thee.

    Adah. I will not leave thee lonely with the dead;
Let us depart together.

    Cain.   Oh! thou dead
And everlasting witness! whose unsinking
Blood darkens earth and heaven! what thou *now* art

I know not! but if *thou* see'st what *I* am,
I think thou wilt forgive him, whom his God
Can ne'er forgive, nor his own soul. – Farewell!
I must not, dare not touch what I have made thee.
I, who sprung from the same womb with thee, drain'd
70   The same breast, clasp'd thee often to my own,
In fondness brotherly and boyish, I
Can never meet thee more, nor even dare
To do that for thee, which thou shouldst have done
For me – compose thy limbs into their grave –
The first grave yet dug for mortality.
But who hath dug that grave? Oh, earth! Oh, earth!
For all the fruits thou hast render'd to me, I
Give thee back this. Now for the wilderness.

                     [ADAH *stoops down and kisses the body of* ABEL.

80   *Adah.* A dreary, and an early doom, my brother,
Has been thy lot! Of all who mourn for thee,
I alone must not weep. My office is
Henceforth to dry up tears, and not to shed them;
But yet of all who mourn, none mourn like me,
Not only for thyself, but him who slew thee.
Now, Cain! I will divide thy burden with thee.
    Cain. Eastward from Eden will we take our way;
'Tis the most desolate, and suits my steps.
    Adah. Lead! thou shalt be my guide, and may our God
90   Be thine! Now let us carry forth our children.
    Cain. And *he* who lieth there was childless. I
Have dried the fountain of a gentle race,
Which might have graced his recent marriage couch,
And might have temper'd this stern blood of mine,
Uniting with our children Abel's offspring!
O Abel!
    Adah. Peace be with him!
    Cain.   But with *me!* –

                                   [*Exeunt.*

from The Vision of Judgment

[A Celestial Bore]

XCV

Then Michael blew his trump, and still'd the noise
    With one still greater, as is yet the mode
On earth besides; except some grumbling voice,
    Which now and then will make a slight inroad
Upon decorous silence, few will twice
    Lift up their lungs when fairly overcrow'd;
And now the bard could plead his own bad cause,
With all the attitudes of self-applause.

XCVI

He said – (I only give the heads) – he said,
    He meant no harm in scribbling; 'twas his way
Upon all topics; 'twas, besides, his bread,
    Of which he butter'd both sides; 'twould delay
Too long the assembly (he was pleased to dread),
    And take up rather more time than a day,
To name his works – he would but cite a few –
'Wat Tyler' – 'Rhymes on Blenheim' – 'Waterloo.'

XCVII

He had written praises of a regicide;
    He had written praises of all kings what ever;
He had written for republics far and wide,
    And then against them bitterer than ever
For pantisocracy he once had cried
    Aloud, a scheme less moral than 'twas clever;
Then grew a hearty anti-jacobin –
Had turn'd his coat – and would have turn'd his skin.

He had sung against all battles, and again
   In their high praise and glory; he had call'd
Reviewing 'the ungentle craft,' and then
   Become as base a critic as e'er crawl'd –
Fed, paid, and pamper'd by the very men
30   By whom his muse and morals had been maul'd:
He had written much blank verse, and blanker prose,
And more of both than anybody knows.

XCIX

He had written Wesley's life: – here turning round
   To Satan, 'Sir, I'm ready to write yours,
In two octavo volumes, nicely bound,
   With notes and preface, all that most allures
The pious purchaser; and there's no ground
   For fear, for I can choose my own reviewers:
So let me have the proper documents,
40   That I may add you to my other saints.'

C

Satan bow'd, and was silent. 'Well, if you,
   With amiable modesty, decline
My offer, what says Michael? There are few
   Whose memoirs could be render'd more divine.
Mine is a pen of all work; not so new
   As it was once, but I would make you shine
Like your own trumpet. By the way, my own
Has more of brass in it, and is as well blown.

CI

'But talking about trumpets, here's my Vision!
50   Now you shall judge, all people; yes, you shall
Judge with my judgment, and by my decision
   Be guided who shall enter heaven or fall.

I settle all these things by intuition,
  Times present, past, to come, heaven, hell, and all,
Like King Alfonso. When I thus see double,
I save the Deity some worlds of trouble.'

CII

He ceased, and drew forth an MS.; and no
  Persuasion on the part of devils, saints,
Or angels, now could stop the torrent; so
60 He read the first three lines of the contents;
But at the fourth, the whole spiritual show
  Had vanish'd, with variety of scents,
Ambrosial and sulphureous, as they sprang,
Like lightning, off from his 'melodious twang.'

CIII

Those grand heroics acted as a spell:
  The angels stopp'd their ears and plied their pinions;
The devils ran howling, deafen'd, down to hell;
  The ghosts fled, gibbering, for their own dominions –
(For 'tis not yet decided where they dwell,
70 And I leave every man to his opinions);
Michael took refuge in his trump – but, lo!
His teeth were set on edge, he could not blow!

CIV

Saint Peter, who has hitherto been known,
  For an impetuous saint, upraised his keys,
And at the fifth line knock'd the poet down;
  Who fell like Phæton, but more at ease,
Into his lake, for there he did not drown;
  A different web being by the Destinies
Woven for the Laureate's final wreath, whene'er
80 Reform shall happen either here or there.

206

He first sank to the bottom – like his works,
　But soon rose to the surface – like himself;
For all corrupted things are buoy'd like corks,
　By their own rottenness, light as an elf,
Or wisp that flits o'er a morass: he lurks,
　It may be, still, like dull books on a shelf,
In his own den, to scrawl some 'Life' or 'Vision,'
As Welborn says – 'the devil turn'd precisian.'

As for the rest, to come to the conclusion
90　Of this true dream, the telescope is gone
Which kept my optics free from all delusion,
　And show'd me what I in my turn have shown;
All I saw farther, in the last confusion,
　Was, that King George slipp'd into heaven for one;
And when the tumult dwindled to a calm,
I left him practising the hundredth psalm.

Don Juan

from CANTO THE FIRST

[A Romantic Letter]

CXCI

She had resolved that he should travel through
    All European climes, by land or sea,
To mend his former morals, and get new,
    Especially in France and Italy
(At least this is the thing most people do).
    Julia was sent into a convent: she
Grieved, but, perhaps, her feelings may be better
Shown in the following copy of her Letter: –

CXCII

'They tell me 't is decided you depart:
10   'T is wise – 't is well, but not the less a pain;
I have no further claim on your young heart,
    Mine is the victim, and would be again:
To love too much has been the only art
    I used; – I write in haste, and if a stain
Be on this sheet, 't is not what it appears;
My eyeballs burn and throb, but have no tears.

CXCIII

'I loved, I love you, for this love have lost
    State, station, heaven, mankind's, my own esteem,
And yet cannot regret what it hath cost,
20   So dear is still the memory of that dream;

Yet, if I name my guilt, 'tis not to boast,
    None can deem harshlier of me than I deem:
I trace this scrawl because I cannot rest –
    I've nothing to reproach or to request.

'Man's love is of man's life a thing apart,
    'T is woman's whole existence; man may range
The court, camp, church, the vessel, and the mart;
    Sword, gown, gain, glory, offer in exchange
Pride, fame, ambition, to fill up his heart,
30   And few there are whom these cannot estrange;
Men have all these resources, but we one,
To love again, and be again undone.

'You will proceed in pleasure, and in pride,
    Beloved and loving many; all is o'er
For me on earth, except some years to hide
    My shame and sorrow deep in my heart's core:
These I could bear, but cannot cast aside
    The passion which still rages as before, –
And so farewell – forgive me, love me – No,
40   That word is idle now – but let it go.

'My breast has been all weakness, is so yet;
    But still I think I can collect my mind;
My blood still rushes where my spirit's set,
    As roll the waves before the settled wind;
My heart is feminine, nor can forget –
    To all, except one image, madly blind;
So shakes the needle, and so stands the pole,
As vibrates my fond heart to my fix'd soul.

'I have no more to say, but linger still,
50   And dare not set my seal upon this sheet,
And yet I may as well the task fulfil,
    My misery can scarce be more complete:
I had not lived till now, could sorrow kill;
    Death shuns the wretch who fain the blow would meet,
And I must even survive this last adieu,
And bear with life to love and pray for you!'

CXCVIII

This note was written upon gilt-edged paper
    With a neat little crow-quill, slight and new;
Her small white hand could hardly reach the taper,
60   It trembled as magnetic needles do,
And yet she did not let one tear escape her:
    The seal a sun-flower; '*Elle vous suit partout*,'
The motto, cut upon a white cornelian;
The wax was superfine, its hue vermilion.

from CANTO THE SECOND

[Lovers in Paradise]

CLXXXIII

It was the cooling hour, just when the rounded
    Red sun sinks down behind the azure hill,
Which then seems as if the whole earth it bounded,
    Circling all nature, hush'd, and dim, and still,
With the far mountain-crescent half surrounded
    On one side, and the deep sea calm and chill,
Upon the other, and the rosy sky,
With one star sparkling through it like an eye.

And thus they wander'd forth, and hand in hand,
   Over the shining pebbles and the shells,
Glided along the smooth and harden'd sand,
   And in the worn and wild receptacles
Work'd by the storms, yet work'd as it were plann'd,
   In hollow halls, with sparry roofs and cells,
They turn'd to rest; and, each clasp'd by an arm,
Yielded to the deep twilight's purple charm.

CLXXXV

They look'd up to the sky, whose floating glow
   Spread like a rosy ocean, vast and bright;
They gazed upon the glittering sea below,
   Whence the broad moon rose circling into sight;
They heard the waves splash, and the wind so low,
   And saw each other's dark eyes darting light
Into each other – and, beholding this,
Their lips drew near, and clung into a kiss;

CLXXXVI

A long, long kiss, a kiss of youth, and love,
   And beauty, all concentrating like rays
Into one focus, kindled from above;
   Such kisses as belong to early days,
Where heart, and soul, and sense, in concert move,
   And the blood's lava, and the pulse a blaze,
Each kiss a heart-quake, – for a kiss's strength,
I think It must be reckon'd by its length.

CLXXXVII

By length I mean duration; theirs endured
   Heaven knows how long – no doubt they never
      reckon'd;
And if they had, they could not have secured
   The sum of their sensations to a second:

211

They had not spoken; but they felt allured,
    As if their souls and lips each other beckon'd,
Which, being join'd, like swarming bees they clung –
40 Their hearts the flowers from whence the honey sprung.

CLXXXVIII

They were alone, but not alone as they
    Who shut in chambers think it loneliness;
The silent ocean, and the starlight bay,
    The twilight glow, which momently grew less,
The voiceless sands, and dropping caves, that lay
    Around them, made them to each other press,
As if there were no life beneath the sky
Save theirs, and that their life could never die.

CLXXXIX

They fear'd no eyes nor ears on that lone beach,
50 They felt no terrors from the night; they were
All in all to each other; though their speech
    Was broken words, they *thought* a language there, –
And all the burning tongues the passions teach
    Found in one sigh the best interpreter
Of nature's oracle – first love, – that all
Which Eve has left her daughters since her fall.

CXC

Haidée spoke not of scruples, ask'd no vows,
    Nor offer'd any; she had never heard
Of plight and promises to be a spouse,
60 Or perils by a loving maid incurr'd;
She was all which pure ignorance allows,
    And flew to her young mate like a young bird,
And never having dreamt of falsehood, she
Had not one word to say of constancy.

She loved, and was beloved – she adored,
    And she was worshipp'd; after nature's fashion,
Their intense souls, into each other pour'd,
    If souls could die, had perish'd in that passion, –
But by degrees their senses were restored,
70   Again to be o'ercome, again to dash on;
And, beating 'gainst *his* bosom, Haidée's heart
Felt as if never more to beat apart.

Alas! they were so young, so beautiful,
    So lonely, loving, helpless, and the hour
Was that in which the heart is always full,
    And, having o'er itself no further power,
Prompts deeds eternity cannot annul,
    But pays off moments in an endless shower
Of hell-fire – all prepared for people giving
80 Pleasure or pain to one another living.

Alas! for Juan and Haidée! they were
    So loving and so lovely – till then never,
Excepting our first parents, such a pair
    Had run the risk of being damn'd for ever;
And Haidée, being devout as well as fair,
    Had, doubtless, heard about the Stygian river,
And hell and purgatory – but forgot
Just in the very crisis she should not.

They look upon each other, and their eyes
90   Gleam in the moonlight; and her white arm clasps
Round Juan's head, and his around her lies
    Half buried in the tresses which it grasps

213

She sits upon his knee, and drinks his sighs,
    He hers, until they end in broken gasps;
And thus they form a group that's quite antique,
Half naked, loving, natural, and Greek.

[Love of Woman]

CXCIX

Alas! the love of women! it is known
    To be a lovely and a fearful thing;
For all of theirs upon that die is thrown,
    And if 'tis lost, life hath no more to bring
To them but mockeries of the past alone,
    And their revenge is as the tiger's spring,
Deadly, and quick, and crushing; yet, as real
Torture is theirs, what they inflict they feel.

CC

They are right; for man, to man so oft unjust,
10   Is always so to women; one sole bond
Awaits them, treachery is all their trust;
    Taught to conceal, their bursting hearts despond
Over their idol, till some wealthier lust
    Buys them in marriage – and what rests beyond?
A thankless husband, next a faithless lover,
Then dressing, nursing, praying, and all's over.

CCI

Some take a lover, some take drams or prayers,
    Some mind their household, others dissipation,
Some run away, and but exchange their cares,
20   Losing the advantage of a virtuous station;

214

Few changes o'er can better their affairs,
　　Theirs being an unnatural situation,
From the dull palace to the dirty hovel:
Some play the devil, and then write a novel.

CCII

Haidée was Nature's bride, and knew not this:
　　Haidée was Passion's child, born where the sun
Showers triple light, and scorches even the kiss
　　Of his gazelle-eyed daughters; she was one
Made but to love, to feel that she was his
30　　Who was her chosen: what was said or done
Elsewhere was nothing. She had nought to fear,
Hope, care, nor love beyond – her heart beat *here*.

CCIII

And oh! that quickening of the heart, that beat!
　　How much it costs us! yet each rising throb
Is in its cause as its effect so sweet,
　　That Wisdom, ever on the watch to rob
Joy of its alchemy, and to repeat
　　Fine truths; even Conscience, too, has a tough job
To make us understand each good old maxim,
40　So good – I wonder Castlereagh don't tax 'em.

CCIV

And now 'twas done – on the lone shore were plighted
　　Their hearts; the stars, their nuptial torches, shed
Beauty upon the beautiful they lighted:
　　Ocean their witness, and the cave their bed,
By their own feelings hallow'd and united,
　　Their priest was Solitude, and they were wed:
And they were happy, for to their young eyes
Each was an angel, and earth paradise.

215

[The Isles of Greece]

1

The isles of Greece, the isles of Greece!
   Where burning Sappho loved and sung,
Where grew the arts of war and peace,
   Where Delos rose, and Phœbus sprung!
Eternal summer gilds them yet,
But all, except their sun, is set.

2

The Scian and the Teian muse,
   The hero's harp, the lover's lute,
Have found the fame your shores refuse:
   Their place of birth alone is mute
To sounds which echo further west
Than your sires' 'Islands of the Blest.'

3

The mountains look on Marathon –
   And Marathon looks on the sea;
And musing there an hour alone,
   I dream'd that Greece might still be free:
For standing on the Persians' grave,
I could not deem myself a slave.

4

A king sate on the rocky brow
   Which looks o'er sea-born Salamis;
And ships, by thousands, lay below,
   And men in nations; – all were his!
He counted them at break of day –
And when the sun set where were they?

5

And where are they? and where art thou,
  My country? On thy voiceless shore
The heroic lay is tuneless now –
  The heroic bosom beats no more!
And must thy lyre, so long divine,
Degenerate into hands like mine?

6

'T is something, in the dearth of fame,
  Though link'd among a fetter'd race,
To feel at least a patriot's shame,
  Even as I sing, suffuse my face;
For what is left the poet here?
For Greeks a blush – for Greece a tear.

7

Must *we* but weep o'er days more blest?
  Must *we* but blush? – Our fathers bled.
Earth! render back from out thy breast
  A remnant of our Spartan dead!
Of the three hundred grant but three,
To make a new Thermopylæ!

8

What, silent still? and silent all?
  Ah! no; – the voices of the dead
Sound like a distant torrent's fall,
  And answer, 'Let one living head,
But one arise, – we come, we come!'
'T is but the living who are dumb.

9

In vain – in vain: strike other chords;
50   Fill high the cup with Samian wine!
Leave battles to the Turkish hordes,
    And shed the blood of Scio's vine!
Hark! rising to the ignoble call –
How answers each bold Bacchanal!

10

You have the Pyrrhic dance as yet;
    Where is the Pyrrhic phalanx gone?
Of two such lessons, why forget
    The nobler and the manlier one?
You have the letters Cadmus gave –
60   Think ye he meant them for a slave?

11

Fill high the bowl with Samian wine!
    We will not think of themes like these!
It made Anacreon's song divine:
    He served – but served Polycrates –
A tyrant; but our masters then
Were still, at least, our countrymen.

12

The tyrant of the Chersonese
    Was freedom's best and bravest friend;
That tyrant was Miltiades!
70   Oh! that the present hour would lend
Another despot of the kind!
Such chains as his were sure to bind.

Fill high the bowl with Samian wine!
  On Suli's rock, and Parga's shore,
Exists the remnant of a line
  Such as the Doric mothers bore;
And there, perhaps, some seed is sown,
The Heracleidan blood might own.

Trust not for freedom to the Franks –
  They have a king who buys and sells;
In native swords, and native ranks,
  The only hope of courage dwells:
But Turkish force, and Latin fraud,
Would break your shield, however broad.

Fill high the bowl with Samian wine!
  Our virgins dance beneath the shade –
I see their glorious black eyes shine;
  But gazing on each glowing maid,
My own the burning tear-drop laves,
To think such breasts must suckle slaves.

Place me on Sunium's marbled steep,
  Where nothing, save the waves and I,
May hear our mutual murmurs sweep;
There, swan-like, let me sing and die:
A land of slaves shall ne'er be mine –
Dash down yon cup of Samian wine!

80

90

[Ave Maria]

CII

Ave Maria! blessed be the hour!
   The time, the clime, the spot, where I so oft
Have felt that moment in its fullest power
   Sink o'er the earth so beautiful and soft,
While swung the deep bell in the distant tower,
   Or the faint dying day-hymn stole aloft,
And not a breath crept through the rosy air,
And yet the forest leaves seem'd stirr'd with prayer.

CIII

Ave Maria! 'tis the hour of prayer!
10   Ave Maria! 'tis the hour of love!
Ave Maria! May our spirits dare
   Look up to thine and to thy Son's above!
Ave Maria! oh that face so fair!
   Those downcast eyes beneath the Almighty dove –
What though 'tis but a pictured image strike,
That painting is no idol, – 'tis too like.

CIV

Some kinder casuists are pleased to say,
   In nameless print – that I have no devotion;
But set those persons down with me to pray,
20   And you shall see who has the properest notion
Of getting into heaven the shortest way;
   My altars are the mountains and the ocean,
Earth, air, stars, – all that springs from the great Whole,
Who hath produced, and will receive the soul.

Sweet hour of twilight! – in the solitude
  Of the pine forest, and the silent shore
Which bounds Ravenna's immemorial wood,
  Rooted where once the Adrian wave flow'd o'er,
To where the last Cæsarean fortress stood,
30 Evergreen forest! which Boccaccio's lore
And Dryden's lay made haunted ground to me,
How have I loved the twilight hour and thee!

CVI

The shrill cicalas, people of the pine,
  Making their summer lives one ceaseless song,
Were the sole echoes, save my steed's and mine,
  And vesper bell's that rose the boughs along;
The spectre huntsman of Onesti's line,
  His hell-dogs, and their chase, and the fair throng
Which learn'd from this example not to fly
40 From a true lover, – shadow'd my mind's eye.

CVII

Oh, Hesperus! thou bringest all good things –
  Home to the weary, to the hungry cheer,
To the young bird the parent's brooding wings,
  The welcome stall to the o'erlabour'd steer;
Whate'er of peace about our hearthstone clings,
  Whate'er hour household gods protect of dear,
Are gather'd round us by thy look of rest;
Thou bring'st the child, too, to the mother's breast.

CVIII

Soft hour! which wakes the wish and melts the heart
50 Of those who sail the seas, on the first day
When they from their sweet friends are torn apart;
  Or fills with love the pilgrim on his way

As the far bell of vesper makes him start,
  Seeming to weep the dying day's decay;
Is this a fancy which our reason scorns?
Ah! surely nothing dies but something mourns!

[Slaughter at Ismail]

CXXI

In the mean time, cross-legg'd, with great sang-froid,
  Among the scorching ruins he sat smoking
Tobacco on a little carpet; – Troy
  Saw nothing like the scene around; – yet looking
With martial stoicism, nought seem'd to annoy
  His stern philosophy; but gently stroking
His beard, he puff'd his pipe's ambrosial gales,
As if he had three lives, as well as tails.

CXXII

The town was taken – whether he might yield
10   Himself or bastion, little matter's now:
His stubborn valour was no future shield.
  Ismail's no more! The crescent's silver bow
Sunk, and the crimson cross glared o'er the field,
  But red with no *redeeming* gore: the glow
Of burning streets, like moonlight on the water,
Was imaged back in blood, the sea of slaughter.

CXXIII

All that the mind would shrink from of excesses;
  All that the body perpetrates of bad;
All that we read, hear, dream, of man's distresses;
20   All that the devil would do if run stark mad;

All that defies the worst which pen expresses;
 All by which hell is peopled, or as sad
As hell – mere mortals who their power abuse –
Was here (as heretofore and since) let loose.

CXXIV

If here and there some transient trait of pity
 Was shown, and some more noble heart broke through
Its bloody bond, and saved, perhaps, some pretty
 Child, or an aged, helpless man or two –
What's this in one annihilated city,
30 Where thousand loves, and ties, and duties grew?
Cockneys of London! Muscadins of Paris!
Just ponder what a pious pastime war is,

CXXV

Think how the joys of reading a Gazette
 Are purchased by all agonies and crimes:
Or if these do not move you, don't forget
 Such doom may be your own in after-times.
Meantime the Taxes, Castlereagh, and Debt,
 Are hints as good as sermons, or as rhymes.
Read your own hearts and Ireland's present story,
40 Then feed her famine fat with Wellesley's glory.

CXXVI

But still there is unto a patriot nation,
 Which loves so well its country and its king,
A subject of sublimest exultation –
 Bear it, ye Muses, on your brightest wing!
Howe'er the mighty locust, Desolation
 Strip your green fields, and to your harvest cling,
Gaunt famine never shall approach the throne –
Though Ireland starve, great George weighs twenty stone.

223

But let me put an end unto my theme:
50 There was an end of Ismail – hapless town!
Far flash'd her burning towers o'er Danube's stream,
  And redly ran his blushing waters down.
The horrid war-whoop and the shriller scream
  Rose still; but fainter were the thunders grown:
Of forty thousand who had mann'd the wall,
Some hundreds breathed – the rest were silent all!

from CANTO THE NINTH

[End of the World]

XXXVII

But let it go: – it will one day be found
  With other relics of 'a former world,'
When this world shall be *former*, underground,
  Thrown topsy-turvy, twisted, crisp'd, and curl'd,
Baked, fried, or burnt, turn'd inside-out, or drown'd,
  Like all the worlds before, which have been hurl'd
First out of, and then back again to chaos,
The superstratum which will overlay us.

XXXVIII

So Cuvier says: – and then shall come again
10 Unto the new creation, rising out
From our old crash, some mystic, ancient strain
  Of things destroy'd and left in airy doubt;
Like to the notions we now entertain
  Of Titans, giants, fellows of about
Some hundred feet in height, *not* to say *miles*,
And mammoths, and your winged crocodiles.

XXXIX

Think if then George the Fourth should be dug up,
   How the new worldlings of the then new East
Will wonder where such animals could sup!
   (For they themselves will be but of the least:
20 Even worlds miscarry, when too oft they pup,
   And every new creation hath decreased
In size, from overworking the material –
Men are but maggots of some huge Earth's burial).

from CANTO THE THIRTEENTH

[Newstead Abbey Remembered]

LV

To Norman Abbey whirl'd the noble pair, –
   An old, old monastery once, and now
Still older mansion, – of a rich and rare
   Mix'd Gothic, such as artists all allow
Few specimens yet left us can compare
   Withal: it lies perhaps a little low,
Because the monks preferr'd a hill behind,
To shelter their devotion from the wind.

LVI

It stood embosom'd in a happy valley,
10   Crown'd by high woodlands, where the Druid oak
Stood, like Caractacus, in act to rally
   His host, with broad arms 'gainst the thunderstroke,
And from beneath his boughs were seen to sally
   The dappled foresters; as day awoke,
The branching stag swept down with all his herd,
To quaff a brook which murmur'd like a bird.

LVII

Before the mansion lay a lucid lake,
    Broad as transparent, deep, and freshly fed
By a river, which its soften'd way did take
20   In currents through the calmer water spread
Around: the wildfowl nestled in the brake
    And sedges, brooding in their liquid bed:
The woods sloped downwards to its brink, and stood
With their green faces fix'd upon the flood.

Its outlet dash'd into a deep cascade,
    Sparkling with foam, until again subsiding,
Its shriller echoes – like an infant made
    Quiet – sank into softer ripples, gliding
Into a rivulet: and thus allay'd,
30   Pursued its course, now gleaming, and now hiding
Its windings through the woods; now clear, now blue,
According as the skies their shadows threw.

LIX

A glorious remnant of the Gothic pile
    (While yet the church was Rome's) stood half apart
In a grand arch, which once screen'd many an aisle.
    These last had disappear'd – a loss to art:
The first yet frown'd superbly o'er the soil,
    And kindled feelings in the roughest heart,
Which mourn'd the power of time's or tempest's march,
40   In gazing on that venerable arch.

Within a niche, nigh to its pinnacle,
    Twelve saints had once stood sanctified in stone;
But these had fallen, not when the friars fell,
    But in the war which struck Charles from his throne,

When each house was a fortalice – as tell
    The annals of full many a line undone, –
The gallant cavaliers, who fought in vain
For those who knew not to resign or reign.

But in a higher niche, alone, but crown'd,
50   The Virgin-Mother of the God-born Child,
With her Son in her blessed arms, look'd round;
    Spared by some chance when all beside was spoil'd;
She made the earth below seem holy ground.
    This may be superstition, weak or wild,
But even the faintest relics of a shrine
Of any worship wake some thoughts divine.

LXII

A mighty window, hollow in the centre,
    Shorn of its glass of thousand colourings,
Through which the deepen'd glories once could enter,
60   Streaming from off the sun like seraph's wings,
Now yawns all desolate: now loud, now fainter,
    The gale sweeps through its fretwork, and oft sings
The owl his anthem, where the silenced quire
Lie with their hallelujahs quench'd like fire.

But in the noontide of the moon, and when
    The wind is winged from one point of heaven,
There moans a strange unearthly sound, which then
    Is musical – a dying accent driven
Through the huge arch, which soars and sinks again.
70   Some deem it but the distant echo given
Back to the night wind by the waterfall,
And harmonised by the old choral wall:

Others, that some original shape, or form
    Shaped by decay perchance, hath given the power
(Though less than that of Memnon's statue, warm
    In Egypt's rays, to harp at a fix'd hour)
To this grey ruin, with a voice to charm
    Sad, but serene, it sweeps o'er tree or tower;
The cause I know not, nor can solve; but such
80   The fact: – I've heard it, – once perhaps too much.

LXV

Amidst the court a Gothic fountain play'd,
    Symmetrical, but deck'd with carvings quaint –
Strange faces, like to men in masquerade,
    And here perhaps a monster, there a saint:
The spring gush'd through grim mouths of granite made,
    And sparkled into basins, where it spent
Its little torrent in a thousand bubbles,
Like man's vain glory, and his vainer troubles.

LXVI

The mansion's self was vast and venerable,
90   With more of the monastic than has been
Elsewhere preserved: the cloisters still were stable,
    The cells, too, and refractory, I ween:
An exquisite small chapel had been able,
    Still unimpair'd, to decorate the scene;
The rest had been reform'd, replaced, or sunk,
And spoke more of the baron than the monk.

[Night Thoughts]

XCVII

The night – (I sing by night – sometimes an owl,
  And now and then a nightingale) – is dim,
And the loud shriek of sage Minerva's fowl
  Rattles around me her discordant hymn:
Old portraits from old walls upon me scowl –
  I wish to heaven they would not look so grim;
The drying embers dwindle in the grate –
I think too that I have sat up too late:

XCVIII

And therefore, though 'tis by no means my way
  To rhyme at noon – when I have other things
To think of, if I ever think – I say
  I feel some chilly midnight shudderings,
And prudently postpone, until mid-day,
  Treating a topic which, alas! but brings
Shadows; – but you must be in my condition
Before you learn to call this superstition.

XCIX

Between two world life hovers like a star,
  'Twixt night and morn, upon the horizon's verge.
How little do we know that which we are!
  How less what we may be! The eternal surge
Of time and tide rolls on, and bears afar
  Our bubbles; as the old burst, new emerge,
Lash'd from the foam of ages; while the graves
Of empires heave but like some passing waves.

On This Day I Complete My
Thirty-Sixth Year

'Tis time this heart should be unmoved,
  Since others it hath ceased to move:
Yet, though I cannot be beloved,
    Still let me love!

My days are in the yellow leaf;
  The flowers and fruits of love are gone;
The worm, the canker, and the grief
    Are mine alone!

The fire that on my bosom preys
10   Is lone as some volcanic isle;
No torch is kindled at its blaze –
    A funeral pile.

The hope, the fear, the jealous care,
  The exalted portion of the pain
And power of love, I cannot share,
    But wear the chain.

But 'tis not *thus* – and 'tis not *here* –
  Such thoughts should shake my soul, nor *now*,
Where glory decks the hero's bier,
20   Or binds his brow.

The sword, the banner, and the field,
  Glory and Greece, around me see!
The Spartan, borne upon his shield,
    Was not more free.

Awake! (not Greece – she *is* awake!)
    Awake, my spirit! Think through *whom*
Thy life-blood tracks its parent lake,
      And then strike home!

Tread those reviving passions down,
30   Unworthy manhood! – unto thee
Indifferent should the smile or frown
      Of beauty be.

If thou regrett'st thy youth, *why live?*
    The land of honourable death
Is here: – up to the field, and give
      Away thy breath!

Seek out – less often sought than found –
    A soldier's grave, for thee the best;
Then look around, and choose thy ground,
40   And take thy rest.

Missolonghi, 22, January 1824.

231

Textual Notes

The poems are arranged in chronological order of publication, except that the extracts from *Don Juan* are grouped together.

DAMAETAS (1807). Included in *Hours of Idleness*, Byron's first published volume of poems (though an earlier volume had been printed privately and anonymously a year previously). Damaetas was the name of a shepherd in the *Idylls* of the ancient Greek poet Theocritus (third century B.C.). The poem shows Byron already at an early age obsessed with a sense of guilt and disillusion – and at the same time already cultivating the legend of Byronic wickedness.

1. Byron's own note explains the legal position in his day: 'In law every person is an infant who has not attained the age of twenty-one.'

14. 'bane' – an old word for evil or harm.

I WOULD I WERE A CARELESS CHILD (1807). Also from *Hours of Idleness*. This poem again shows how early the main outlines of the Byronic Byron began to form. In its reiterated call to find refuge from pain and disillusionment in childhood and in scenes of wild and picturesque natural beauty it is a typical poem of the Romantic period. But a rejection of easy romantic escapes is also implicit in it. Already, too, there are premonitions of the loneliness and exile that Byron would be called upon to endure and of the elements in his own nature that can be said to have 'invented' them.

2. A reference to the fact that much of Byron's early childhood was spent in Scotland.

9. cultured lands, a reference to the estates in England (including Newstead Abbey) which Byron inherited.

10. name of splendid sound, that of *Lord* Byron.

[FAREWELL TO ENGLAND] from *Childe Harold's Pilgrimage*, Canto the First (1812), stanzas I–XIII

1. Hellas: Greece. The fact that Byron chose to begin the Canto in this way is, of course, prophetic of his future involvement with Greece.

4. sacred hill: Mt Parnassus, a mountain in Greece a few miles north of Delphi, was the sacred hill of the nine Muses.

5. i.e. the Castalia, a spring on Mt Parnassus, sacred to Apollo (the god of music and poetry) and to the Muses.

6. Delphi: in a deep, rocky cleft on the south-west slopes of Mt

Parnassus, was in classical times the seat of a temple to Apollo and of a famous oracle.

8. mote: archaic word for 'must'; *shell:* conch-shell – used in some parts of the world as a musical instrument; *weary Nine:* the nine Muses.

10. whilome: archaic word for 'once upon a time'; *Albion:* England.

11. ne: archaic form of the negative.

14. sooth: archaic word for 'truth'; *wight:* archaic word for 'person'.

18. wassailers: archaic word for revellers.

19. hight: archaic word for 'named' or 'called'.

20–2. A reference to Byron's own ancient lineage.

23. losel: archaic word for a profligate or ne'er-do-well.

36. Eremite: archaic word for 'hermit'.

37–45. Although *Childe Harold* is undoubtedly autobiographical in spirit, it is not always possible to find exact parallels in Byron's own life. For example, the character of Childe Harold probably owes as much to Byron's great-uncle 'the wicked Lord' from whom he inherited his title, as to Byron himself. On the other hand, we know that Byron was fascinated by his great-uncle, felt that he shared with him an 'ancestral curse' – and in moments of cynicism or bravado felt impelled to imitate him.

39. The theme of unrequited love is part of the Romantic pose, and the 'one' whom Childe Harold loved is in part a composite, generalised figure. In addition, however, Byron had in mind Mary Chaworth, a distant relation and heiress to an estate neighbouring Newstead Abbey. Byron had fallen in love with her in 1803 when he was sixteen years old, and Mary two years older. The man whom the wicked Lord Byron had killed in a duel was a member of the Chaworth family, and Byron had the romantic idea that if he married Mary (who did not return his feelings) the bad blood between the two families would be wiped out and his inherited guilt expiated.

47. bacchanals: followers of Bacchus, the Greek god of wine.

49. ee: archaic form of 'eye'.

55–9. References to Byron's ancestral home of Newstead Abbey.

61. Paphian: devoted to the service of love, after Paphos, in Cyprus, which in ancient times contained a famous temple of Aphrodite, the goddess of love.

64–5. A typical example of the early Byronic Byron in its posturing, melodramatic phase, before self-awareness and irony had begun to temper the rhetoric.

66. Probably a reference to the 'bad blood' between the Byrons and the Chaworths (see above).

67. Probably a reference to his unrequited passion for Mary Chaworth (see above).

73–6. Byron himself did in fact hold a riotous house-party at Newstead Abbey before he set out on his tour.

77. lemans: archaic word for 'sweethearts' or 'mistresses'.

79. Eros: the Greek god of (sexual, as opposed to 'ideal') love; *feere:* archaic spelling of 'fear'.

81. Mammon: a personification of great wealth (after the Aramaic word for 'riches', used in the Greek text of two of the Gospels, and taken by medieval writers to be the proper name of a devil of covetousness); *Seraph*: a type of angel.

82. Byron loved his mother but was often on very bad terms with her.

84. A reference to Byron's half-sister, Augusta (the daughter of his father's first marriage).

99. Paynim: archaic word for 'pagan'.

118–97. This inset poem calls to mind the early Scottish *Ballad of Sir Patrick Spens*, which was well known at the time, because it was included in the *Reliques of Ancient English Poetry*, edited and 'restored' by Thomas Percy in 1765 – one of the 'key books' of the Romantic Revival. The poem is also a good example of Byron's love of the sea.

175. paramour: 'mistress'.

196. deserts and *caves* are images Byron frequently uses to express loneliness and separation.

[GREEKS, ARISE!] from *Childe Harold's Pilgrimage*, Canto the Second, (1812), stanzas LXIII–LXXVI. This address to the Greeks, who at the time were subjects of the Turkish Empire, is to all intents and purposes, a call to arms – some thirteen years before they in fact rose in revolt and sixteen before Byron himself died on their behalf. It is an obvious example of Byron's 'prophetic' utterances.

3–4. Here Byron compares the Greeks with the tribes of Israel whom Moses led out of their bondage to the Egyptians, to 'the promised land'. Byron was deeply read in the Old Testament and frequently drew on its stories.

6–9. In 480 B.C. three hundred Spartans under Leonidas, the vanguard of the small Greek army, held at bay a vast invading Persian army under Xerxes, in the narrow pass of Thermopylae. The Spartan warriors – *hopeless* because the odds were so great, but willingly facing their *doom* – are contrasted with the modern Greeks. Byron, in effect, is asking where, in the Greece of his day, is a leader to be found who can call back into existence the spirit of the Spartans who fought at Thermopylae.

10–14. At the end of the Peloponnesian War, the victorious Spartans imposed on the defeated Athenians an oligarchy of thirty magistrates – known as the 'Thirty Tyrants'. Thrasybulus was an Athenian General and statesman who organised a band of exiles against the 'Thirty Tyrants', and after occupying first Phyle (404 B.C.) and then Piraeus (the harbour of Athens) he eventually overthrew 'the Thirty' and restored democracy to Athens.

13. Attic: Athenian. Attica is another name for Athens.

15. carle: archaic word for an ordinary person (cf. the word 'churl').

31. Gaul: France.

34. Helots: the serfs of ancient Sparta.

[LAMENT FOR GREECE – AND YOUTH] from *Childe Harold's Pilgrimage,* Canto the Second (1812), stanzas LXXXVIII–XCVIII. This is one of the most interesting sections of the first two Cantos, bringing together a number of important themes. It will be noted that the lament for Greece's departed glories after the stirring description of the battle of Marathon, becomes more elegaic and historical in tone and less of a rallying cry. Greece emerges as a kind of lost 'wonder land' of nobility and heroism, though, of course, this doesn't exclude the political implications.

It is interesting to note, too, that stanza XCIV contains the clear hint that Childe Harold is on his way out as a separate *persona*, though Byron does not finally dismiss him until the Fourth Canto – and exactly at the point where the whole tone and mood deepen, as Byron the poet, struggling with his own personal emotions, begins taking command.

A specific personal grief, in fact, lies behind stanzas XCV to XCVIII, which were added to Canto the Second after Byron's return to England – the death of John Edleston in October 1811. Edleston had been a choirboy at Trinity College, Cambridge, when Byron was an undergraduate there, and there had been a strong romantic attachment between them. The stanzas also reveal Byron's more general melancholy and his persistent feeling that his capacity for happiness had been prematurely exhausted.

9. Athena: or Athene, patron goddess of Athens; *Marathon*: a plain near the east coast of Attica, the scene of the historic defeat of the Persian army in 490 B.C.

19. Mede: another word for Persian.

25. Asia's fear: Asia's, because Persia is part of Asia. The battle of Marathon saved Greece from becoming an Asiatic principality and thus enabled her to continue laying the foundations of European culture.

30. Ionian blast: the wind from the Ionian Sea.

36. Pallas: another name for the goddess Athene.

37–45. A typical evocation of Childe Harold's – and Byron's – feelings of loneliness and exile.

48–54. A reference to those who appropriated relics of Ancient Greece, and especially to Lord Elgin, who when he was envoy to the Turkish Government (1799–1803) conveyed to England the Elgin Marbles (as they came to be known) which included parts of the frieze and pediment of the Parthenon in Athens, the work of the great sculptor Pheidias (*c.*440 B.C.)

90. A good example of the 'bad' Byron: a typically stagey touch to the portrait of the Byronic hero.

99. Eld: archaic word for 'age'.

[HYMN TO LIBERTY] from *The Giaour* (1813). This is the first of Byron's 'Eastern Tales' drawing, like the first two cantos of *Childe Harold,* upon his travels in Asia Minor and the Balkans. These tales were just as popular, and eight editions of *The Giaour* appeared in the last seven months of 1813, in the course of which it increased in length from 685 to 1,334 lines. The word 'Giaour' (pronounced 'dja-oor') is a term or reproach applied by the Turks to non-Muslims, and especially Christians.

The tale is about a female slave, Leila, who because she has been unfaithful to her Turkish lord, Hassan, is bound and thrown into the sea. Her young Venetian lover, the Giaour, avenges her by killing Hassan. The narrative structure is interesting because, as in *Childe Harold,* Byron makes use of more than one narrator. At first the story is told by a Turkish fisherman, who witnesses some of the events, and finally in the Giaour's confession to a monk. This device does not interfere with the stirring pace of the octosyllabic couplets (four beats to a line, and not the five of the heroic couplet). This particular passage about Greece (more forthright than the similar ones in *Childe Harold*) helps to explain why Byron, even at this stage, was seen throughout Europe as a forceful and invigorating champion of liberty.

11. Salamis: an island in the Saronic Gulf, scene of the crushing defeat of the Persian fleet by the Greeks in 480 B.C.

[WHO THUNDERING COMES] from *The Giaour* (1813). This passage typifies the Byronic hero in action and shows Byron's narrative gifts – speed, economy of effect, immediacy – at their best. The character, mood and appearance of the Giaour are conveyed to us not by static description, but in continuous motion. There are some obvious touches from Byron's own personality, but it is also a genuine piece of characterisation – and one of the most telling of the earlier descriptions of 'the Byronic Hero'.

12. I loathe thy race: the narrator at this point is the Turkish fisherman, and he hates the Giaour as a Christian, while admiring him as a man.

20. Othman's sons: Ottomans or Turks (after Othman, the third of the Mohammedan Caliphs, a kinsman and son-in-law of Mohammed).

23. like a demon of the night: a typically 'Byronic' image.

33. ween: archaic word for 'know'.

46. tophaike: Byron's own note reads: ' "tophaike", musket. The Bairam is announced by the cannon at sunset: the illumination of the mosques, and the firing of all kinds of small arms, loaded with *ball*, proclaim it during the night.'

72. Jereed: Byron explains in his notes: 'Jereed, or Djerrid, a blunted Turkish javelin, which is darted from horse-back with great force and precision. It is a favourite exercise of the Mussulmans.'

82–97. A fine passage, in which the Giaour's state of mind, Byron's own, and some of the characteristic Byronic themes are fused together. It is full of the kind of images Byron used to convey a sense of moral – and cosmic – devastation: 'Winters of memory'; 'time's record'; 'Eternity of thought'; 'infinite as boundless space'.

[PIRATE'S SONG] from *The Corsair* (1814), Canto the First, stanza I. This was the third of Byron's Turkish Tales, following *The Bride of Abydos*, which was published in November 1813. Unlike the other two, which were composed in octosyllabic couplets, *The Corsair* uses what Byron (in his dedication to his friend, the Irish poet Tom Moore) called 'the good old and now neglected heroic couplet', the verse form of his revered 'master', Alexander Pope – the first time Byron had used it since *English Bards and Scotch Reviews* (1809). The more measured beat of the heroic couplet, however, doesn't in the least detract from the verve and colour of the narration – which this time is direct, without the intervention of another narrator besides the poet.

The Corsair took the reading public by storm almost as much as the first two Cantos of *Childe Harold*. Murray, Byron's publisher wrote: 'I sold, on the day of publication – a thing perfectly unprecedented – 10,000 copies.' Part of its success was due to the swift, vivid narrative, the fine descriptive passages, and the knowledge that the exotic background was authentic – and part to the fact that the public believed that Conrad, the very Byronic hero of the poem, was a self-portrait. The poem can also be seen, however, as Byron's first full-scale attempt to depict, through Conrad, the 'condition of man', as he saw it.

The Story. Conrad is a pirate chief in the Aegean Sea. He receives information that Seyd, the Turkish Pasha, is preparing a fleet for a descent on his island. He determines to anticipate him, takes his leave of his beloved mistress, Medora, makes his way to the Pasha's rallying-point at night, and introduces himself to his presence as a dervish who has escaped from the pirates. The premature firing of the Pasha's galleys by Conrad's men gives warning of the *coup*, which is in consequence only partially successful. Conrad is wounded, and taken prisoner, but not before he has rescued Gulnare, the chief slave in the Pasha's harem, from imminent death. She falls in love with Conrad, manages to obtain the postponement of his execution, and finally brings him a dagger with which to kill the Pasha in his sleep. Conrad revolts from the cold-blooded murder of an unprepared enemy, whereupon Gulnare kills the Pasha herself and escapes with Conrad. But her deed has turned him against her. They reach the pirate island, where Conrad finds Medora dead from grief at the reported slaying of her lover. Heart-stricken, Conrad disappears.

This first extract is a kind of pirates' chorus. Its effectiveness is due to the tension generated between the apparent exultation in a life of action, courage and freedom, and the implicit moral condemnation of its evil basis.

'Corsair' – was, strictly speaking, a privateer or pirate ship, especially off the Barbary Coast, but is often loosely used not for a ship but for a pirate.

[PORTRAIT OF CONRAD] from *The Corsair* (1814), Canto the First, IX–XII. Here we have the very epitome of the 'Byronic hero' (except perhaps, that the villainy is more stressed than usual for the sake of the story) – the dark secrets, the pride, the defiance, the courage, the ferocity, and above all the suggestion that his behaviour is the result of wrongs and injustices inflicted by others on a fundamentally good and sensitive nature.

There are a number of obvious points of resemblance in the portrait between Conrad and Byron himself – and it was this that thrilled Byron's contemporary readers.

1–4. Note that Byron does not say that Conrad is anything out of the ordinary: he wishes us to take his hero as a kind of 'everyman', but one whose early ideals have been frustrated, and who is condemned to a life of evil and violence. We must not overlook the wider significance in these heroes of Byron: they are all part of his vision of the human condition.

11–12. Another obvious touch of self-portraiture.

53–4. There are autobiographical elements here, especially in the hint of dark secrets in the past, and in the sense of blighted promise and happiness.

57–62. Another autobiographical passage, stressing once more Byron's pervasive sense of disillusionment.

69. A reference to Byron's own feeling of having prematurely 'anticipated life'.

89–94. In the same way Byron himself clung to the ideal of a perfect love that would redeem past sufferings.

STANZAS FOR MUSIC 1814 ('I speak not, I trace not, I breathe not thy name'). These impassioned stanzas were written for a song, at Tom Moore's request. At first some people thought they were addressed to Lady Frances Webster, with whom Byron had shared a romantic (but platonic) passion. In fact they were written for his half-sister Augusta Leigh, and they reveal both the force of his feelings for her and the emotional turmoil their relationship was causing him.

[LARA'S HOMECOMING] from *Lara, A Tale* (1814), Canto the First, Stanzas I-VIII. At the end of *The Corsair*, Conrad disappears. But now we meet him again; for *Lara* is a sequel to *The Corsair*, and its hero is Conrad returned to his ancestral home in Spain, which he had left in bitterness as a youth. He is accompanied by a page named Kaled – who is Gulnare in disguise. For a time Lara lives aloof from his neighbours. Then he is recognised, and becomes involved in a feud in which he is finally killed, dying in the arms of 'Kaled'.

The tale was popular for the same reason as *The Corsair* – it appeared to throw further light on Byron's mysterious and fascinating personality; and there is no doubt that to some extent it does represent, as do most of the verse tales, another of Byron's explorations into the Self, another of his attempts to discover his identity. The tone and mood, however, though the heroic couplet is again used, are more serious and sombre than those of *The Corsair*.

The poem is a throw-back to the first canto of *Childe Harold* in that it makes great use of Gothic background – detail – knights, ladies, baronial halls and so on.

In other ways, though, *Lara* looks forward to *Don Juan*, for Lara (or Conrad) has returned from his adventurous, blood-thirsty past to a highly formalised Spanish society – the kind of society which Byron was later to call 'The World' with a capital W.

After the stanzas printed in this section, the structure of the poem becomes more and more chaotic, though the narrative-line remains clear. But this is really Byron's main point, and probably what he had in mind when he told Tom Moore that the poem was more 'metaphysical' than narrative. For what he is showing us in *Lara* is that the past always lives in the present, that the world, however it is lived, remains basically the same, and that man is inescapably bound to his hell within.

13–20. This is one of the few occasions when Byron's bitterness about his father's abandonment of him when he was still a small child finds expression.

67–84. Another telling portrait of the 'Byronic hero', in his withdrawn, brooding mood of 'all passion spent'.

130. A rhetorical but intensely moving line, expressive again of Byron's bitterness and disillusionment in the face of a world where all dreams, the good and the bad alike, eventually fall apart.

THE WILD GAZELLE (1815). From a collection of poems entitled *Hebrew Melodies*, mostly written in the autumn of 1814 (when Byron was engaged to be married to 'Annabella' Milbanke). They were set, by I. Nathan, to airs sung in the Jewish religious services. Most of them deal with Old Testament subjects. *The Wild Gazelle*, with its reference to 'Israel's scatter'd race' condemned to 'wander witheringly' makes it very clear why Byron should have had a strong fellow feeling for the Jews. The poem, and especially the second stanza, is also a most apt illustration of the 'lost Eden' motif – or 'lost delight' as it appears in the poem – which runs through all Byron's poetry.

1. Judah: an area of ancient Palestine, from which the name 'Jews' is derived, and whose capital was Jerusalem.

11. Lebanon: mountain range of south-west Syria, famous in ancient times for its cedar trees.

23. The Temple of the Jews was destroyed by the Romans in A.D. 135 after their defeat of the Jewish uprising against their rule.

24. Salem: another word for Jerusalem.

THE DESTRUCTION OF SENNACHERIB (1815). Also from *Hebrew Melodies.* Sennacherib was a King of Assyria (705–681 B.C.) who invaded Palestine, but was forced to retire because of a pestilence among his troops – brought about, the Old Testament Jews believed, by the intervention of their Lord Jehovah.

4. Galilee: Northern province of Palestine, now in Israel.

9–10. A reference to the pestilence which assailed Sennacherib's troops.

21. Ashur: the ancient capital of Assyria.

22. Baal: a 'false god' worshipped by the Assyrians.

23. Gentile: a person not of Jewish blood; *unsmote by the sword,* because the Assyrians were defeated not in battle but by pestilence.

STANZAS FOR MUSIC 1815 ('There's not a joy the world can give like what it takes away'). One of the most direct expressions of Byron's basic theme of the 'lost Eden'.

4. . . . 'ere youth itself be past: another reference to Byron's feeling that he had prematurely exhausted life's potentialities.

9–12. Byron often had the feeling that – acceptance of the world as it is could only be achieved by destroying part of one's humanity. There are characteristic pairs of images to express this feeling – *chill* opposed to *fountain, sparkle* opposed to *ice.*

13. Byron himself was frequently a gay and witty companion – as his letters bear witness.

18. many a vanish'd scene: once again the characteristic yearning for a 'golden past'.

19–20. Further typical Byronic images – *springs, deserts* and *wither'd waste.*

WHEN WE TWO PARTED (1816). Written in February 1816 (and published with some alterations in *Poems, 1816*) after Byron had heard that a libel suit had been won against the *Morning Chronicle* for slanderously associating Lady Frances Webster's name with that of the Duke of Wellington. And yet the lines seem too passionate for an affair that was apparently never consummated, and one cannot help wondering whether Byron, in some of the lines at any rate, really had Augusta in mind.

14–16. This refers to the gossip attending the libel suit against the *Morning Chronicle.*

STANZAS FOR MUSIC 1816 ('There be none of beauty's daughters . . .'). One of the most beautiful of Byron's lyrics. As it was published in 1816 not long after Byron had met Shelley's sister-in-law Jane 'Claire' Clairmont, who became his mistress, it was generally assumed that the poem was addressed to her. But it is quite likely that it was written earlier for John Edleston, and the reference to 'thy sweet voice' (bearing in mind that Edleston was a choir boy when Byron first met him) bears out this supposition.

STANZAS TO AUGUST 1816 ('When all around grows drear and dark'). Byron wrote this moving poem to his half-sister, Augusta in April 1816, as a token of gratitude to her for standing by him so loyally after the break-down of his marriage.

DARKNESS (1816). Written in Switzerland during the first year of Byron's exile, when his spirits were at their lowest. Leslie A. Marchand (one of Byron's most distinguished biographers) has described this poem as 'a terrifying vision of man's last days in a dying universe – in which all civilisation has crumbled in the primordial struggle for existence' and the 'altruistic instinct' has disappeared from every living creature, except one dog. It is an important poem because it reveals that the 'hell' that existed in Byron's soul was related not only to his personal life but was also a vision of the 'chaos of hard clay', which he felt surrounded the whole life of man. It can be regarded as the first of the truly 'metaphysical' poems, a prelude to *Prometheus, Manfred* and *Cain*. It is full of the 'cosmic imagery' Byron uses in this kind of context. It is, too, a remarkably modern poem – and might almost be regarded as a vision of a world laid waste by nuclear warfare.

PROMETHEUS (1816). Written about the same time as *Darkness*. Prometheus – the Titan chained eternally to a rock, with vultures gnawing his vitals, as a punishment for bringing fire and other benefits to mankind – had been one of Byron's defiant heroes, ever since as a schoolboy at Harrow he had written a paraphase of a chorus of the *Prometheus Vinctus* of Aeschylus. In Byron's poem Prometheus becomes not only a symbol of his own suffering (which he always felt was not altogether deserved) but also of the only course, it seemed to him, open to a 'doomed' humanity – a defiant refusal to surrender either to self-pity, madness, or death.
24. Byron, although he was condemned by many as an atheist, believed strongly in the concept of Eternity.
26. thunderer: Jupiter, the king of the Gods, whose main weapon was a thunderbolt.
31–34. God himself, Byron is to tell us in *Cain*, was not truly 'free', and was himself wretched.
47. Byron also believed that man partook of divinity.

A FRAGMENT (1816). Another product of the first year of exile, revealing a similar metaphysical depth as Byron probes deeper into his experience and, in so doing, deeper into what seemed to him the sad reality of human life. It is full of images of loss, evanescence, death and chaos.

LINES ON HEARING THAT LADY BYRON WAS ILL (1816). Although Byron was increasingly probing into the nature of his own experience and that of mankind in general, the more purely personal poems must not be overlooked. This poem certainly displays bitterness and revengefulness, but the wounded feelings it reveals also make it clear that Byron felt deeply for his wife and was shocked by her decision to break up their marriage.

15. Nemesis: goddess of divine vengeance.
36. Clytemnestra: in Greek legend, the wife of Agamemnon, King of Argos and leader of the Greek armies which besieged Troy, whom she murdered on his return from the war, with the help of her lover, Aegisthus. She was in turn slain by her son, Orestes, in revenge for the murder of his father.
51. Averments: positive statements, affirmations.
53. Janus- spirits: people who are changeable, or two-faced. In Roman mythology Janus was a deity who guarded gates and doors, especially those of the State in times of war. He was always represented in statuary as having two faces, one at the front and one at the back of his head.

[EXILES] from *Childe Harold's Pilgrimage,* Canto the Third (1816) stanzas I–XVI. The third Canto of *Childe Harold* was one of the major products of Byron's stay in Switzerland during his first year of exile. It is instructive to read the separate Cantos in the chronological order in which they appeared because they have a habit of gathering up and developing the motifs of the intervening poems, and because they serve as a register of Byron's progress – though this third canto is the most directly related of all of them in mood and feeling to events in Byron's life. At the same time it must be remembered that *Childe Harold* can be read as a continuous poem, the four cantos in some ways resembling the separate movements of a symphony.

It is interesting to note that Byron begins the poem in his own direct voice, with an address, in the first stanza, to Ada, the daughter he had left behind and whom he was never to see again. But he soon brings Childe Harold back into the picture, and in

243

commenting on him adopts the narrator's tone. In other words, he again feels the need to use three different voices. The point is that at this stage he has not absorbed his experience to the extent of wishing to be dogmatic about it and he is still drawing back from some of its implications, especially the grimmer philosophical ones. Although, therefore, Childe Harold is very close to Byron, we must not assume that they are always identical. Sometimes Childe Harold's emotions and reactions are more extreme, for example, than those of Byron himself. Often, in fact, he is using him as a kind of scout, pushing him out ahead to test out the emotional climate, so that he himself can make up his mind what he feels and thinks about it at a different level of his being.

5. Byron splits the line in order to convey that his reverie about Ada has been taking place on board ship – when his speculations are already in vain.

9. This echoes the farewell lines in the first Canto – 'Adieu, adieu! my native land . . .' – and reminds us that they were indeed prophetic.

19. The *One* is, of course, Childe Harold.

29. The reference to the *harp* suggests that Byron is now merging into the 'minstrel' or narrator – as distinct from the Byron who spoke to us directly in the first stanza.

46–55. One of the first formulations of Byron's belief that creativity – however vain – was the only means of asserting the spirit's defiance against man's essential nothingness. The beginning of this stanza contains touches that remind one of Shelley, who was Byron's companion in Switzerland (together with his wife and his sister-in-law Claire Clairmont). The two poets influenced each other in a number of ways during this period.

55–63. It is exactly this overwrought frame of mind that made the fiction of Childe Harold a useful 'filter'.

66. And it is at this point, when Byron most needs a control, that Harold *does* reappear.

87. Childe Harold, in other words, has reached a point of imperviousness to grief which Byron longs for, but has not attained.

90. wonder-works of God: this seems to suggest that Harold was seeking comfort in religion – and there is also a hint of this in line 76.

97–8. Here Harold (somewhat like the wandering Jew, in the medieval legend, who was condemned to wander the earth without rest till the Day of Judgment, as a punishment for insulting Christ on his way to the Crucifixion) becomes a universal symbol of loss and exile. He is a cosmic symbol, too, in that he is caught up in the 'vortex' of the universe, bound in 'a giddy circle, chasing Time'. *105–6*. We shall find the same attitude exemplified in *Manfred*.

109–17. Harold momentarily tries to absorb himself in nature as Wordsworth and other Romantics had done.

118. The Chaldean: the Chaldeans were a race of Semitic Babylonians originating from Arabia, who in ancient times were famous as astronomers and astrologers.

122–3. In other words, the Wordsworthian religion of Nature was not for him.

[WATERLOO] from *Childe Harold's Pilgrimage*, Canto the Third, stanzas XVII–XXVIII. These stanzas, which run on from the previous passage, include some of Byron's most famous lines. He visited Brussels, the Belgian capital, and the field of Waterloo, on his way to join the Shelleys and Claire Clairmont in Switzerland. The battle of Waterloo, in which Napoleon Bonaparte was finally defeated, was of course, the most momentous historical event of Byron's life to date. The battle had been fought on 18 June 1815 – not much more than a year before Byron's visit, and Byron's description has the freshness and vividness of contempory reporting. The suddenness with which these Waterloo stanzas are introduced does not mean that they have no connection with what had gone before. On the contrary – for Byron and Childe Harold have just been talking about personal lives laid waste, in which the main lesson has been that 'all is vanity' – and now the same theme is displayed on a public and vaster stage. The beauty and gaiety of the ball on the eve of the battle are just as transient as Byron's or Childe Harold's moments of hope and happiness – and they, too, are doomed. Waterloo, in fact, is one of Byron's 'extended metaphors', standing for the chaos that he felt was always waiting to swallow up the dreams, hopes and aspirations of mankind. Byron saw Napoleon as a potential Prometheus who *might* have brought benefit to mankind, but who had not only betrayed his trust but also, by continuing to remain alive after defeat, failed to maintain his Promethean defiance.

9. king-making: because with the defeat of Napoleon the corrupt and reactionary monarchs he had deposed were restored to their thrones.

10. Golgotha, where Christ was crucified, was also called 'the place of skulls' – and at Waterloo, too, many brave men were 'crucified'.

12–13. A statement of the general theme governing the whole Canto so far. 'Fame' is just as 'fleeting' as the hope, for example, that Childe Harold might find a respite in the beauties of Nature.

14. Byron explains the inverted commas in a note: ' "Pride of place" is a term of falconry, and means the highest pitch of flight.'
19. Gaul: France.
20. France is 'in fetters' because the king, Louis XVIII, has been restored to his throne.
25–7. the *Lion* is Napoleon and Byron is castigating England for supporting the *Wolf* – that is, the restored King.
36. Harmodius: with his friend Aristogiton attempted to assassinate Hippias, tyrant of Athens, in 514 B.C.
82. The Cameron Highlanders fought at Waterloo.
83. war note of Lochiel: the battle – tune for the pipers of the Clan Cameron; *Albyn:* Albion, or England.
85. pibroch: series of martial variations for bagpipes.
90. Sir Ewen (or Evan) Cameron of Locheil (1629–1719) was a famous chief of the clan Cameron (described by Sir Walter Scott as 'the Ulysses of the Highlands'). His grandson Donald, known as 'gentle Lochiel', was wounded at the battle of Culloden in 1745.
91. Ardennes: hilly, forested region in Belgium and north-east France.

[ON THE RHINE] from *Childe Harold's Pilgrimage*, Canto the Third, stanzas LI–LV. After leaving Belgium, Byron visited the famous beauty spots of the Rhine. His sister Augusta was very much in his mind; there are a number of references to her and the tender and charming Drachenfels poem was really written for her, though it is noticeable that Byron is careful to conceal himself under Childe Harold's cloak – not because he thought the disguise would not be penetrated, but because it helped to distance his own suffering.

We see, too, from stanza LIV that his infant daughter, Ada, was still very much in his mind.

Drachenfels is a mountain peak on the Rhine near Königswinter.

[ESCAPE INTO NATURE] from *Childe Harold's Pilgrimage*, Canto the Third, stanzas LXVIII–LXXV. These stanzas show the remarkable effort Byron was making to adapt himself to his new situation. Again it should be noticed that he does not write of nature with the calm confidence that Wordsworth does. Thus (in the first line of the passage) Lake Leman (another name for Lake Geneva) has to 'woo' him to set aside his sorrows. The numerous question-marks are those of a man seeking to convince himself of something he is secretly doubtful about.
30. The River Rhône flows through Lake Geneva.

[A TRUCE WITH THE WORLD] from *Childe Harold's Pilgrimage*, Canto the Third, stanzas CXIII–CXVIII. These are the concluding stanzas of the Canto. As far as Byron's feelings during this first year of his exile are concerned, they represent the reverse-side of the coin to the utter despair of *Darkness*. They suggest a mood not only of acceptance of his lot, but of modest hopefulness for the future and the survival of love, represented perhaps by Augusta and certainly (he still hoped at this stage) by his infant daughter Ada (though he suspects he will never see her again), and it is Ada who begins and ends the Canto.

THE PRISONER OF CHILLON (1816). Byron wrote this poem, too, in Switzerland. It centres on the imprisonment of François de Bonnivard in the castle of Chillon, on the Lake of Geneva. Bonnivard (who was born in 1496) was prior of the monastery of St Victor near Geneva, and conspired with a band of patriots to throw off the yoke of the Duke of Savoy and to establish a free republic in Geneva. For this he was twice imprisoned by the duke, his second imprisonment being in the Castle of Chillon, from 1530 to 1536, when he was released by the neighbouring Bernese. He lived for a long time after this, dying probably in 1570.

In a note at the beginning of the first section of the poem Byron apologises for not having known all the facts at the time he wrote it. But this is really irrevelant to the main theme underlying the poem. At one level the Promethean figure of Bonnivard is a poetic symbol – of resistance to tyranny. At another, he stands for defiance of the human spirit in general. At yet a deeper level his imprisonment symbolises the whole human condition, confined to the 'dungeon' of the world, haunted by illusory gleams of beauty and hope of deliverance.

The two brothers who share Bonnivard's imprisonment can also be seen as 'symbols': the one gentle and compassionate, standing for what might be called the 'feminine principle' in Byron's nature – and in life in general; the other, virile, strong and active, standing for the 'masculine principle'. The juxtaposition of heart and mind, love and war, is common throughout Byron's verse tales.

One of the reasons why the poem is generally regarded as the best of all his narrative poems, is that the oblique methods of narration which Byron used in his other verse tales have been discarded and the poem is in the form of a dramatic monologue, with everything concentrated on the plight of the prisoner and his reactions to it. It will be noted that Byron does not use rhymed couplets throughout, but varies his rhyme scheme and the length of his lines. This, too, makes for a greater density of effect.

The 'Sonnet on Chillon', which prefaces the poem has been omitted; otherwise it is printed entire.

80. The typical Byronic yearning note for a 'golden past' is heard here.

136–7. This makes it clear that the dungeon stands for a whole world in which men do evil to each other.

270–2. There is a certain ambivalence of feeling about the bird: it brings back the stir of life – but it is a gleam of hope that finally vanishes, and in any case with the death of his brothers – the two 'principles' of life – the prisoner himself is to all intents and purposes dead himself.

322–3. The dungeon has now indeed become a metaphor of the whole world and of the human condition in it.

392. He regained his freedom 'with a sigh' because he has learned the bitter 'Byronic' lesson that the whole of life is a prison.

SONG FOR THE LUDDITES (1816). Two other aspects of Byron we must not lose sight of appear here – the gay and witty companion, and the liberal who retained a vivid interest in political events in England even after he had left it for good.

The Luddites were bands of artisans who between 1811 and 1816 were attacking the new weaving and spinning machines which were robbing them of their livelihood (named after Ned Ludd). The incident that sparked off this particular political 'squib' took place in Nottinghamshire, where Newstead Abbey is situated; it was the introduction of a Bill to hang machine breakers that inspired Byron's brilliant maiden speech in the House of Lords in 1812. Byron abhorred political violence, but he had strong sympathies for the Luddites.

1. the Liberty lads o'er the sea: the French revolutionists who had guillotined their king, Louis XVI.

6–7. Appropriate images, of course, for weavers.

MANFRED (1817), Act II, Scene IV to end of Act III, Scene II. The first two Acts of Byron's tragedy *Manfred* were written during 1816 when Byron was still in Switzerland. The third and final Act was written after he had settled in Venice. The play is written in both blank verse and rhymed verse and interspersed with a number of Shelley-like songs.

The play, which is probably the most powerful of all the 'Byronic' Byron's evocations of 'Promethean' man, is set in the Alps. There

Manfred, guilty of some mysterious and inexpiable crime, an outcast from society and tortured by remorse, wanders among the Swiss Alps, whose icy peaks correspond with the ice in his heart, and contrast with his hopeless yearning for the warmth of human love.

In the first act Manfred, after being refused the boon of 'oblivion' by the Spirits of the Universe, wanders on the Jungfrau, where a chamois hunter prevents him from hurling himself to his death. In the second Act Manfred, after having accompanied the chamois hunter to his cottage and having recovered from the impulse to destroy himself, goes into an Alpine valley, where the Witch of the Alps appears to him. Manfred tells her of his quest for knowledge and of the woman who had been destroyed by his love. She offers to help him to find forgetfulness if he will submit to her, but he proudly rejects the offer. In the third scene of this Act various Destinies and Spirits describe the disasters they have inflicted on mankind and welcome the arrival of Nemesis.

Now follows the fourth scene in which Manfred visits Arimanes (or Ahriman), who, in the Zoroastrian system, is the principle of evil, in perpetual conflict with Ormazed the god of goodness and light. The scene contains echoes from the scene in the first part of Goethe's great drama *Faust* (published in 1808), where Faust enters into a compact with Mephistopheles.

ACT II, Scene IV
31. A Magian: a follower of the Magi, an ancient Persian priestly caste, skilled in magic and astrology.
49. Worm is used several times in this scene, together with *clay* and other of Byron's characteristic images for denoting 'man'.
60-3. The mind of man is no more effective than his heart, Byron implies, in achieving a permanent state of happiness.
83. Astarte: the eastern equivalent of Aphrodite, goddess of love. But here she also represents Augusta Leigh.
98-105. These lines echo those in *Dr Faustus*, the blank-verse tragedy by the Elizabethan playwright Christopher Marlowe, where Mephistopheles conjures up a vision of Helen of Troy at Dr Faustus's request.

ACT III, Scene I
12. schoolman's jargon: the Schoolmen were the writers and university teachers of the Middle Ages who taught logic, metaphysics and theology, seeking to reconcile the Ancient Greek philosopher Aristotle and the doctrines of Christianity.
13. Kalon: the 'beautiful', or 'golden mean' – the point of perfect

equipoise between opposing emotions, advocated by Aristotle as the ethical goal of civilised man.

88. 'Rome's sixth emperor' – the Emperor Nero, who committed suicide in A.D. 68.

128. simoom: or 'simoon', the hot, dry and suffocating wind of the desert.

136. gin: short poetic form of 'begin'.

138–41. So Byron felt of himself. And he died in Greece, not in battle but of a fever. Another prophetic note.

ACT III, Scene II

4–8. A striking instance of the way in which the idea of a purer, more innocent state of mankind constantly exercised Byron's imagination. Byron in his notes quotes: "'And it came to pass, that the *Sons of God* saw the daughters of man that they were fair', etc. 'There were giants in the earth in those days; and also after that, when the *Sons of God* came in unto the daughters of men, and they bore children to them, the same became mighty men which were of old, men of renown', Genesis 6: 2 and 4."

From, ACT III, Scene IV (Manfred has ascended the tower of his castle to contemplate the heavens. The Abbot makes a second attempt to persuade him to accept the consolations of religion. As he talks to him, a spirit of terrifying aspect approaches Manfred.)

40. Byron once again reverts to the myth of a purer and wiser time before man was corrupted by sin.

46–63. In this important passage Manfred (or Byron) spurns the spirit, proclaiming that he has no power over him and that he alone is responsible for his choices between good and evil. He may have committed sins – but they were not the result of external temptations or an external destiny. This defiant assertion of man's 'free will' is in direct opposition to the Calvanist idea of 'predestination' which he had probably been taught as a child. It is here that Manfred reaches the fullest stature of 'Promethean man', accepting suffering, evil and death as man's inevitable lot, but refusing to bow to any of them. It is, indeed, almost as if he refuses to yield to death itself, choosing his own moment to die.

SO, WE'LL GO NO MORE A ROVING (1817.) Written in Venice (where Byron settled in November 1816 for several years) after a spell of exhausting dissipation. The realisation that Carnival in Venice was not long over when he wrote the poem perhaps adds an additional touch of magic to the brightness of the moon in the poem. The

actual poetic constituents may not be out of the ordinary (apart from
the erotic nature of the image in line 5), and yet somehow the poem
has a spell which only Byron could have woven. This lies partly in
the wry, worldly-wise tone of a man who has won through to some
kind of wisdom and maturity, and partly in a deeper melancholy that
we sense below the surface.

TO THOMAS MOORE (1817). These stanzas were added to a poem
which Byron had apparently begun to Moore just before he set
sail from England – hence the shipboard references – and included
in one of Byron's many letters to his friend and fellow poet. They
are a useful corrective to any exaggeratedly gloomy picture of
Byron, showing how disengaged and even flippant he could be
about his misfortunes. The typically Byronic images are there,
including the juxtaposition of 'desert' and 'springs', but lightened
by gaiety.

CHILDE HAROLD'S PILGRIMAGE, Canto the Fourth. This great
concluding movement to the choral or symphonic structure that is
Childe Harold's Pilgrimage is the culmination of most of the develop-
ments we have seen in the earlier Cantos, in the tales, and in *Man-
fred*. The major theme of disenchantment, together with all the
subsidiary Byronic themes, rises to a powerful climax. The material
however, is so close-knit that it is best to leave comment to the
notes. In the Dedication to his friend John Cam Hobhouse, Byron
explained: 'There will be found less of the pilgrim than in any of the
preceding, and that little slightly, if at all, separated from the author
speaking in his own person.' In other words the 'I' of the poet has
finally taken over and we are now primarily listening to his voice,
not that of either Byron the private individual or Byron the legend.

[VENICE] from *Childe Harold's Pilgrimage*, Canto the Fourth, stanzas
I-XVIII.
1-9. Venice, too, is one of Byron's 'extended metaphors' for a
glorious but mythical past.
1-2. Bridge of Sighs: joining the old ducal palace and the State prison.
5. a Thousand years: the first doge, or Chief Magistrate, of Venice
was elected in A.D. 697, though Venice had existed as a city for many
years before that.
7. For centuries Venice, as the chief European port for trade with
the East, was rich and powerful, and controlled a considerable
empire.

8. the winged Lion: the emblem of St Mark, the patron saint of Venice.

10. Cybele: a goddess representing the fecundity of Nature.

19. Tasso: Torquato Tasso (1544–95), great Italian poet, whose most famous work was *La Gerusalemme Liberata* (Jerusalem Delivered), published in 1581 and 1593. He lived for some time in Venice.

33. Shylock and the Moor: Shylock in Shakespeare's *The Merchant of Venice;* and the 'Moor of Venice' or Othello, who, in Shakespeare's famous tragedy of that name was a general employed by the Venetian state.

34. Pierre: a character in *Venice Preserved*, a tragedy in blank verse by Thomas Otway, first produced in 1682.

37-45. An important passage in which Byron states one of his main themes in the fourth Canto, and one that was already coming to the fore in the third – that creativity represents the only real defence against complete nihilism and despair.

46-7. But even creativity is no more than a *refuge* for the excessive hopefulness of youth, and the *vacancy* of old age.

48. It is only a *worn* feeling.

49. Byron can be no more certain than a 'may be'.

50-4. The artist's world, in any case, is only a romantic *fairy-land*, a *fantastic sky*, and there may be truths far deeper than those the artist can show.

55-6. But do these *truths* really exist – or are they, too, only *dreams?*

71. the inviolate island: England.

91-3. In the days of Venice's independence there used to be an annual ceremony to signify the sea-power of Venice. The Doge, in his state barge, the *Bucentaur*, would put out to sea on Ascension Day, and drop a ring into the water as a symbolic marriage of Venice and the sea.

97-8. Frederick I (*c.*1123–90), the Holy Roman Emperor, after a long quarrel with Pope Alexander III, who excommunicated him, eventually made peace by the Treaty of Venice (1177), kneeling before the Pope and kissing his feet as a token of submission.

100. The Emperor Frederick I, was also Duke of Swabia in Germany: at the time Byron was writing the whole of Italy, including Venice, was part of the Austrian empire.

106. lauwine: an avalanche.

107-8. Enrico Dandolo, elected Doge of Venice in 1193; although over seventy and nearly blind he proved one of Venice's most able rulers. In 1203 (when he was over eighty) he commanded the fleet which took part in the capture of Constantinople (then known as Byzantium), capital of the Eastern division of the Roman Empire.

109–10. Four colossal bronze horses, belonging to a Graeco-Roman triumphal quadriga, which Dandolo brought to Venice from Constantinople in 1204.

111. Doria's menace: Andrea Doria (1466–1560), a Genoan admiral who achieved many notable victories against the Turks, but who hated Venice.

118. Tyre: ancient and once powerful seaport of the Phoenicians on the Lebanon coast.

120. Byron explains – 'that is, the Lion of St Mark, the standard of the republic . . .'

123. the Ottomite: the Turks.

124. Candia: large city of Crete, on the site of the ancient Heracleon, the seaport of Cnossus; once part of the Venetian empire.

125. Lepanto's fight: the battle of Lepanto (entrance to Gulf of Corinth in Greece) in which the Turkish fleet was defeated by a 'Holy League' which included Venice.

136. Syracuse: city in Sicily, scene of a battle in 413 B.C. (during the war between Athens and Sparta) in which the Athenians were defeated in their attempt to take the city, and their fleet destroyed.

138–44. The thousands of Athenian prisoners after the battle consoled themselves by reciting passages from their great poets and tragedians and especially Euripides. The Tyrant of Syracuse is said to have been so impressed when he heard some of the Athenian slaves that he released them.

151. Byron blames England for allowing Venice to be restored to Austria after the defeat of Napoleon.

154. a fairy city of the heart: an apt illustration of Byron's use of Venice as one of his 'extended metaphors' for the perpetual fading of hope and beauty.

158. Authors of works in which Venice figured.

[SUFFERING AND RUIN] from *Childe Harold's Pilgrimage*, Canto the Fourth, stanzas XXI–XXV.

10–26. In part a personal statement of Byron's own suffering – and its inevitable return after the illusory moments of hope.

27. The 'we' transfers the personal suffering to that of all humanity.

31. blight and blackening: characteristic images of the decay of hope.

37. This line marks the transition to a widening of the theme to take in the whole of Italy, as an even larger extended metaphor.

39. A ruin amidst ruins: Byron himself – and the whole human condition.

[THOUGHTS ON ITALY] from *Childe Harold's Pilgrimage*, Canto the Fourth, stanzas XLIII–XLVII.

15. The Po: The Italian river which flows from Monte Viso, through Piedmont and Lombardy to the Adriatic.

20–1. Servius Sulpicius, Roman poet and friend of Marcus Tullius (*Tully*) Cicero, the great Roman orator and philosopher (106–43 B.C.). Sulpicius wrote a letter to Cicero describing a journey he had made through the places mentioned in the stanza.

23–5. Ancient Greek cities. Byron is recalling his earlier travels in Greece.

44. Titanic form: Ancient Rome is like a Titan Prometheus who has fallen.

46–54. Evidence of Byron's growing concern with the cause of Italian independence.

[ROME] from *Childe Harold's Pilgrimage*, Canto the Fourth, stanzas LXXVIII–LXXXII.

1. Rome is another of Byron's images for the state of his own soul and that of mankind in general.

10. Niobe: in Greek legend she boasted that she was superior to the mother of Apollo and Artemis, who as a punishment slew her six sons and five of her six daughters. Niobe herself was then changed into a rock and her tears for her children became streams which trickled from it.

14. Scipios' tomb: tomb of an ancient Roman family which produced many heroes, including Publius Cornelius Scipio, the conqueror of Spain, and victor over Hannibal at the battle of Zama (202 B.C.).

17. Tiber: the river which runs through Rome.

19. The Goths, under Alaric, sacked Rome in A.D. 410.

23. the Capitol: The great national temple of Ancient Rome, regarded as the hub of the empire.

35. Eureka: The cry of exultation 'I have found it!' or 'It is clear to me', made by Archimedes of Syracuse, the Greek mathematician (287–214 B.C.), when he discovered means of determining, by specific gravity, the proportion of base metal in the crown of Hiero, the Tyrant (or king) of Syracuse.

39. Brutus: one of the conspirators who assassinated Julius Caesar, in the hope of restoring republican government to Rome.

41. Virgil: the great Roman poet (70–19 B.C.), author of *The Aeneid*, the epic of the Roman people.

42. Livy: famous Roman historian (59 B.C.–A.D. 17).

44–5. Even if Rome *were* liberated it would be in a world less 'bright' than that of Ancient Rome. In other words, even man's aspirations to freedom are doomed from the start.

[FREEDOM FOR ITALY] from *Childe Harold's Pilgrimage*, Canto the Fourth, stanzas XCVI-XCVIII.

3. Columbia: America, who won independence from the British in 1776.

10. Napoleon liberated Italy, but himself became a tyrant.

11. Saturnalia: a Roman festival in honour of the God Saturn, usually accompanied by riotous debauchery.

17-18. Here we have the image of the 'fall' in the Garden of Eden related to the collapse of the hopes for mankind, apparently embodied in the French Revolution.

19-22. A defiant assertion of Byron's faith in liberty in spite of everything.

23-7. The image of the Tree of Knowledge in the Garden of Eden is continued. Byron's belief in political liberty is here seen as analagous to his Promethean defiance in general.

[EGERIA – AND HUMAN LOVE] from *Childe Harold's Pilgrimage*, Canto the Fourth, stanzas CXV–CXXVII.

1-3. Egeria, a fountain-goddess, was says Byron, the ideal creation of someone who had found the actuality of love, in the real world, a disappointment.

4. Aurora: the Greek goddess of the dawn.

5. nympholepsy: the *Concise Oxford Dictionary* defines this word (very aptly for Byron's case) as 'ecstasy or frenzy caused by desire of the unattainable'.

11. Elysian: belonging to Elysium, which in Greek mythology was the happy abode of the blessed after death.

30. In Roman myth, Egeria became the counsellor and wife of King Numa, legendary second King of Rome, and successor to Romulus, its founder.

39-45. An eloquent expression of the Byronic dream of a perfect human love, freed from the inexorable law of impermanence – contrasted with the reality.

46. A powerful evocation of the 'waste land' which Byron sees as the human condition.

58. The kind of love Byron dreams of is for ever unattainable – existing only in the creative imagination.

64-9. And the creations of the imagination are false, as are all human aspirations. Even so (lines 76–9) we still follow them.

70. An explicit statement of the concept of the irreversible expulsion from Eden which lies at the heart of all Byron's poetry.

80. Only the stubbornness of the heart remains constant.

81. wealthiest when most undone: because, Byron suggests, striving for ideal love sustains the illusion of hope, whereas the attainment of love reveals its worthlessness.

82–90. One of Byron's bleakest and most uncompromising poetic statements of the valuelessness of all aspirations for a humanity doomed from the start.

102. There is no escape from man's 'original sin'.

103. upas: a poisonous tree, whose juice was supposed to have been used by the natives of Java to envenom their darts, and which is reputed to kill all animal life within a radius of fifteen miles.

109–12. Byron reasserts the defiance of the creative mind as the only positive act allowed to man – even if it cannot alter the stark reality.

115–16. Does Byron mean here that if the *faculty divine* (line 113) *were* vouchsafed man it would be a comforting revelation – or that it would finally confirm his terrible vision, and so be too painful to bear?

[VENGEANCE – OR FORGIVENESS?] from *Child Harold's Pilgrimage*, Canto the Fourth, stanzas CXXX–CXXXVII.

1–2. It is the ruins of Rome which have inspired Byron's train of thought.

6. sophists: teachers of rhetoric and philosophy in Ancient Greece: but the word often implies pedantry and arid hair-splitting.

10–13. Byron here explicitly identifies himself and his case with the ruins of Rome.

18–45. In these lines Byron's personal bitterness and his feeling that he has been wronged (by his wife and by the scandalmongers) probably breaks out more fiercely than anywhere else.

21–3. Nemesis: In Greek mythology Nemesis, the instrument of the gods' vengeance, has the power of calling up the Furies, or avenging deities, to carry out the gods' decrees. They assailed Orestes when he murdered his mother Clytemnestra and her lover Aegisthus, who had in their turn murdered his father Agamemnon.

29. A reference to the crimes of his forebears of which Byron was morbidly conscious.

46. But he has reached a stage where forgiveness can take over from bitterness.

67–8. An utterance of 'Promethean' defiance.

[THE LAST OF CHILDE HAROLD] from *Child Harold's Pilgrimage*, Canto
Fourth, stanzas CLXIV–CLXVI.
1–9. Byron no longer has any need of an intermediary: the fiction of
Childe Harold has finally been absorbed into the experience of the
poet.
10–27. One of the most impressive – and terrible – of all Byron's
evocations of the 'waste land' of a human existence lost in the chaos
of the universe.
27. fardels: burdens.

[NATURE, OCEAN – AND FAREWELL] from *Childe Harold's Pilgrimage*,
Canto the Fourth, stanzas CLXXVII – CLXXXVI.
1–9. The poet clutches at the hope that, even now, he will find a
love that is not flawed. The question-marks signify his doubt.
10–18. He tries once more the Wordsworthian refuge.
19–63. The vastness – and indifference – of the Ocean show up
man's wickedness and puny pretences to power and glory.
64–72. A measure of Byron's triumph in *Childe Harold* is that after
such a pitiless exposure of the vanity of all human wishes, after such
a terrible, nihilistic vision, he should still be capable of such
buoyancy of spirit.
84. the Pilgrim: Childe Harold.
80. shoon: an archaic word for 'shoes'; *scallop-shell:* the emblem of
the pilgrim in the Middle Ages. These echoes of the medievalism
of the first two Cantos are a reminder that the four Cantos of *Childe
Harold's Pilgrimage* constitute one complete poem.

[MAZEPPA'S RIDE] from *Mazeppa* (1819). One of Byron's most vivid
verse tales (composed in octosyllabic couplets), as full of energy and
narrative verve as the earlier ones, but more controlled and therefore
even more compelling.
   In history the hero of the poem was Ivan Stepanovitch Mazeppa,
a Polish nobleman, born about 1645, who became hetman (military
chief) of the Eastern Ukraine. He abandoned his allegiance to the
Russian Tsar, Peter the Great, and fought on the side of Charles
XII of Sweden at the battle of Pultova (1709), in which Charles was
defeated. The first part of the poem, which is based on passages in
Voltaire's *Charles XII*, tells how the king and his followers rest
under an oaktree after their defeat. To rouse them out of their
despair, Mazeppa begins to tell them about an incident in his youth
when he had a love affair with the wife of a local count. The intrigue

was discovered and Mazeppa seized – and he now goes on to describe the Count's revenge.

37–49. A savagely brilliant description of devastation.

60. The old hetman is seeking to encourage the defeated Charles XII.

80. Spahi: Turkish irregular cavalry.

262. ignis-fatuus: will o' the wisp, or phosphorescent light on marshy ground.

307. werst: or 'verst', a Russian (and Polish) measure of length – 3,500 feet.

341–52. In this fine contrast between the freedom of the wild horses and Mazeppa's plight, as the victim of human wickedness (his own as well as the Count's) a characteristic Byronic motif emerges again.

365–405. These reflections of Mazeppa's are of course typically Byronic ones, upon the vanity of the thoughtful man's aspirations and his dream of a 'lost Eden'.

395. The Tree of Knowledge that would – he imagines – take him into a Paradise or Eden.

397. repair'd his fall: once more the imagery of the 'Fall'.

426–7. At the point of death Mazeppa has his *latest dream* – and imagines he sees *a lovely star* – that is he experiences man's perennial dream.

490. When, that is, Mazeppa became hetman of the Cossacks of the Ukraine.

498. The Borysthenes: a tributary of the Dnieper.

510–12. So even the hetman's efforts were wasted – a neat ironic touch.

STANZAS (1820) – 'When a man hath no freedom to fight for at home. To change the mood – and to show Byron commenting flippantly on his devotion to the cause of freedom. The lines were contained in a letter to Tom Moore, at a time when Byron was in considerable personal danger because of his complicity in the Carbonari conspiracy.

STANZAS WRITTEN ON THE ROAD BETWEEN FLORENCE AND PISA (1821). Byron in another lighthearted mood; he wrote these stanzas in his coach on his way to join his mistress Teresa Guiccioli.

3. myrtle and ivy: both sacred to Venus, goddess of love.

13. i.e. he only looked for fame and found it in the eyes of his beloved.

15–16. In other words, in this mood, he can still believe in love.

From CAIN, A MYSTERY (1821). In this three-act blank verse tragedy (or 'Mystery', as Byron called it) we are taken right into the Old Testament myth of the Fall – at a point in the story some time after the expulsion of Adam and Eve from the Garden of Eden. They and their family have reconciled themselves to the fact that the lost Eden is lost for ever – all except Cain, who bitterly challenges the justice of God's decree, and who as a result of his challenge introduces a worse evil into the world.

In some respects Cain's plight is similar to that of Byron's – also expelled, both from his childhood dream of Eden and from his native land, fiercely questioning the justice of his fate and yet haunted by the feeling that he has brought harm to others, as well as by a more pervasive and unidentifiable sense of sin.

Cain is the highwater mark of Byron's metaphysical and theological exploration (though *Heaven and Earth*, a play that followed, a year later, continued the process). Many critics accused *Cain* of atheism, but the fact that Byron went on struggling with these problems rather discounts the criticism. Byron in fact does not query the existence of God. What he *does* do is to question God's justice, and to assert that man had the right to do so, whatever the cost.

ACT I, SCENE I

4. Jehovah: principal and personal name of God in the Old Testament.
30. forbidden tree: the tree of the knowledge of good and evil in the Garden of Eden, the fruit of which Adam and Eve were forbidden to eat. It was because Eve broke this injunction, tempted by the serpent, that she and Adam were expelled.
32. tree of life: this tree, too, grew in the Garden of Eden and was also forbidden. One of the reasons why God expelled Adam and Eve was that he feared that they might eat its fruit as well – which conferred immortality.
47. orisons: prayers.
83. other spirits: the angels with the flaming swords whom God stationed to prevent Adam and Eve and their family from re-entering the Garden of Eden.
90. cherubim: plural of 'cherub': an order of angels gifted with knowledge.
99. Master of Spirits: Lucifer, or Satan, the rebel archangel who was hurled from heaven, was the commander of the fallen angels.
104–9. In Byron's imaginative world only the stupid, the ignorant and the unthinking can experience unalloyed happiness. Knowledge,

259

because it reveals the injustice at the basis of the universe, inevitably brings suffering – and also defiant revulsion against this injustice.

116–19. Byron always believed in the 'life after death' – but he thought it would be no better and no juster than mortal existence.

133. seraphs: or seraphim: the first order of angels (above the cherubim, that is), gifted with love.

137–63. The kind of utterance which struck many of Byron's contemporaries as shocking blasphemy.

147–51. God is in no better plight than the poet – both turn to creation as a refuge from misery.

184. matins: morning prayers or hymns.

191. a serpent: the form Lucifer took to appear to Eve in the Garden of Eden.

193–5. Man is not tempted to evil, Lucifer argues, but by acquiring knowledge learns that evil exists.

204. In the Book of Genesis God speaks to his 'children' through thunder.

270. umbrage: shade.

315. Like Manfred, Cain defiantly refuses to bow to any power. To Byron man was himself part-divinity, and must therefore be his own arbiter, standing or falling by the decisions he makes.

360–77. Byron, of course, has in mind his own relationship with a sister.

397–400. This is indeed the whole human condition, as Byron sees it.

538. save ONE: perhaps this is a reference to the myth (as in the medieval poem *The Harrowing of Hell*) that at the end of things Christ will descend into Hell to reclaim Adam and Eve and others from Satan's clutches. The use of capitals suggests this: on the other hand Christ is not 'mortal', so Byron may also have himself in mind, as a man who has dared descent into hell.

From ACT II, SCENE I. (Lucifer has taken Cain into 'the Abyss of Space'. He has shown him the distant globe Earth, and told him that it is but one of countless myriads. Cain then asks to be shown 'the mysteries of death'.)

11. Is but the wreck: even the world – like Greece, or Rome, or the fallen Napoleon – is only a ruin of a former and more splendid state.

28. And Edens in them? . . .: Eden, and its loss, are not only the condition of mankind, but of all things.

From ACT III, SCENE I. (After Cain's return to Earth, Adah persuades him to join his brother Abel in offering up sacrifices to God. The brothers take their offerings to their respective altars, but whereas that of Abel 'kindles into a column of the brightest flame', that of Cain, together with the altar upon which it is placed, is scattered by a whirlwind. In anger at God's rejection of his own sacrifice Cain seeks to throw down his brother's altar – and when Abel tries to stop him, deals him his death-blow. A little later Abel's wife Zillah arrives on the scene, to find Cain standing beside her slaughtered husband, and cries 'Death is in the world!' She brings Adam, Eve, and Adah to the scene. Eve curses Cain, and Adam tells him he must leave for ever. Cain and Adah are left together.)

28–30. The sign which the Lord orders the angel to put on Cain's brow (known as 'the mark of Cain') was not only to signify his curse, but also to be a protection to him: for the Lord promises that if Cain should be slain in spite of the mark, he would be avenged 'sevenfold'.

57. the four rivers: Byron says in his notes: ' "The four rivers" which flowed round Eden, and consequently the only waters with which Cain was acquainted on earth.'

87. Eastward from Eden: the lot of man is to travel ever farther away from his dream.

96. But with me!: Cain sets out on his exile with foreboding – but he is a less heroically defiant figure than Manfred, in that he accepts the Lord's decree and his own destiny with comparative meekness.

[A CELESTIAL BORE] from *The Vision of Judgment* (1822). It is the object of this selection to draw attention away from the satirical Byron – but here is a taste of his manner in this vein. The poem from which it is taken was published in *The Liberal*, Byron's shortlived magazine, and was a devastating travesty of another poem called *A Vision of Judgment*, in which the poet laureate, Robert Southey, had lauded the late King George III (who had died in 1820) and (in its preface) had attacked Byron. In Byron's poem King George III arrives at the gates of heaven, but is denied admission by St Peter, while the Archangel Michael and Satan argue as to who should take charge of the new arrival. Southey is summoned as a witness: he begins an oration in ponderous verse, until the listeners shout out in protest . . .

16. Poems by Southey.

17. regicide: one who kills or connives at the killing of a king. In his youth Southey had been an ardent supporter of the French Revolutionaries who had guillotined their king, Louis XVI.

18. Byron had a special hatred for Southey because he had 'turned his coat' and become a staunch supporter of the Establishment.

21. *pantisocracy:* a form of communism which Southey and Coleridge had, in their revolutionary youth, planned to set up in America.

23. *anti-Jacobin:* a Jacobin was a supporter of the French Revolution.

33. *Wesley's life:* Southey, among other biographies, wrote a 'Life' of John Wesley, one of the founders of Methodism.

55. *King Alfonso:* Alfonso X, King of Leon and Castille (1252–82), known as 'The Wise' and 'The Astronomer'.

55–6. In his notes Byron tells us that Alfonso had said: ' "Had *he* been consulted at the creation of the world he would have spared the Maker some absurdities." '

63. *ambrosial:* divinely fragrant (ambrosia in Greek mythology was the food of the gods); *sulphureous* – the smell of hell-fire emanating from Satan and his attendants.

64. *melodious twang:* Byron explains in his notes: 'See Aubrey's account of the apparition which disappeared "with a curious perfume and a most melodious twang". . .'

76. *Phaeton:* the son of Helios, the Sun God. Allowed one day by his father to drive the sun chariot across the sky, he lost control of it, and was killed by Jupiter, his body falling into the river Po.

87. *'Life'* or *'Vision':* references to Southey's many biographies, and to his poem *A Vision of Judgment.*

88. *Welborn:* a theologian.

96. 'the hundredth psalm' – or 'the old hundredth'; best known in the hymn version that begins 'All people that on earth do dwell . . .'

DON JUAN (1819 – 1824). *Don Juan*, the crown of Byron's poetic achievement, was composed over a number of years (and left unfinished at his death) – but it is more convenient here to group the selected stanzas together.

Byron's hero has little in common (apart from his Spanish blood and his amours) with the Don Juan of legend, the most famous version of which is Mozart's opera *Don Giovanni*. He is, rather, a vehicle for Byron's mature and considered judgments on men's affairs. Although much of the poem is comic satire, and Byron's tone is often witty, caustic or flippant, his vision of the futility and ultimate meaninglessness of man's life within a universe of chaos has not been modified, and there are many passages of great bitterness, both poetical and personal, as well as passages as grim in their metaphysical implications as any in *Manfred* or *Cain*. The basic, underlying theme of his work – that of man's expulsion from an Eden which in any case only existed in his imagination – is more powerfully expressed than ever, especially in the way Byron juxtaposes passages of idyllic beauty and scenes of horror which inevitably swallow them up. There are differences though: in *Don Juan* Byron's own emotions are under complete control, and in consequence he is able to contemplate human existence with a new detachment – and, above all, with a deep compassion.

The first Canto of the poem describes Juan's birth and upbringing, culminating in an amorous adventure with Dona Julia, one of his priggish mother's friends. Julia's husband discovers the affair and Don Juan's mother decides to hustle her son out of the country. The farewell letter which Julia sends him from the convent where her angry husband has locked her up, is a subtle blend of genuine feeling and excess of romantic sensibility, reminding us that Byron was an 'anti-Romantic' in so far as Romanticism was an evasion of reality.

[A ROMANTIC LETTER] from *Don Juan*, Canto the First, stanzas CXCI – CXCVIII.
57–64. It is this stanza, with its suggestion of a certain sentimental contrivance on Julia's part, that contains Byron's ironic comment, driven home by the mocking tone of the final couplet.
62. '*Elle vous suit partout*': the sunflower will turn towards him wherever he goes.
63. cornelian: semi-precious stone.

[LOVERS IN PARADISE] from *Don Juan*, Canto the Second, stanzas CLXXXIII – CXCIV. The ship in which Don Juan is sailing is wrecked. All perish except Juan, who is cast up on a Greek island, the base of a pirate, whose innocent young daughter Haidée finds Juan and (in the absence of her father) nurses him back to health. The love of Juan and Haidée is a beautiful idyll – and Byron handles it with great tenderness. But the whole point about an idyll is that it is a 'time out of time', and Byron is at pains to check any over-emotionalism by all kinds of disconcerting interpolations and asides – while eventually the idyll dissolves into violence and the death of Haidée.
1–10. There are echoes here from the fourth book of Milton's *Paradise Lost* where Adam and Eve wander innocently through the Garden of Eden.
55–6. Only in first love, Byron says, does man approach the pure bliss that belongs to the vanished Eden.
79–80. A comic-bitter intrusion of cynicism.
86. Stygian: belonging to the Styx, the river which, in Greek mythology, surrounds Hades or Hell.

[LOVE OF WOMAN] from *Don Juan*, Canto the Second, stanzas CXCIX-CCIV.

1–8. These famous lines show how far Byron was from being the heartless profligate of legend.

9–24. The compassion suddenly passes into a savage onslaught on the values of 'the World' (as Byron usually – and ironically – calls Society with a capital S) that recalls Alexander Pope.

25–32. It is astonishing that Byron is able to make such sudden and startling transitions of mood without destroying the spell of this idyll of Juan and Haidée.

40. Castlereagh: Chief Secretary for Ireland (1799–1801); Foreign Secretary (1812–22) and leading British representative at the Congress of Vienna, which settled the affairs of Europe after the defeat of Napoleon; a special object of Byron's hatred, because he saw him as the prime initiator of reactionary policies both in Ireland and in Europe.

The suddenness of the transition to Castlereagh is, at the same time, a measure of the pain Byron feels at the thought that love like that of Juan and Haidée cannot last.

41–8. But immediately Byron returns to the Paradise or Eden of first love: it represents a dream he doubts, but can never let go.

[THE ISLES OF GREECE] from *Don Juan*, Canto the Third, following stanza LXXXVI. This lyrical poem, inserted into the body of the Canto, is a reminder that the 'Byronic Byron' of the first Canto of *Childe Harold* is still very much alive. It is as if the emotion Byron has felt in describing the love of Juan and Haidée reminded him of the earlier emotion he felt when he first saw Greece – an emotion analogous to first love. The poem is also another rousing call to the Greeks to free themselves from the Turks.

2. Sappho: Greek lyrical poetess of Lesbos (flourished *c.*610 B.C.)

4. Delos: island in the Aegean, an important centre of the worship of Apollo, the god of music and poetry. *Phoebus* – another name for Apollo.

5–6. The glory, like that of man's longed for Eden – has vanished.

7. References to islands in the Ionian Sea, famous for their poetic associations.

12. In Greek legend, islands of the Western Ocean where favourites of the gods dwell after death.

19. i.e. Xerxes, the king of the Persians, who watched his fleet being defeated by the Greeks at Salamis.

30. Even here Byron's sense of guilt appears.

50. Samian: belonging to Samos, a large island in the Aegean.

55. Pyrrhic dance: a war dance of the ancient Greeks.

56. Pyrrhic phalanx: battle formation used by Pyrrhus, King of Epirus, who fought a series of campaigns against Rome.

59. Cadmus: in Greek legend the founder of Thebes in Boetia, reputed to have introduced the alphabet to Greece.

63. Anacreon's song: Anacreon was a Greek lyric poet (*c.*563–478 B.C.)

64. Polycrates: – a tyrant of Samos who made his island a great naval power.

67. the Chersonese: the Thracian peninsula west of the Hellespont.

69. Miltiades: Athenian statesman and general, victor of Marathon.

73. Suli; Parga: places in the Aegean.

78. Heracleidan: belonging to Heracles (or Hercules), the mythical ancient hero.

79. Franks: the French.

91. Sunium: a promontory at the southern apex of Attica; *marbled* because Sunium is the site of a marble temple to Poseidon, god of the sea.

[AVE MARIA] from *Don Juan*, Canto the Third, stanzas CII – CVIII. Another example of the more romantic Byron, returning us to the idyll of Juan and Haidée – but note that Byron does not allow it to become too lush, and that the note of personal loneliness and homelessness at the end of the passage prevents it from becoming too 'literary' a set-piece.

1. Ave Maria: 'Hail Mary' – a devotional recitation and prayer to the Virgin in the Roman Catholic religion, especially associated with evening services.

10. Byron switches the emotion to earthly love.

27. Ravenna: city in north-east Italy, famous for its pine forests. Ravenna became the western capital of the empire after the fall of Rome; it, too, eventually fell to the Goths.

28. Adrian: Adria was a Greek colony on the Po estuary (not far from Ravenna) dating back to the sixth century.

30. Boccaccio: great Italian poet and story-teller (1313–75) author of the *Decameron*, a famous collection of tales.

31. Dryden: English poet, dramatist, critic and translator (1631–1700). His works included verse paraphrases of tales of Boccaccio.

33. Cicalas: or 'cicadas', insects which make shrill sounds, found chiefly in hot climates.

36. vesper bell: bell for evensong (vespers).

37–40. In one of Boccaccio's stories Nastagio degli Onesti of Ravenna is scorned by the woman he loves: in a vision he sees a woman chased and torn to pieces by hounds, which are urged on by the lover she had rejected; Onesti arranges that his beloved shall also see the vision, and as a result she is cured of her haughtiness.

41. Hesperus: the evening star, Venus.

[SLAUGHTER AT ISMAIL] from *Don Juan*, Canto the Eighth, stanzas CXXI – CXXVII. After numerous adventures Juan finds himself fighting with the Russian army in its bloody onslaught on the Turkish held fortress-town of Ismail in Bessarabia, on a tributary of the Danube (1790). As the town falls, with the exception of a solitary bastion, where the Turkish Pasha, or governor, has his headquarters, Byron himself launches into a savage onslaught – on the futility and falsity of military glory.

7. The pasha is smoking a Turkish pipe, or hookah.

12–13. The Turkish flag was replaced by the Russian one.

31. Muscadins: slang word for inhabitants of Paris (cf. 'Cockneys')

33. Gazette: government publication which lists promotions, honours, decorations, casualties, etc.

39. Byron was strongly opposed to England's oppressive policy in Ireland where there was recurrent famine.

40. Wellesley: Arthur Wellesley (1769–1852) first Duke of Wellington, and victor of Waterloo.

48. great George: the Prince Regent became King George IV in 1820 (to 1830). He was a man of great corpulence.

[END OF THE WORLD] from *Don Juan*, Canto the Ninth, stanzas XXXVII – XXXIX. Byron interrupts his account of the sacking of Ismail with some mock-solemn reflections, in one of which he pretends to have lost the thread. The important stanzas that follow can be seen as a comic counterpart to the earlier poem *Darkness*, which also envisages the end of the world. Not altogether comic though: there is often a note of desperation in Byron's laughter, and there is certainly nothing funny in the last line of the extract, which sums up Byron's disenchantment at its blackest and most nihilistic.

9. Cuvier: Georges Léopold Cuvier, Baron – a famous French naturalist (1769–1832), who conducted important researches into palaeontology (i.e. the study of extinct life forms in fossil remains, etc.), founded a system of classification in zoology and originated the science of comparative anatomy.

[NEWSTEAD ABBEY REMEMBERED] from *Don Juan*, Canto the Thirteenth, stanzas LV–LXVI. After the capture of Ismail Juan becomes a favourite of the Russian Empress, Catherine the Great. She sends him on a mission to England, which gives Byron ample opportunity, in the last cantos of the work, to conduct a devastating satire on contemporary English society. In doing so, however, other feelings are aroused, among them nostalgia for his old Gothic home of Newstead Abbey – in the poem called 'Norman Abbey', the seat of Lord and Lady Amundeville.

10. Druid oak: the oak was sacred to the Druids, an order of priests or magicians among the ancient Celts of Gaul and Britain.

11. Caractacus: ancient British chieftain who put up a heroic resistance against the Romans.

34. While yet the church was Rome's: before the break with the Roman Catholic Church and the foundation of the Church of England.

44. Charles: Charles I, defeated by Cromwell in the Civil War.

75-6. In Greek legend Memnon was an Ethiopian prince slain at Troy. There was a colossal statue which tradition assigned to him (in reality it was that of one of the Pharaohs Amenhotep) at Thebes, in upper Egypt, which gave out a musical note when struck by the rising sun.

[NIGHT THOUGHTS] from *Don Juan*, Canto the Fifteenth, stanzas XCVII – XCIX. Don Juan, while a guest at Norman Abbey, receives a visitation from what he believes to be a ghost (in fact it is a female fellow-guest in disguise). This leads to these reflections by Byron, a characteristic blend of the flippant and the serious, with a final stanza (the last of the Canto) which is one of the saddest and most profound statements of his pitiless vision of the littleness and futility of the human lot.

3. sage Minerva's fowl: the screech-owl, associated with Minerva, Roman goddess of wisdom.

ON THIS DAY I COMPLETE MY THIRTY-SIXTH YEAR, 1824. The poem was written at Missolonghi in Greece, less than six months before Byron's death. Touching as it does on so many of the themes that made up his life it forms a brave and fitting epitaph.

Further Reading

Editions
Byron: *Poetical Works* (Oxford University Press: Standard Authors, 1904, reset 1945)
Poetical Works of Lord Byron, ed. E. G. Coleridge (Murray, 1947)
Byron: *A Self-Portrait: Letters and diaries*, ed. Peter Quennell (Murray, 1950), 2 vols.

Life
MARCHAND, LESLIE A., *Byron: a biography* (Murray, 1958), 3 vols.
MAYNE, ETHEL C., *Byron* (2nd edn., Methuen, 1924)
ORIGO, IRIS. *The Last Attachment* (Murray, 1949)
PARKER, DEREK. *Byron and His World* (Thames & Hudson: Pictorial Biography series, 1968)
QUENNELL, PETER. *Byron: The Years of Fame* (Collins, 1935)
QUENNELL, PETER. *Byron in Italy* (Collins, 1941)

Critical Studies
BLACKSTONE, BERNARD. *Byron: I. Lyric and Romance; II. Satiric, Reflective and Descriptive* (Longman for British Council: Writers and their Work, 1970)
BLOOM, HAROLD. *The Visionary Company* (Faber, 1962)
CHEW, S. C. *Byron in England: his fame and after-fame* (Murray, 1924)
GLECKNER, ROBERT F. *Byron and the Ruins of Paradise* (John Hopkins Press; Oxford University Press, 1968)
JOSEPH, M. K. *Byron the Poet* (Gollancz, 1964)
KNIGHT, G. WILSON. *The Burning Oracle* (Routledge, 1939)
KNIGHT, G. WILSON. *Lord Byron: Christian Virtues* (Routledge, 1952)
LOVELL, ERNEST J. *Byron: The Record of a Quest* (Texas University Press; Shoe String Press, 1949)
READ, HERBERT. *Byron* (Longmans for British Council: Writers and their Work, 1951; with a revised bibliography, 1966)
ROBSON, W. W. *Critical Essays* (Routledge, 1966)
RUTHERFORD, ANDREW. *Byron: A Critical Study* (Oliver & Boyd, 1962)

RUTHERFORD, ANDREW, ed. *Byron: The Critical Heritage* (Routledge, 1970)

Background

ALLEN, B. S. *Tides in English Taste, 1619–1800* (Harvard University Press, 1937)

BOWRA, C. M. *The Romantic Imagination* (Oxford University Press, 1961)

CLARK, KENNETH M., *The Gothic Revival: an essay in the history of Taste* (2nd ed., Constable, 1950; Penguin)

ELTON, OLIVER. *A Survey of English Literature, 1780–1830* (Edward Arnold, 1912), 2 vols.

GRIGSON, GEOFFREY. *The Harp of Aeolus and other essays* (Routledge, 1948)

HOUGH, GRAHAM. *The Romantic Poets* (Hutchinson University Library 1953; n.e. 1967)

JONES, J. *The Egotistical Sublime* (Chatto & Windus, 1954)

LEAVIS, F. R. *Revaluation* (Chatto & Windus, 1936)

PRAZ, MARIO. *The Romantic Agony*, trans. A. Davidson (Oxford University Press, 1951; Fontana)

READ, HERBERT. *The True Voice of Feeling: studies in English Romantic poetry* (Faber, 1953; paperback 1968)

RODWAY, A. E. *Godwin and the Age of Transition* (Harrap, 1952)

WILLEY, BASIL. *The Eighteenth-Century Background* (Chatto & Windus, 1940)

WILLEY, BASIL. *Nineteenth-Century Studies* (Chatto & Windus, 1949)